JOHN M. McDERMOTT S.J.
(editor)

THE THOUGHT OF POPE JOHN PAUL II

A Collection of Essays and Studies

EDITRICE PONTIFICIA UNIVERSITÀ GREGORIANA
ROMA 1993

IMPRIMI POTEST

Romae, die 3 novembris 1992

R. P. Giuseppe Pittau, S.J.
Rector Universitatis

IMPRIMATUR

Dal Vicariato di Roma, 19 gennaio 1993

ISBN 88-7652-656-0

Editrice Pontificia Università Gregoriana
Piazza della Pilotta, 35 - 00187 Roma, Italia

TABLE OF CONTENTS

LIST OF CONTRIBUTORS

JOHN J. CONLEY, S.J., is currently assistant professor of philosophy at Fordham University. With a good background of modern philosophy and the Thomistic tradition his chief interests are in moral philosophy and aesthetics, on which he has written several articles.

BRIAN E. DALEY, S.J., after serving as acting rector, is currently professor of historical theology at the Jesuit School of Theology, Cambridge, MA. His books and articles are mainly in the field of patristic theology.

AVERY DULLES, S.J., after a long teaching career at many distinguished universities, is currently Lawrence J. McGinley Professor of Religion and Society at Fordham University, New York. Internationally renowned for his numerous books and articles, he has just been named a member of the International Theological Commission by Pope John Paul II.

BENJAMIN FIORE, S.J., is professor of Sacred Scripture at Canisius College, Buffalo, N.Y. He has published on various New Testament themes.

RAYMOND T. GAWRONSKI, S.J., has just been appointed assistant professor at the Pontifical Oriental Institute, Rome. His doctoral dissertation was a study of the theology of Hans Urs von Balthasar, *Word and Silence: Christian Obedience and Mystical Experience.*

GARY GURTLER, S.J., is associate professor of ancient philosophy at Boston College. He has published a book and several articles on Plotinus.

ROBERT F. HARVANEK, S.J., past provincial of the Chicago Province, currently rector of the Jesuit Community and professor of philosophy at Loyola University of Chicago, has published widely on St. Thomas and modern philosophy.

PAUL V. MANKOWSKI, S.J., though still a graduate student in Semitic Languages at Harvard University, Boston, MA., has written many articles on feminist theology.

GERALD A. McCOOL, S.J., professor emeritus of philosophy at Fordham University, New York, has been invited since his retirement to teach as visiting professor at various American universities. His field of expertise is the history of modern Thomistic philosophy and theology, especially transcendental Thomism.

JOHN M. MCDERMOTT, S.J., is professor of dogmatic theology at the Pontifical Gregorian University, Rome. He has published widely on the New Testament, modern Thomism, and moral questions.

JOSEPH MURPHY, S.J., is professor of sacramental theology at Kenrick-Glennon Seminary in St. Louis, MO. He is also interested in moral issues.

JOHN H. NOTA, S.J., professor emeritus of philosophy at Brock University, Ontario, has taught at numerous universities in North America and Europe. An internationally recognized Scheler scholar, he has written a great many books and articles on phenomenology and modern philosphy.

VINCENT G. POTTER, S.J., past rector of the Jesuit Community, chairman of the philosophy department, and Vice President for Academic Affairs at Fordham University, is currently professor of philosophy at Fordham and editor of *International Philosophical Quarterly*. His interests lie in modern American pragmatism, especially C.S. Pierce, and transcendental Thomism, especially B. Lonergan. He has published widely on those topics as well as on the relation between philosophy and the natural sciences.

TERRENCE PRENDERGAST, S.J., is past rector of the Jesuit community and currently dean of theology at Regis College, Toronto, Ontario, where he teaches Sacred Scripture. He has published various articles on New Testament themes.

MOST REV. JOHN R. SHEETS, S.J., recently consecrated auxiliary bishop of Fort Wayne, IN., long taught theology at Marquette University and Creighton University, where he founded and directed the Institute of Christian Spirituality. He has published widely on theology and spirituality.

DAVID STAGAMAN, S.J., is dean of theology and associate professor of systematic theology at the Jesuit School of Theology at Berkeley (CA). There he had previously served as acting rector and chairman of .the department of historical/systematic theology. He has published on questions of theological method and linguistic analysis.

JAMES SWETNAM, S.J., past dean of the Pontifical Biblical Institute, Rome, is currently its past dean and vice-rector secretary as well as professor of biblical languages. His publications are primarily on New Testament topics.

Frequently Used Abbreviations for the Papal Writings
of John Paul II:

CA - *Centesimus Annus* [*On the Hundredth Anniversary of "Rerum Novarum"*] Encyclical Letter (1991)

DIM - *Dives in Misericordia* [*On the Mercy of God*] Encyclical Letter (1980)

DEV - *Dominum et Vivificantem* [*On the Holy Spirit in the Life of the Church and the World*] Encyclical Letter (1986)

FC - *Familiaris Consortio* [*The Role of the Christian Family in the Modern World*] Apostolic Letter (1981)

LE - *Laborem Exercens* [*On Human Work*] Encyclical Letter (1981)

MD - *Mulieris Dignitatem* [*Dignity and Vocation of Women*] Apostolic Letter (1988)

MR - *Mater Redemptoris* [*Mother of the Redeemer*] Encyclical Letter (1987)

RD - *Redemptionis Donum* [*The Gift of Redemption*] Apostolic Exhortation (1984)

RH - *Redemptor Hominis* [*The Redeemer of Man*] Encyclical Letter (1979)

RM - *Redemptoris Missio* [*On the Permanent Validity of the Church's Missionary Mandate*] Encyclical Letter (1990)

SD - *Salvifici Doloris* [*On the Christian Meaning of Human Suffering*] Apostolic Letter (1984)

SRS - *Sollicitudo Rei Socialis* [*On Social Concern*] Encyclical Letter (1987).

INTRODUCTION

As the successor of Peter and vicar of Christ, Pope John Paul II deserves attention at least for the influence his thought and action have over millions of Roman Catholics and other Christians who look to Rome for spiritual guidance. *De facto* this Slav Pope, the first in history, has already effected epoch-making changes in world history. General Jerozielski admitted that John Paul II's return to Poland raised the level of consciousness of the Polish people, inspiring them with the sense of destiny and courage that gave rise to the Solidarity movement. Lech Walesa attributed essential support to the Pontiff that not only inspired Solidarity but encouraged it during the dark days of its apparent demise. Not without reason then the French secular weekly *L'Express* hailed on its front cover the destruction of the Berlin wall and the dismantling of the Communist empire as "the victory of the Pope". Where the pacific Paul VI was inclined to compromise with the Communist regimes of Eastern Europe, John Paul II had lived under their rule and had known their interior corruption. He held to a course of firm opposition and provided a beacon of moral uprightness and hope to millions of oppressed peoples, and history has already proven him right. With Mikhail Gorbachev's pilgrimage to the Vatican a power was acknowledged which far transcends the quantified mass of tank divisions. Indeed, since his enforced retirement from active politics, the former president of the Soviet Union has paid homage to the outstanding spiritual personality of the Pope and attributed to his inspiration a good part of the success in the opening of Europe to a greater freedom.

That political victory seems only a small part of the Pope's wider strategy. The opening of the East has nourished his hopes for reunion with the Eastern Orthodox Churches, a constant theme of his pontificate. Not only is the schism between East and West in Christendom a scandal that Christ wants to abolish but also the Pope sees the necessity of the "two lungs" of Christianity breathing in unison to resist the main danger threatening mankind in the twenty-first century, or perhaps in the third millennium after Christ. Materialism, aided by the technological revolution which often submits màn to its impersonal sway, now stands revealed as the common foe in East and West. Communism had provided an ideological cover to materialism in the East and gave rise, in reaction, to an ideological anti-Communism in the West. But with the crumbling of ideologies, man's spiritual predicament in the wake of the Enlightenment must now be faced. What answer can respond to the deepest yearnings of the human heart for meaning? For the Pope, despite the theological disarray within Christianity, this is the opportune moment for the rechristianization of Europe and the world. Here Eastern and Western Churches can provide invaluable assistance to each other. The Western Church, enfeebled by too facile an "adaptation to the modern world", needs a revitalization of its spirituality. This the Eastern Churches, purified by decades of resistance to materialism when they relied only on spiritual resources, can offer the West. Yet the withdrawal into themselves by the Eastern Churches in order to preserve the essentially Christian as well as the official Communist persecution which drove intellectual life underground left them without many of the intellectual tools to affront the challenges of the secular materialism now so dominant in the West. Here the Western experience can mediate to the Eastern Churches not only a knowledge of dangers to be avoided but also instruments of intellectual analysis. With reason the Pope looks toward the ecumenical movement as the fulfillment of a prayer in Christ's and the Church's efforts to bring salvation to all men.

    Indeed the Pope's vision is vaster than the reunion of Western and Eastern Churches; it is as vast as the world. His

journeys into every part of the world are meant to preach his
vision of man and to defend human rights before every type of
dehumanizing oppression. Man must be respected as the indispensable soil for the fruitful reception of the Christian message.
By preaching his Christian humanism the Pope both fulfills the
Church's moral obligation to defend the human and prepares for
the future spiritual union of all men under Christ's headship.

In accomplishing what he considers his God-given mission
the Pope has been indefatigable. Besides the journeys that would
bring many a younger man to an early grave, a stream of all sorts
of pronouncements, encyclicals, apostolic letters, instructions,
and even the weekly Wednesday talks at general papal audiences
have poured forth from the papal pen and mouth. Surely a bevy
of speech writers must be employed in the papal chanceries, yet
all the pronouncements manifest the unmistakable tone of John
Paul II. He is orthodox in theology, considering himself a
guardian of the Church's spiritual heritage, the gospel message,
which has been proclaimed through the centuries. Yet one does
not find the categories of the traditional Thomistic orthodoxy
that dominated Catholic theology in the century before Vatican
II and that was taught to him at the Angelicum in Rome by
Garrigou-Lagrange, his doctoral director. The traditional doctrine has clearly been rethought by a very perceptive, active mind
in touch with the concrete reality of faith, fascinated by the
experience of the mystics, and trained in a personalist philosophy. Out of that lived matrix of experience and thought the Pope
seems to draw the inspiration for his spiritual doctrine.

With his world-wide vision and his strong positions the Pope
has also found himself at the center of controversy. This could
hardly be avoided in the aftermath of Vatican II, a time of chaos
for traditional Catholic theology in which many self-proclaimed
prophets have been loudly selling their wares. The Pope, while
listening for the signs of the times, certainly does not give way
easily to the fads and fashions of the day. Stolidly orthodox in
theology, he maintains the tradition strongly in family and
personal morality while radically rethinking social doctrine. No

pope has ever been so trenchant in his criticism of materialism and capitalism as John Paul II.

Who then is this man and what is his doctrine? That question has been posed by the *Realpolitiker* and by the theologians as well as by ordinary faithful desirous of finding some mooring for their faith in a time of turbulence. The question is all the more crucial for members of the Society of Jesus, a religious order bound by special vow and tradition to the successor of Peter. Yet even a cursory reading of newspapers would reveal that Jesuits have found themselves engaged in controversy on various sides of issues raised by the Pope. In order to deal with the question about the Pope's person and message and the underlying tensions besetting the Society of Jesus (as well as many other religious families) a conference on the Pope's thought was held for Jesuits at Loyola University of Chicago on August 11-13, 1990.

The purpose of the conference was to study respectfully, yet critically the bases of the Pope's thought. It is beyond doubt that Karol Wojtyla possessed an outstanding intellect even before he was elected bishop of Rome. Behind the strong expressions of doctrine one finds careful nuances and stimuli to further reflection. Yet so massive is the Pope's production of documentation that it often seems most difficult to grasp the essential core of his thought. Surely there are tensions in his thought as there are in his practical positions. But what exactly are they? And what are their theoretical and practical bases? After the tensions and their foundations are uncovered, the further question of consistency must be raised. Only in that way may an adequate judgment about their validity and feasibility be attained. The Jesuit participators in the conference were well aware of their owed loyalty to the successor of Peter as well as of their obligations to truth and to the rigor of intellectual honesty. Yet it is only by a critical, albeit reverential, approach to the Pope's thought that his positions may be adequately understood, applied, and complemented. It was the hallmark of the Society of Jesus' success through the centuries that its leaders and thinkers knew how to interpret and apply intelligently and creatively papal directives. This not only gave the papal position a flexibility in being adapted to diverse circumstances but also assured a solid unanimity essential for effective practical action. It was in the hope of reattaining that unity of minds and wills that the Jesuit participants at the conference dedicated their energies. The success of that undertaking must be judged by the readers of the essays and papers which follow in this volume. Yet the participants at the conference were very pleased with the results of the presentations and discussions. Unanimously they voted for a subsequent conference to be sheduled two years later. That conference, sponsored by the Jesuit Community of Fordham University (August 8-10, 1992), centered on the theme of ecclesiology. Although that conference ranged beyond an immediate study of the papal documents, two of the main papers presented there actually fit perfectly into the scope of the present volume presenting the thought of Pope John Paul II. That conference was successfull enough to raise the request for another, this time on morality and sexual ethics, in two more years (1994). The success of the conferences encouraged the organizers and the editor to publish these papers with the hope that others might also profit by the wisdom and insights of the participants.

The first conference was structured around four major presentations handling the philosophy, theology, exegesis, and spirituality of John Paul II. These represent more than the traditional divisions of Catholic thought. They reflect well the lived emphases of the Pope. His spirituality provides the foundation as well as the culmination of his doctrine. Nurtured in Poland during the Nazi occupation, Karol Wojtyla sought the spiritual strength to resist that totalitarian oppression in his faith. This turn into interiority, however, did not cut him off from his Polish people but deepened his sense of solidarity with them and with the Church that fought with and for them. It was the universal dimension of the Church that enabled him to raise his eyes even beyond Poland and seek strength and intelligence in the many Catholic thinkers and saints from other lands. This spirituality grounded and was doubtless strengthened by his many papal voyages and ecumenical interests. Not without reason then did John Sheets, S.J., recently named auxiliary bishop of Fort Wayne, emphasize the Pauline character of the Pope's spirituality. Paul's vision that submitted the universe to Christ shows remarkable similarities with the Pope's dynamic vision.

It would be impossible to ignore the Pope's philosophy. His second doctorate concentrated on the ethics of Max Scheler, and for years he served as a seminary professor of philosophy. Indeed, he continued to teach there after his nomination as bishop and archbishop. Without doubt *The Acting Person* stands as his major scientific work, which would rank high on any philosophical list and certainly had an influence upon his theology. In *Love and Responsibility* and often in his encyclicals Karol Wojtyla employed a phenomenological method of description to lay bare the underlying structures of reality and argue his points. It is doubtless from his phenomenological personalism that the Pope transferred many personalist terms and categories to theology to produce that rethinking of the tradition which is so fascinating to the theologian. By trying to uncover the roots of the Pope's phenomenological method Robert Harvanek, S.J., rendered a service to future discussion.

Since the Pope is the bishop of Rome, entrusted with preserving and proclaiming the faith of the Church, Karol Wojtyla must be judged as a theologian. Although it may be possible to some extent to distinguish the pristine message of the gospel from later theologizing and the Pope is responsible for preaching the gospel, not for publicizing his private theological insights, surely the Pope's theological perspective strongly influences his preaching and practice. A central place had therefore to be attributed to a consideration of Karol Wojtyla's theology. Gerald McCool, S.J., tried to locate him with respect to the major schools of twentieth century Catholic theology even while outlining the major emphases of his theology.

Since Catholic teaching rests on Scripture and tradition and some theologians even understand tradition as the ambient in which scriptural revelation is read and interpreted, the Pope's exegetical method in his use of Scripture deserves to be analyzed. It had become a commonplace in antipapal circles to criticize Karol Wojtyla on account of his lack of appreciation for modern biblical exegesis. Though it is foolish to take modern exegesis as the ultimate norm of truth when there is no unanimity among the exegetes on essential questions and many Protestant presuppositions dividing the historical Jesus from the Christ of faith have become embedded in modern scriptural methodology, nonetheless the charge raised against the Pope bears serious consideration. For not only are exegetes striving to find truth and should be taken seriously in their endeavor but also, because they represent so much of the modern, skeptical mentality, their problems deserve a hearing and response. Perhaps the state and presuppositions of their hypothetical science do not at present allow such a total, convincing response. In any case one would be interested to know John Paul's attitude to modern biblical exegesis. Terrence Prendergast, S.J., studied the papal exegesis on the basis of certain key encyclicals and then tried to broaden his results by taking note of other pontifical writings and discourses. His suggestions stimulate thought, raising questions not only about papal exegesis but also about the purpose and method of exegesis itself.

The first conference noted many vital tensions in the Pope's thought, not the least of which concerned the natural and supernatural orders. Though the Pope rarely discusses that problem directly, the underlying question invariably manifests itself to anyone attempting to understand the relation between humanity, created in the image and likeness of God, and the Church, a supernatural reality. These two central themes of the papal writings constantly meet and cross each other, yet their relationship is rarely spelled out clearly. So this topic provided the matter for the first presentation of the second conference, intended to bridge the endeavors of the future to the success of the past. Joseph Murphy, S.J., accepted the challenge. In his paper he noted a shift in perspective from the earlier Karol

Wojtyla, who concentrated upon the individual person, to the later John Paul II, who placed the marital juncture of Christ and His Church, imaged in the union of husband and wife, at the center of his Christocentric universe. From that axis he handled the relation of natural and supernatural orders, going beyond the Pope's explicit position to develop his own interesting hypotheses.

The role of the Church itself has often been placed into question by the modern world's preferences for individuality, autonomy, and interiority. Not surprisingly theologians form and lend themselves to the expression of such doubts about the necessity of the Church. Yet the Catholic Church has consistently insisted that it is the unique mediator of Christ's salvation and the necessary means of salvation. The tension between the Church's spatio-temporal limitations and the universality of God's salvific will has exercised the ingenuity of many a modern thinker. John Paul II has also taken a stand on the necessity of the Church for salvation. So from another perspective, that of salvation, Avery Dulles, S.J., has analysed John Paul II's pronouncements to capture his vision of the relation of the Church to the human race. His care in handling texts and prudence in coming to a balanced judgment indicate how the mind of a theologian works who desires to remain faithful to the truth of the Catholic tradition while facing the problems and questions of the current age.

The main presentations were followed by critical commentaries and the raising of questions from the floor. These discussions were lively and interesting — we shall touch later upon some of the points emphasized. But another means of coming to grips with the Pope's thought was explored in a round table conversation. Given the centrality of *The Acting Person*, it seemed imperative to study that work in some depth. Various experts tackled various tensions and problems within the work and tried to relate it to their own fields of expertise. Although the discussion was far-ranging and stimulating, the experts were asked to restrict their reflections, in view of publication, to the relation between *The Acting Person* and their own specialities. Thus John Nota, S.J., shed light upon the phenomenological tradition of Scheler from whom the Pope borrowed much in his method and noted various misinterpretations as well as mistranslations of his work. Vincent Potter, S.J., showed remarkable similarities among Wojtyla, C.S. Pierce, and B. Lonergan, and argued that their mutual corroboration, despite their different philosophical backgrounds, greatly supported his strong suspicion about the correctness of their views. David Stagaman, S.J., was concerned to underline the theological implications of *The Acting Person* and noted how the image of the self-sacrificing Christ actually provided the guiding ideal of Wojtyla's anthropology. The present editor had composed the panel for the discussion from experts from diverse fields in the hope of stimulating strong criticism and discussion among the panel members themselves. He was surprised by the amount of unanimity manifested by the members and their high praise for the quality of thought in *The Acting Person*. All agreed that the work held great potentialities for further development in metaphysics and theology as well as in phenomenological analysis. It is hoped that the readers of this volume will find their vision broadened by these short essays and be stimulated to develop some of the insights sketched out.

Most participants found that the discussion groups established to study various major papal writings were the most helpful part of the conferences. In this way the suggestions of the main presentations and the round table discussion were applied to concrete documents and through the exchange of ideas an appreciation of the Pope's thought in its strengths and weaknesses emerged. This result was facilitated by the excellent preparation of the discussion leaders and the knowledge of the document in question shown by the participants. Three main writings were chosen at the first conference. *Redemptor Hominis*, the Pope's first encyclical, spelt out the program of John Paul II's papacy and laid its theological and anthropological foundation. *Laborem Exercens*, previous to the most recent *Centesimus*

Annus, represented the most elaborate version of the Pope's social teaching about the value of human work, a point on which he expended much energy in order to meet the challenge of Marxism, technology, and modern materialism. It also exhibits him at his most creative in reformulating the Catholic tradition. Finally *Mulieris Dignitatem* was chosen for its importance for the ecclesiological discussion in the United States and Canada. The role of woman in the Church and the world, a subject that easily arouses intense passions, deserves a dispassionate study, and the Pope's position on the issue was clearly spelled out. For him the question of liberation is grounded in an ontological and theological dignity which should be preserved against many false ideologies that one-sidedly reduce the role of woman. Yet others would see the ontological distinction between man and woman as a block to true liberation. Since the relation of man to woman involves a question of self-identity that is second only to man's identity before God, the question of the role of the sexes has to be posed and answered by any serious thinker today. The various discussion leaders were kind enough not only to summarize their own presentations of the papal writings but also to indicate the points of agreement and debate among the discussion participants. These summaries may well serve the reader as indicators of issues that are not yet fully defined and need clarification for the sake of inner-ecclesial unity.

The original intention of the conferences included the assembly of reputable, balanced scholars who would exhibit the critical, yet respectful, distance required of Jesuit professors and teachers. The quality of the scholars who responded positively to the requests for contributions was very gratifying and augured well for the conference. Many had obtained a national or international fame, and others had been entrusted with positions of responsibility and honor by both their scholarly colleagues and their superiors in the Society of Jesus or in the Church. Younger scholars of promise were generally asked to respond to the major papers or lead discussion groups. Not infrequently, it was hoped, their questions and insights might prove more fruitful and stimulating than the main talks. The present volume shows how favorably that augury was realized.

The approaches to the Pope's thought adopted in the various contributions to this volume differ widely. Part of that is due to their various tasks. Those summarizing group discussions tried to outline the content of the papal writings and the issues at stake before indicating the various reactions to them, whereas the respondents in the round table discussion, presupposing a good knowledge of *The Acting Person*, developed personal insights and indicated in what areas further research might profitably be carried on. Yet among these respondents J. Nota also made exact remarks about textual mistranslations that might mislead the unwary into a false idea of Wojtyla's notion of experience. The main presentations all attempted straightforwardly to develop a thesis. Yet even here there was much room for diversity of presentation. R. Harvanek and J. Sheets first examined the wider background against which the papal philosophy and spirituality were to be understood. G. McCool, with a plethora of footnotes, laid out the Pope's theology before relating it to other movements in Catholic thought. In that sense his contribution was much more technical than the others. (At the conference he read only a shortened version of the paper presented in this volume). A. Dulles placed John Paul II's thought about the necessity of the Church for salvation within the broader Catholic tradition, especially as spelled out by recent popes and the Second Vatican Council. He sought the unity and continuity in that tradition in order to respond to questions raised by modern theologians. T. Prendergast hewed out a middle way, analyzing in detail various encyclicals before developing a wider hypothesis. J. Murphy similarly joined speculation to papal documents, but whereas Prendergast "speculated" about the reasons for John Paul's adoption of a particular exegetical method, Murphy sought to unify and develop the whole speculative *Weltanschauung* of the Pope by discovering and deepening his speculative presuppositions. Whatever the approach employed, the papers and other contributions to this volume are intended to stimulate reflection and send the reader back to the original documents. It is also hoped that the reader will achieve a greater appreciation of the Pope's intellectual positions in all their complexity. That should overcome too facile categorizations of his positions and help to promote an authentic dialogue serving a greater unity in the Church and in mankind.

With all due respect for the Pope's intelligence and position it must nonetheless be noted that the many tensions in his thought gave rise to diverse interpretations. These appeared in the conference presentations and discussions. Basic to the diverse interpretations of R. Harvanek and G. McCool was the decision whether to interpret Wojtyla's thought as fundamentally phenomenological, borrowing elements from Thomism, or as metaphysical and Thomistic, expanding Thomism with insights from phenomenology. Floor discussion brought out clearly the differences between these two scholars but the perceptive reader will doubtless note how the original option formed their diverse presentations. Closely linked to that question was the interpretation of the Pope's positions as staunchly traditional or involving a radical rethinking of elements of Catholic theology. Does the Pope's view of the Church regard it primarily as a community of believers joined in solidarity to God and each other through a series of personal relations or as institutional authority responsible for passing on the heritage of the gospel message? How does the Pope's strong Christocentrism in theology let itself be reconcilied with the universal anthropology that seems to form the basis of his thought? So often in his writings philosophy, theology, and social analysis seem to flow into each other, yet at other times he can insist strongly upon their clear distinction, as in his insistence on the necessity for seminarians of studying philosophy before theology or in the exclusion of clerics from direct political involvement. J. Murphy attempted to cut the Gordian knot by stressing the change from the earlier philosopher of the individual person to the Pope proposing a metaphysical, nuptial theology in such a way that the natural-supernatural distinction was surpassed in a unified Christocentric

universe. Though his identification of the early Wojtyla's emphasis on the person as individual agreed with Harvanek's analysis,
both the response and the floor discussion questioned the
radicality of the shift from a personal, or individual, to a
co-personal emphasis as well as the resulting absorption of the
natural into the supernatural order. In moral questions the Pope
might be interpreted as an innovator, intent on rethinking
morality in modern, personalist terms, or as a staunch upholder
of the tradition of natural law with its prescriptive, universal
norms. By highlighting these and other tensions the contributions in this volume intend to promote the ongoing discussion in
the Church and world about the thought of Karol Wojtyla.

The discovery of tensions in any person's thought does not
of itself imply a rejection of that thought. The inability to make a
final synthesis may lie in the limitations of the interpreters. In
such a case the thinker studied may be kind enough to enlighten
his bemused commentators. Whether Pope John Paul II has time
for that task is another question. Moreover the discovery of
tensions does not imply that the basic insights of a thinker are
incorrect. On the contrary, too often a false, rationalistic consistency can lead superficial thinkers to ignore whole aspects of
reality and excogitate terribly mangled imitations of reality.
Various insights are usually necessary to balance each other off
in polar tension in order that the real might be more adequately
approached through theory. If the final, synthetic ground of the
Pope's synthesis has not yet been manifested to the contributors
to this volume, that need not prove disastrous. Rather they are
encouraged to probe deeper for the basis of that synthesis. Surely
it cannot escape notice that many of the intellectual issues
troubling the Church and Western society actually derive from
oppositions such as are discovered in John Paul II's thought.
Whereas many have despaired of discovering any unity and sense
in the contradictory play of position and counterposition —
witness the current vogue of deconstructionalist criticism in so
many fields of study at American universities — the Pope tries to
hold the oppositions in vital tension. In that he may best be

fulfilling his role as center of unity for the Church and the world. This vital center, mediating extremes, may also encourage various, opposed "schools" within the Church to go beyond too facile opposition, to reexamine their own positions, and to strive for a more complex, more adequate vision of reality. The current stand-off in Catholic theology is not healthy for the Church or for the disputing theologians and philosophers. An advance must be made, and perhaps the thought of John Paul II can serve as a basis for further discussion in mutual respect. Certainly the Jesuits participating in the conferences found ground for dialogue and unity in the Pope's thought. If their efforts, reproduced in this volume, can be of assistance to others in their ultimate quest for truth, then this volume will have achieved its purpose.

A final word of gratitude should be expressed to all those who contributed financially to the achievements of both conferences. They include the following provinces of Society of Jesus: Upper Canada, New York, California, Maryland, Chicago, New England, Missouri, as well as the legacy of Mrs. E. McDermott. The first conference was originally organized by T. Prendergast, S.J., and J. McDermott, S.J., and was greatly assisted at Loyola University of Chicago by R. Harvanek, S.J., and G. Gurtler, S.J. When the election of T. Prendergast to the position of dean of Regis College, Toronto, turned his attention to more pressing tasks, J. McDermott took responsibility for organizing the second conference. In that undertaking he received great support from B. Fiore, S.J., and from various members of the Jesuit Community at Fordham University. Several students of the Scots, Irish, English, and North American Colleges in Rome were kind enough to help the editor with correcting the proof sheets. Last, but not least, the Rev. Joseph Pittau, S.J., has merited our thanks for his encouragement of the Conferences and support of this publication.

JOHN M. McDERMOTT, S.J.

THE PHILOSOPHICAL FOUNDATIONS
OF THE THOUGHT OF JOHN PAUL II

Robert F. Harvanek, S.J.

Pope John Paul II (Karol Wojtyla) is both a theologian and a philosopher, but his teaching career was as a philosopher, that is, as professor of ethics at the University of Lublin. Though it is true that he had previously studied under Garrigou-Lagrange at the Angelicum in Rome and written his dissertation on St. John of the Cross, and his undisturbed professorship at Lublin was for only three years (1954/5 to 1957/8), his immediate preparation for the post at Lublin was a second doctorate in the ethics of Max Scheler. This had a dominant influence on his teaching and on his major philosophical work, *The Acting Person*[1]. Lublin, the only independent university in Poland at the time, was also a center of thomism. There are certainly aspects of thomism in Pope John Paul's thought.

This double background has given rise to a controversy about Karol Wojtyla's philosophical allegiance. Is he a Lublin Thomist (Andrew Woznicki) or a Schelerian phenomenologist (Anna Tymieniecka)? The obvious ploy is to say that he is both. But that still leaves the question as to how the two fit together. In any event, it is my view that one cannot understand Pope John Paul II unless he understands Max Scheler and the phenomenological movement of which he was part. I plan therefore to spend a large part of this paper in presenting the thought of Scheler as

---

[1] K. Wojtyla, *The Acting Person*, tr. A. Potocki (Boston: Reidel, 1979).

found in his major work, *Formalism in Ethics and the Non-Formal Ethics of Values*[2]. I will then show how Karol Wojtyla deals with Scheler in his own work, *The Acting Person*. This should lay the foundations for interpreting his later writings as Pope.

I. Scheler and Phenomenology

a) *Life and Influences*

Max Scheler was considered a genius in his own time. He was born in 1874 and died in 1928. He was a star in German philosophy and in the Catholic revival in Munich. He was eventually eclipsed by Heidegger, but his reputation was also affected by the political currents of the times. Part Jewish and also a Catholic for a number of years, he was opposed by the Nazis and not accepted by the scholastic philosophers and theologians in the Church. His personal life was not edifying and he eventually moved out of Catholicism.

His mother was a Jew and his uncle a rabbi. This was the strong religious influence from his parents which eventually seemed to show in his last years when Spinoza seemed to color his thought. His father was a negligent Lutheran. He himself became a convert to Catholicism in his teens and a leader of the Catholic revival that sprang from a group that formed around Husserl in his first period. Prominent names in that group were Dietrich von Hildebrand and Edith Stein. Others were the Jesuit, Caspar Nink, and Hedwig Conrad-Martius, a Protestant. Perhaps Romano Guardini belongs to the movement. As already mentioned, Scheler was not fully accepted by the Catholic philosophy and theology professors because he was not a thomist or scholastic. He had more affinity with Augustine and was

---

[2] M. Scheler, *Formalism in Ethics and Non-Formal Ethics of Values*, tr. M. Grings and R. Funk (Evanston: Northwestern U., 1973).

spoken about as Augustinus Redivivus, though he himself resented that tag. By the time he was mistakenly called to Cologne by Adenauer to buttress the Catholic thought in that university he had begun to move out of the Catholic Church and towards a kind of dualism and panentheism which is presented in his programmatic *Man's Place in Nature*[3], the one work that was broadly circulated in the United States in paperback. He was a volatile personality and his marital and women problems scandalized the German academic community, but his productivity was astonishing and most of it was produced during his Catholic period.

Scheler had earlier thought of studying medicine and had begun to do so. As a result he developed a background in science as applied to man. This explains his interest in the philosophy of human nature. When he switched to philosophy at Berlin, he studied under Dilthey, a move that further set his focus on philosophical anthropology. Dilthey was known as a vitalist who built an anti-Cartesian reaction to conceiving the human being as a union of spirit and matter. Descartes had mechanized life and life-functions and had effectively eliminated life from the plant, animal and human world except insofar as it was included in spirit. Dilthey reinstated life as a level of reality, and hence the vitalism category.

The other influence on Scheler was Husserl. He is sometimes spoken of as a disciple of Husserl but he certainly did not study under Husserl. Husserl is said to have repudiated Scheler and his type of phenomenology. Nevertheless Scheler can best be described as a phenomenologist, but he developed a style of phenomenology which may best be characterized as his own and which helped to locate him in the Augustinian tradition. He may have been influenced by and also influenced the Munich phenomenologists mentioned above who were disciples of Husserl's

---

[3] M. SCHELER, *Man's Place in Nature*, tr. H. Meyerhoff (New York: Farrar, Straus and Cudahy, 1979).

first period and critics of his later transcendental phenomenology period.

These phenomenologists saw Husserl as a response to the associationist psychology (Max Wundt) that dominated the philosophical scene at the time. It was a return, they thought, to the objective philosophy of essences that formed the staple of philosophy from the time of Plato's ideas. These essences as present in our minds and produced by us could be reflected upon and described. The strength of the movement was the talent the practioners had in recovering and describing the content of the ideas that our words expressed. The truth of the essence was in its own consistency (Spinoza) and it governed our thinking and judgments. One could distinguish between true and false essences somewhat the way Aristotle did between moral virtue and the vices at the extremes. The methodology had little use for logic of the Aristotelian-Stoic type or of the Frege style. Logic was useful for demonstration but not for discovery, nor did it really govern our intellectual life, especially the life of values. These are given to us as essences which command our response.

This Munich group of disciples of Husserl was dismayed when he continued his work in logic (he was a mathematician originally) and developed his transcendental phenomenology which showed him as a disciple of Kant's apriorism and not at all the objectivist they had first understood him to be. The true *a priori*s according to the Munich phenomenologists were the essences presented to the mind which needed experiences perhaps to bring them forward but not to validate them. The whole system of Scheler's philosophy of values places values in an in-between area between mind and sense and finds them present in all experience. Empiricism, as presented by Locke and Hume, and even Aristotle, is not the initiating experience out of which ideas emerge, but an abstraction from a holistic experience that already included values. Central to Scheler's philosophy was his theory of values. We will discuss that later.

b) *Contrast of Scholasticism and Munich Phenomenology*

Let me exemplify the above, especially the difference between scholasticism and Munich phenomenology, with a couple of anecdotes.

I had studied during regency under von Hildebrand at Fordham. Once during my theology studies at West Baden College, Indiana, I stopped in the office of our dean, Edwin Healy, S.J., who taught moral theology and had written a manual of scholastic moral theology. I noticed on his desk a book of von Hildebrand's which had just been published in English, *Fundamental Moral Attitudes*[4]. It was a slender volume which presented in the phenomenological mode five moral or ethical attitudes. I asked Fr. Healy how he liked the book. His response was that it had some interestings insights, but did not prove anything. For von Hildebrand the insights were the proof.

Some years later John Connery, who had replaced Healy in the chair of moral theology, came into my room with von Hildebrand's *Christian Ethics*[5] in hand. He had been asked to review it, but he could not get a handle on it. I tried to explain phenomenology to him and also show him how von Hildebrand was using it. John himself was in the tradition of the casuistry of Jesuit Moral Theology of the times. In the end John excused himself from the review.

Dietrich von Hildebrand was a disciple of Husserl and loved to recount how Husserl had said that of all his students he, von Hildebrand, best understood Husserl. At the same time von Hildebrand maintained that Husserl had switched directions and betrayed the movement and receded into Kantianism. Von Hildebrand had done his own dissertation in the realm of values. Dietrich on the other hand was a friend of Scheler's, perhaps

---

[4] D. VON HILDEBRAND, *Fundamental Moral Attitudes*, tr. A. Jourdain (New York: Longmans, Green, 1950).
[5] D. VON HILDEBRAND, *Christian Ethics* (New York: McKay, 1953).

Scheler's closest friend. His conversion to Catholicism had been influenced by Scheler, and this embarassed him when Scheler moved out of the Catholic faith. His philosophy was also influenced by Scheler. In fact, it could be argued that von Hildebrand's philosophy was the result of the harmonization of Scheler with contemporary thomism of the Maritain variety.

I believe that Dietrich von Hildebrand can be used as a model for understanding Karol Wojtyla. Wojtyla's philosophy can be understood as another version of the harmonization of Scheler with thomism, or at least Aristotelianism. And Wojtyla's method, as von Hildebrand's, was an adaptation of Scheler's phenomenology to thomistic and religious themes. Von Hildebrand was a much clearer writer than Wojtyla, possibly because he was more consistently a phenomenologist, whereas Wojtyla tends to mix phenomenology and metaphysics. For a time von Hildebrand was very popular in the Catholic community in the United States. His books were quickly translated into English and were easily read by the non-academic public. Wojtyla on the other hand is ponderous in his style and writes in the mode of Polish academics. His writings did not get translated until he became famous for other reasons, and he was not initially well served by his translators. Though he is sometimes identified with Lublin Thomism, he was strongly influenced by Scheler. Karol Wojtyla is not a pure thomist.

c) *Scheler's Philosophy*

Let me turn then to a summary presentation of Scheler's major work, *Der Formalismus in der Ethik und die materiale Wertethik (Formalism in Ethics and Non-Formal Ethics of Values)*. This is the work which Karol Wojtyla had in mind when he wrote *The Acting Person*. It should be kept in mind that Scheler was primarily an anthropologist in the European mode of philosophical anthropology. He revived interest in anthropology in Germany and can be seen as the influence behind Karol Wojtyla's promotion of the philosophy of human nature as the

primary need of our times. Though Wojtyla places his anthropology, in a good thomistic spirit, within the context of a philosophy
of being, I think it is more clarifying to relate him to neo-
Aristotelians like Alisdair McIntyre, or neo-Kantians like John
Macmurray, and to another admirer of Scheler, Charles Taylor,
for whom ethics is the primary discipline and anthropology takes
the place of metaphysics. *Formalism* both accepts Kant and
rejects him. It accepts Kant's thesis that ethics cannot be
teleological but must be founded in the immediacy of the
noumenal self. Consequently Scheler rejects Aristotelian and
scholastic ethics which is based on the end of man, whether
happiness or the glory of God. He also rejects or at least modifies
the scholastic philosophy of the good by drawing a distinction
between value and good. This is at the heart of his philosophy of
ethics. Value becomes a somewhat autonomous sphere which
governs the whole ethical realm. Values are not things; goods on
the other hand are things which possess values. I will return to
this topic later.

By the same token, Scheler rejects Kant's formalism of
practical reason. Scheler argues that values are given in intentionality and have a content by which they are diversified. He
presents a scale of values, each of which can be described
phenomenologically. As a result, ethics has a material dimension, that is, an objective content which can be compared to
Aristotle's and Aquinas' virtues. He also changes Kant's notion
of the *a priori* from the structure of reason forming the manifold
of experience to the intrinsic essence of each value. One can see
how his thought could be compared to Plato's, or to Augustine's,
and even to the thomistic notion of essence, though there are
many differences.

Scheler's theory of values needs a brief explanation. Values
are distinct from goods. They exist in a sphere of their own.
Scheler explains this sphere by referring to the Cartesian distinction between primary and secondary qualities. You will remember that Descartes reduced the physical world to extension which
he identified with primary qualities, since in his analysis, exten-

sion does not depend upon perception. The trees are still "out there real" (Lonergan's phrase) whether one sees or hears them or not. On the other hand, secondary qualities, e.g., color and sound, are dependent upon perception. In like manner things are independent of perception, but values are only given in intentionality. This can be compared in the scholastic system to universals in the absolute state abstracted from both the concrete individuals and from the formal and reflective universals. They are in the intentional order, but neither in the mind nor in the thing. Or it can been compared to the order of possibles which can be analyzed for their essential content which holds them together. They can be objects for the mind even though they may have never been experienced in reality. For example, von Hildebrand draws many of his examples of virtues or traits from literature, especially drama. The compatibility or incompatibility of notes is given in intelligibility.

Intentionality, therefore, is the principal sphere of philosophizing in Husserl's phenomenology and all philosophies influenced by him. In the Munich school, it was the givenness of essences that dominated rather than the constructing or projecting mind. The essences, in fact, commanded the mind.

The theory of values does not take up the whole book. Fully one-third of the 600 pages is given over to a theory of person. As Scheler himself says, the book is not really an ethics in the sense of the resolution of problems of action, but rather it lays the foundations of ethics. The philosophy of person which Scheler develops here is likewise the foundation for the development that is sketched out in *Man's Place in Nature*, and returns to what is probably Scheler's most important work contribution, the development of an anthropology.

In developing his theory of person, Scheler returns to his first interest in medical studies and in Dilthey's initial work in the humane sciences. It is necessary to remember that Scheler is not doing a metaphysics, not even a metaphysical anthropology, but a phenomenology, that is, describing how things are present to the intentional mind. One cannot think of a metaphysics of substance, or of an Aristotelian philosophy of animals and man. This will be a major difference between Scheler and Karol Wojtyla. On the other hand Scheler will be recognized as a kindred soul by people in the Greek tradition of the level theory of reality. All the levels of the cosmos are replicated in man: being, life, sense, reason, spirit. (I do not know how he is related to the *Schichtenlehre* (level theory) of German philosophy in the first half of this century.) The theory is anti-Cartesian in that it rejects the mechanization of life and refuses to reduce human nature to the dualism of mind and body.

Life is a primary category for Scheler. It is from life that energy is supplied to be guided by the mind. Mind on the other hand "comes in from outside" in Aristotle's language, that is, it is separate from life levels somewhat as *nous* is in Aristotle and needs the energy of life to be effective. This is what critics have referred to as the extreme dualism of Scheler, the distinction of spirit and human, or person and nature. Scheler does not treat this distinction under the category of mind itself but rather under that of person, and moral person in particular. "Person" immediately brings to the scholastic mind the rational individual in the tradition of Boethius' definition. That would be a misreading of Scheler. Person is in no way an individual substance. It is rather an act, and the act which unifies all the functions which make up a moral act. Person is not an ontological concept but a dynamic one. As a result, the person is not present until all the conditions for a fully functioning person are present. Thus, a fetus is not a person, nor even is a young child until he or she has become a moral adult.

As indicated already, Scheler's philosophy of person or spirit in man is comparable to Aristotle's *nous*, at least in the Averroistic exegesis. It also can be seen to fit with *Genesis* and the Creator breathing spirit into man and making him in the image and likeness of God. The point of departure for the idea of the divine for Scheler is not motion or change in the universe, or the universe at all, but rather the visage of man whom we encounter and in whom we perceive something that does not derive from the lower levels of man but shows its derivation from above.

Scheler goes on to describe person in its relationship to other persons in community. This is not something that arises in the human context only when adults encounter each other in the realm of justice, but is part of the very constitution of the person. Cartesian egoism and British individualism are unintelligible in the Schelerian analysis. His thought is, I believe, the origin of the notion of solidarity promoted in Poland by Karol Wojtyla and of the notions of I-Thou and We developed in an original fashion by Martin Buber. When we turn to Wojtyla and his *The Acting Person*, we should keep in mind that it was written with Scheler's *Formalism* on his desk. He certainly became acquainted with John of St. Thomas' thomism while doing his first doctorate at the Angelicum under Garrigou-Lagrange. But when he turned to ethics it is obvious that he considered Scheler the philosopher to be dealt with, and he modeled his own book on the second half of *Formalism*, the part where Scheler develops his theory of moral person. The Polish title of *The Acting Person*, literally *Person and Act* clearly shows the relation to Scheler, for whom the person is the act.

Before presenting Wojtyla's thought a brief reference to other similar thinkers may stimulate reflection.

A frequent reference in *The Acting Person* is Maurice Blondel's most influential *Action*[6], another work in foundational ethics and centered on action, that is, moral action, rather than intellect and will.

If one were to turn to Aquinas for parallels, one should not look to Aquinas' metaphysics, or even to his metaphysics of substance and person, but rather to his ethics. The brief prologue to the *Prima secundae* of the *Summa* defines the presupposition of what is the central and major part of the *Summa*; namely, that

---

[6] M. BLONDEL, *L'Action (1983)* (Presses Universitaires de France, 1950).

man is created in the image of God (Creator). As image he is intelligent, has free determination, and *the power to initiate action* (emphasis added), that is, he is an acting person.

One more reference may be helpful, though I am not aware that Wojtyla was acquainted with the work of the Scottish philosopher, John Macmurray. Macmurray's Gifford Lectures, *The Form of the Personal*, published in two volumes as *The Self as Agent* and *Persons in Relation*[7], is comparable to Wojtyla's work. There is the same centering in anthropology, and the same placing of the core of the human person in action. Macmurray goes on to found religion in man rather than in metaphysics. He does not however make use of the phenomenological method as do Scheler and Wojtyla and relies more directly on Kant. Macmurray also approaches interpersonal relationship through communication and language rather than through action and work.

II. WOJTYLA'S PHILOSOPHY

a) *The Action Person*

With this preparation then, it is possible to turn to Wojtyla himself and we can begin with *The Acting Person*. The context and the intent of the work is given in the Preface. Wojtyla follows the Polish style of referring to himself in the third person.

> Granted the author's acquaintance with traditional Aristotelian thought, it is however the work of Max Scheler that has been a major influence upon his reflection. In my overall conception of the person envisaged through the mechanisms of his operative systems and their variations, as presented here, may indeed be seen the Schelerian foundation studied in my previous work.
>
> First of all, it is Scheler's value theory that comes into question. However, in our times, when the differentiation of

---

[7] J. MACMURRAY, *The Self as Agent* (London: Faber and Faber, 1969); ----, *Persons in Relation* (London: Faber and Faber, 1970).

issues concerning man has reached its peak — introducing the
most artificial cleavages into the heart of the issues themselves —
it is the unity of the human being that it seems imperative to
investigate[8].

Clearly Wojtyla is not at all Cartesian, yet Scheler's philosophy of person, as mentioned above, is characterized by an
extreme dualism of spirit-person and life-body, or what comes
from above and what comes from below. While attracted by
Scheler's analyses of person, Wojtyla attacks the central problem
of dualism. He does not do this by refuting Scheler but by
making his own positive analysis. He sets aside Scheler's discussion of value and turns to the question of the person. Like
Scheler, he locates the full expression of the human person in the
human act, that is, the moral act. He does not do this, however,
by way of a scholastic objective and logical analysis of the human
act in the mode of Aristotle and Aquinas, but rather by
phenomenologically reflecting upon and describing the experience a subject person (he himself) has of acting. Hence he begins
his analysis with reflection on consciousness and the experience
of a subject in action. This leads him to a study of the experience
of being an agent, or as he puts it, the experience of efficacy.

His second discussion turns around the personal structure of
self-determination. This of course involves a treatment of will
and free-will. It is in the dynamism of freedom that the transcendence of the person is based. By transcendence, Wojtyla
seems to mean the independence of the person from subjectivity
and determinism. The person stands free of nature in an order of
transcendence. There is a cognitional dimension to the free act
too, of course, and that opens the person to the order of truth.

This is an important element in Wojtyla's analysis, the
position of truth in the human act. It rules, I believe, his
approach to administration and government. To understand this,
consider two approaches to truth, one pragmatic, the other

---

[8] WOJTYLA, *Acting Person*, preface.

cognitive. The pragmatic moves from the good to the true. That is, it determines what is good and proceeds to what will bring it about. This is in general Dewey's approach: we move from where we are to the next best thing, to what will improve our situation, and work to bring it about. Ultimate goals are pushed beyond the horizon. We work from next to next. The cognitive approach to truth is one with which we are all familiar. In the correspondence theory, truth is the correspondence between mind and reality. In cognition the mind judges what is actually the case. If what is asserted is actually the case, then truth is present. The good is a consequence of the truth; the truth is judged antecedently to the good.

An example might be drawn from current controversy over the ordination of women. One argument in favor of ordination is that the equality of women and men is a good, a matter of justice. But real equality will not be achieved if women are not permitted to be ordained. Therefore ordination of women is legitimate and should be permitted. The restrictive view argues in the opposite way. This view accepts as true a prophetic tradition which has not, for over 1900 years, practiced the ordination of women. Therefore it is judged to be part of revelation that the priesthood is restricted to men. But the truth and the good are convertible. Therefore, justice and the equality of the sexes cannot depend on the ordination of women.

Wojtyla's inclusion of truth in his analysis of action is not found, at least with the same emphasis, in Scheler and shows the influence of thomism. It also throws light on Pope John Paul's frequent reference to truth in his governmental policies and decisions.

In the same context of discussing the personal structure of self-determination or moral action, Wojtyla reflects on the character of the self-fulfillment or growth of the person in such moral acts. Aquinas, and the tradition, had pointed out the difference between the goodness of God and the goodness of the human being. God is complete goodness, in Him there is no growth or becoming. The human person however is good as a being, but he or she must become good by his or her moral action. This truth is commonly asserted, but I am not aware that it is explained. Wojtyla enters into the elements of this growth and lays them out. He concludes this discussion with a statement of his project: "The fact that in the performance of the action man also fulfills himself shows that the action serves the unity of the person, that it not only reflects but also actually establishes this unity"[9].

Wojtyla takes up Scheler's dualism of person and humanity under the rubric of transcendence and integration within the unity of person and nature. Transcendence over nature is manifest in free choice and in submission to truth. In Part III of *The Acting Person*, Wojtyla considers the question of integration, the unity of person and nature, the correlate of transcendence. It is here that Wojtyla discusses the classic distinction in the human being between soul and body, or rather, here he presents an alternative to that distinction. Remember that he is operating within his own subjective experience of himself in action. He is not, in other words, analyzing outer experience and from that perspective concluding to a soul within and distinct from his body. Nor is claiming to experience his soul. He is working with consciousness, including his consciousness of his body. Thus, he is closer to the psychophysical category of modern philosophy and psychology, but he finds that too empiricist in the objective sense.

He prefers the term "psychosomatic" to "psychophysical" and the term "*soma*" to "body". *Soma* expresses the experienced living body that the subject has and in some sense is, though he follows Luijpen rather than Marcel in the matter of both being and having one's body. The person is not identical with the body because it always transcends the body. In the process of action the body is not seen as separately and by itself, the container of the soul as in Plato, or even as the container for the guiding mind

---

[9] *Ibid.*, p. 184.

as in Aristotle, but rather as the complexity that is unified in action, and the passive and resistant element in action. In the dynamic perspective of the acting person the dualism appears in tensions such as freedom and determinism rather than in ontic relationships of soul and body. The *soma* expresses the person and at the same time determines many of its features. Wojtyla refers to the anthropological lists of personality types identified from their bodily types. We can think here of the Myers-Briggs characterologies or the Enneagrams, but with explicit correlation with body types. Earlier personality theory from Hippocrates through Kretschmer to Sheldon has tended to relate personalities to bodies. It is this tradition that undoubtedly Wojtyla has in mind[10].

It is in this context of psychosomatic integration that Wojtyla discusses the experience of emotions and their relation to action. It is here too that he briefly touches on the role of emotions in the perception of values and shows the influence of that part of Scheler's treatise.

> Both the emotional stirring and the emotions of the human being always relate to a value and are born out of this relation. This is true when we are angry and it is equally true when we love, mourn, rejoice, or hate. The reference in all these cases is to a value, and the whole emotion may be said to consist of this reference[11].

Yet emotions are "neither cognitive nor appetitive". They are, however, an indication of values that exist apart from emotions, values which exist "outside the subject having that emotional experience"[12]. These remarks reflect the philosophy of Scheler. I am not aware that Wojtyla discusses this topic at length anywhere else.

---

[10] Cf. C. HALL and G. LINDZEY, *Theories of Personality* (New York: J. Wiley & Sons, 1957), ch. 9.

[11] WOJTYLA, *Acting Person*, p. 248.

[12] *Ibid.*

Wojtyla continues to follow the sequence of Scheler's *Formalism*. In his last chapter Scheler takes up the social and historical dimension of person. Wojtyla does likewise and in the last part of *The Acting Person* proceeds to the question of the acting subject's relation to other subjects, that is, to other persons. He does this under the category of participation. However in a lengthy article published in *The Review of Metaphysics*[13] he picks up the same topic and reworks it. It may have been that he had not had time to edit the book before it was published. I take it that the article replaces at least a part of the section of the book dealing with community.

Wojtyla begins his analysis with a strong description of the acting subject or the individual self. It would be incorrect to say that he follows in the path begun by Descartes by making the ego the point of departure of the analysis of experience, but only because he puts the focus on action rather than on cognition. It is not so much that he rejects the starting point of Kant, Hegel, and Kierkegaard, but rather that he does it differently and in his view, of course, correctly; typically he does not debate the philosophers but simply phenomenologically lays out his own description.

b) *Wojtyla and Lubin Thomism*

This starting point with the self is a common position of Lublin Thomism. How much Wojtyla influenced that position I do not know, but it can be found presented in the philosophical anthropology written by M.A. Krapiec, O.P., the leader of Lublin Thomism, published in English in a reduced and edited form under the title *I-Man: An Outline of Philosophical Anthropology*[14]. I see this as a reading of the individual in

---

[13] K. WOJTYLA, "The Person: Subject and Community", *The Review of Metaphysics* 33 (1979), 273-308.

[14] M. KRAPIEC, O.P., *I-Man: An Outline of Philosophical Anthropology*, ed. and tr. M. Lescoe, A. Woznicki, T. Sandok, et al. (New Britain: Mariel, 1983).

Boethius' definition of person. It might be good to recall the scholastic definition of individual: *"indivisum in se et divisum a quolibet alio"* (undivided in itself and divided from everything else). Wojtyla quotes what philosophers say, "The 'I' is, so to speak, constituted by 'you'". However his explanation of that aspect of the "I" is different from that of the philosophers who use the phrase[15].

John Macmurray, for instance, sees consciousness of self as a response to the other who addresses me. In the chapter on Mother and Child in *Persons in Relation* his analysis points out that the child becomes aware of itself in relation to its mother and to the others of the human world who care for it and nurture it. Awareness of identity is a developmental concept which takes time to mature. Children commonly first use their name to identify themselves rather than the pronoun "I". At least that was the case in my own history. I can remember being teased because I said, "Bobby wants", rather than "I want".

Openness to the other in Wojtyla's analysis is, however, a characteristic of the human person, and every person finds himself in a plurality of persons. Nevertheless, that is not enough to understand the union which makes up community, properly speaking, between persons.

Wojtyla analyses the I-Thou and the We relationship to explain this dimension of the human person. Consistent with his focus on action he places communion in the phenomenon of many persons who "exist and act together". He uses the term "participation" to identify this feature of human beings. One should not be misled to understand participation in a Platonic or neo-Platonic sense, or even in a thomistic sense, to mean the creature's participation in the Creator. Here the direction is lateral, or side by side. "We" act together, the way husband and wife, or father and mother, act together to nurture and foster

---

[15] John Macmurray is the only philosopher I know that uses the language of constitution, though Buber and Marcel come close to it.

their family. It is not the external action which is intended, though that is included, but the intentional action of the persons as persons, which produces one common action and works for a common good.

The Lublin philosophers admit the influence of Maritain in this analysis of communion as distinct from simply living together in society. It is what distinguishes Catholic social philosophy from continental totalitarianism and British individualism. Person indicates relatedness while retaining autonomy. The relationship between person and community is dialectical and each must recognize the primacy of the other. This is a distinction which Wojtyla calls upon in all his writings as Pope. It is related obviously to the Solidarity movement in Poland and expresses the strong social sense of Wojtyla. Undoubtedly this has a value in Poland as a counterpart to the social attractiveness of Marxism. I recall a Jesuit provincial, Father Popeil, at an international philosophical meeting in Rome arguing how important it was not merely to refute Marxism but to present a philosophy that responded to Marxist issues and values. Nevertheless, despite this social emphasis, I consider Lublin Thomism's and Wojtyla's strong philosophy of the individual self a distinctive characteristic of the Pope and explanatory of his way of acting. I-Man is a primary category.

Perhaps I should explain my own stance with regard to person, since I suspect that all philosophers in the Aristotelian-scholastic tradition would empathize with the Lublin position once one granted the subject dimensions of the acting person. I understand person to indicate both a uniqueness and a relation, and the uniqueness is a function of the relation.

If one makes use of the etymology of the word, "person", or of the Greek near synonym, *prosopon*, a person is a communicator, an individual subject in dialogue, a member of a community from the start of existence. In fact a person is a respondent. That is, he is born from another person and is held in relationship until he becomes independent. When he develops in his existence, he develops in communication, responding to the affection of parents. brothers, sisters, nurse, responding to their speaking, knowing himself from their naming him. A person is the ultimate subject of rational communication. He grows into the I situation, becomes an isolated I only through alienation, or withdrawal from communion.

The result of this view is that community is a correlative of person, in fact precedes person. This of course may sound like Marxism, the primacy of the group over the individual, but that is true only if one is thinking of individuals and locates the principle of individuation in signate quantity; it is not true if one thinks of a person, that is, a speaker who is face to face with another. The ultimate relationship of course is with the Creator, who calls me by name into existence, and continues to call me into association with Himself in His community. Seeing is only a dimension of ultimate beatitude; the core is communion.

So, from this point of view I find Lublin Thomism excessively individualist and subjectivist. It starts out from the self instead of from the other. This possibly explains John Paul II's great personal strength and approach to his role as chief bishop of Rome and the Church. He is a teacher more than a listener, a decision-maker more than a synthesizer. This may derive from his experience as teacher and professor, but it also harmonizes with his philosophy of man.

III. Summary and Reflection

Let's summarize and reflect on what we have been studying.

1. John Paul II should not be interpreted from the perspective of neo-thomism or neo-scholasticism. He is not working in ontology or metaphysics, nor in Aristotelian epistemology and methodology. Rather, he should be interpreted from the point of view of Munich phenomenology and Scheler. He is working in philosophical anthropology and ethics. For him the philosophy/theology of man is the foundational and all-important discipline of our times, not man in the abstract, but in history and culture. This explains the importance he gives to the category of culture,

for culture is what makes historical man and what is made by historical man.

2. John Paul II gets his problematic and methodology from Scheler. Methodology cannot be completely separated from content. Methodology determines what questions are asked and how they are asked, as well as how they are answered. Ultimately the difference is between British empiricism and analytic philosophy on the one hand and Continental social and dialectical philosophy on the other; the difference is great and it is rooted in methodology.

3. But John Paul II responds to Scheler's reading of man with a knowledge of and sympathy for Aristotelian Thomism. However he approaches Aristotelianism though Schelerian anthropology. In that sense Karol Wojtyla was innovative and non-traditional. All his encyclicals and lectures (for example, his Vatican lectures on *Genesis*) are to be read from that point of view.

4. At the same time there is a conservative tendency in that philosophy, not in the sense of holding onto old teaching, but in the nature of Munich phenomenology itself. It is, as must have become evident from my earlier description, essentialist in its reading of experience and especially in its theory of values, and therefore in its ethics. It tends not to be empiricist. This is to be seen in Dietrich von Hildebrand's reaction to the changes in the Church after Vatican II. Like Maritain, he was very upset by the direction of philosophy and theology in the Church after the Council.

To illustrate this further, it helps to recall that there was, perhaps still is, a group that meets in Rome occasionally to study John Paul II's thought. The convener of the group is Josef Seifert, who was for a while on the faculty of St. Mary's College in Texas. But he was found to be too conservative, or unsympathetic to contemporary movements other than Munich phenomenology, and he eventually moved out to found his own institute and eventually moved back to Europe. He is also one of the principal movers of a Dietrich von Hildebrand Society.

And I have already pointed out the role that the primacy of truth plays in John Paul II's thought. This also is a conservative element in his governance.

5. Finally, I believe nevertheless that John Paul II leads us away from neo-scholasticism and towards contemporary philosophy of man and ethics. The significance and implications of that move remain to be worked out.

THE PHILOSOPHICAL FOUNDATIONS OF THE THOUGHT OF JOHN PAUL II

A Response

JOHN J. CONLEY, S.J.

Father Harvanek's study of the philosophical foundations of the thought of John Paul II convincingly places Karol Wojtyla's philosophy in the phenomenological tradition, more specifically the tradition of Max Scheler. In my remarks, I will apply this phenomenological hypothesis to John Paul II's encyclicals and exhortations. I believe that the pope's phenomenological background clearly shapes the distinctive methodology of his major papal writings. However, I also believe that the pope's philosophy of action owes more to scholasticism than Father Harvanek's analysis suggests.

The phenomenological method of John Paul II is apparent in a number of his major texts. This method differs from the scholastic or rationalist methods of argumentation inasmuch as it does not seek truth by establishing a proposition, proving the proposition through schematic evidence and refuting counterpropositions. The phenomenological method tends to examine a problem by moving from less to more adequate insights as it describes the various dimensions of a particular question.

The pope's phenomenological method clearly emerges in *Salvifici Doloris* (1984), an apostolic exhortation devoted to the question of human suffering. Stressing that suffering is a mystery rather than a problem (along the lines proposed by Marcel), the pope moves progressively from the most superficial to the most profound descriptions of suffering. He examines the technical approach to suffering, exemplified by medical science (SD 5). He examines the various types of suffering described in the Old Testament, with particular attention to the problem of moral suffering (SD 6-7). He describes the social dimensions present in the "world of suffering" (SD 8). He privileges the book of Job as a key witness against simplistic moralistic answers to the suffering of the innocent (SD 11-12). Finally, the pope meditates upon the conquest of suffering through love in the paschal mystery of Jesus Christ (SD 14-18). Even in this ultimate moment of theological analysis, however, the pope stresses that "man, in his suffering, remains an intangible mystery" (SD 4).

The movement of the pope's analysis from the narrowest (technological) to the broadest (the theological) dimensions of the issue indicates his phenomenological method. This successive deepening of the dimensions of suffering clearly differs from the theodicies common to both scholastic and rationalist natural theologies, which attempt to demonstrate the existence and goodness of God, given the data of natural and moral evil. In the pope's phenomenological reasoning, the medical perspective on suffering is not wrong. Rather, it is a partial perspective which, if not complemented by other approaches to suffering, can harden into materialism. Similarly, the argument of certain psalms that suffering is related to moral transgression is not erroneous but unbalanced, if not enhanced by Job's greater grasp of God's transcendence and the opacity of the suffering of the innocent. The phenomenological method moves successively from one perspective to another as the analyst moves to a progressively more "transcendent" (SD 2) consideration of the question.

Given this onion-peeling logic of analysis, the phenomenological method places great values on the attentive description of the various appearances of a question at each step of insight. In *Salvifici Doloris*, for example, the pope identifies no less than thirteen types of suffering present in the Old Testament alone (SD 5). Such careful description not only underlines the mystery and complexity of a question, which eludes reduction to a proposition. It suggests in passing the further insights to be gleaned by subsequent philosophers who ponder this inexhaustible question. This attentive description common to the phenomenological school explains the "meditative" quality which many commentators find in the pope's writings.

This phenomenological method explains in part the bewilderment which many American readers experience in reading the pope's declarations. Critics frequently complain that John Paul II is prolix and repetitious. After the pope released his encyclical on the Blessed Virgin Mary, an editorialist at *America* wondered why the pope had to mention all of these Marian apparitions in order to "prove his point". Of course, for most Americans, accustomed to scholastic and pragmatic reasoning, this meandering style of argumentation may seem tedious. For the phenomenologist, however, there can be no adequate exploration of truth without a patient — and inevitably lengthy — movement of analysis, a movement which progressively broadens the very perspectives of analysis. For a good scholastic like Pius XII, providing a precise definition of the dogma of Mary's Assumption, buttressed by textual proofs and concise refutations, indicates the truth concerning Mary's unique role in salvation. For a good phenomenologist like John Paul II, however, it is impossible to explore Mary's unique role without pondering the appearances of Mary to Catherine Labouré and Bernadette Soubirous. For the phenomenologist, the grasp of the truth concerning a particular question only slowly emerges through extensive rumination on the multiple appearances of the question.

The pope's phenomenological method also shapes his interdisciplinary approach to controverted questions. Earlier Church documents in this century often employed the two-step method of neoscholastic analysis. The question was studied from the viewpoint of natural reason (philosophy), then evaluated from the viewpoint of revelation (theology). Pope John Paul II intertwines the philosophical and theological perspectives in a study of problems rooted in the fundamental framework of anthropology. *Redemptor Hominis* (1979), the pope's inaugural encyclical, illustrates this interdisciplinary method. In meditating upon the mystery of human redemption, the pope interweaves christological (RH 7), soteriological (RH 9-10), anthropological (RH 10, 14), political (RH 17), sacramental (RH 20) and Mariological (RH 22) categories of analysis.

Many readers, especially academics, confess their confusion at the pope's melding of disparate disciplines. This stereophonic use of different disciplines to illumine a given issue seemed somewhat arbitrary. It followed neither the reason/revelation scholasticism of a *Rerum Novarum* nor the see/judge/act pragmatism of a *Progressio Populorum*. This fusion of perspectives especially baffled academics from an analytic background, accustomed to a strict separation of the disciplines and their respective methods. Like many phenomenologists, however, the pope shifts methodically from one perspective to another in order to provide multiple viewpoints on a given issue, since all these disciplines are ultimately united in the single science of anthropology: "Man is the principal route that the Church must travel in fulfilling her mission: he is the primary and fundamental way for the Church, the way traced out by Christ Himself, the way that leads invariably through the mystery of the incarnation and the redemption" (RH 14).

It is striking to note the difference between the kinds of reasoning used by the pope and that used by the Roman Congregations in their respective major texts. Although both reach identical conclusions, their methodologies diverge. The Sacred Congregation for the Doctrine of the Faith's *Quaestio de abortu* (1974) and *Jura et bona* (1980), for example, provide a clear distinction between "natural law" (QA 8-13; JB 13-18) and "divine law" (QA 5-7; JB 19-24) arguments on specific norms concerning respectively abortion and euthanasia. This neoscholastic method of analysis is clearly foreign to the synthetic interdisciplinary perspectives used by John Paul II in his own meditative defenses of traditional Catholic principles.

John Paul II's systematic intertwining of philosophical, theological and historical categories also indicates the influence of *la nouvelle théologie* on his method. Like phenomenologists, the artisans of *la nouvelle théologie* criticized neoscholasticism's nature/supernature dichotomy with its corresponding wall between philosophy and theology.

Despite the patent influence of phenomenology on John Paul II, there are certain neoscholastic influences in his writings. Father Harvanek rightly underlines the importance of Scheler and Blondel in Karol Wojtyla's philosophy of action. However, I think it is crucial to underline the pope's debt to neoscholastic theory in his analysis of the moral act, especially his emphasis upon the intrinsic evil of certain acts.

The pope's insistence that certain human acts are intrinsically wrong, therefore never capable of moral justification, emerges clearly in his analysis of sexual action. In *Familiaris Consortio* (1981), the apostolic exhortation devoted to family issues, the pope categorically condemns the acts of contraception (FC 29), fornication (FC 80) and the remarriage of divorcés (FC 84). The pope supports this critique of specific categories of acts by quoting the thesis of *Gaudium et Spes*: "The moral aspect of any procedure does not depend solely on sincere intentions or on an evaluation of motives. It must be determined by objective standards. These (are) based on the nature of the human person and his or her acts" (FC 32).

Strikingly, the pope's explanation of why these particular acts are morally unacceptable does not follow the teleological arguments of traditional natural-law theory. The pope analyzes artificial contraception thus: "The innate language that expresses the total reciprocal self-giving of husband and wife is overlaid, through contraception, by an objectively contradictory language, namely, that of not giving oneself totally to the other" (FC 32). The categories of culture, in this case language, displace the older categories of biology. Internal contradiction replaces frustration of ends as the *locus* of the moral evil. Nonetheless, in his repeated insistence that specific acts are universally wrong, the pope diverges from many phenomenological (Jankelevitch) and personalist (Janssens) ethicians who easily speak of "conflicts of value" and who refuse to condemn a particular act as wrong apart from the act's context of motive and circumstance.

This insistence upon the innate moral quality of specific acts squarely places John Paul II in the tradition of the neoscholastic manualists. Like the manualists, the pope carefully articulates particular norms of action in precise propositional form: "One may never directly kill an innocent human being" or "One may never directly sterilize a patient". This defense of precise moral norms situates the pope at the center of the dispute between traditionalist (Grisez, Finnis, Boyle) and proportionalist (Fuchs, McCormick) interpreters of natural-law ethics. The pope clearly sides with the traditional school. In his defense of exceptionless norms, the pope routinely rejects appeals to pastoral compassion or lesser evils or conflicts of duties, which would relativize these norms of action. In his philosophy of action, the pope refuses to remain at the level of a general description of moral action or moral values. The pope argues that an adequate grasp of anthropology must yield precise norms on particular categories of human action. The primacy of truth and the effective defense of human rights demand such crystalline clarification of specific human acts, with no concessions to subjectivism or relativism.

I believe that the distinctive union between phenomenological method and neoscholastic analysis of the moral act explains part of the difficulty many of us experience when reading the pope's documents. I often have the impression of banging into scholastic steel as I wander through the phenomenological fog. Not without ambiguity, the pope's distinctive fusion of human mystery and action norm serves his anthropological vision of a humanity summoned to divine communion but capable of Auschwitz.

THE THEOLOGY OF JOHN PAUL II

Gerald A. McCool, S.J.

John Paul II is better known as a philosopher and as a religious leader than he is as a theologian. This is understandable enough, since, before he became a bishop, Karol Wojtyla was a university professor of philosophy, and the best known of his scholarly works, outside of Poland at least, is still his treatise on philosophical anthropology, *The Acting Person*. He had made his reputation at the University of Lublin largely through his work in the area of Christian ethics, and, before he became a leading figure in the Church, it might have been easy enough simply to list him among the Polish Thomists who had managed to retain their influence behind the Iron Curtain after Thomism had ceased to be a major force in Western European thought. Wojtyla, it might then be claimed, had managed to keep his Thomism alive because he had broadened and up-dated it by drawing upon the resources of Scheler's phenomenology of values. Scheler's phenomenology of consciousness and its world of ideal values and Aquinas' realistic metaphysics of being had been incorporated, in different ways, into his personalist metaphysics of the moral agent; and, in the confined intellectual arena of Communist Poland, Wojtyla's personalist metaphysics had enabled Catholic intellectuals to argue for their Christian view of man and society as a philosophical alternative to the materialistic collectivism of their government's Marxist ideology. If Wojtyla's work were looked at from that angle, philosophy and politics would have furnished the points of view from which his writings would have been interpreted.

That way of looking at Wojtyla's thought might be plausible enough, as far as it went, but it could not do justice to the seriousness, unity, and scope of his speculative work. Wojtyla's early interest in culture was literary rather than philosophical in its orientation. In fact, he knew nothing about philosophy until he began his studies for the priesthood in the clandestine seminary linked to the University Faculty of Krakow after his own life of prayer had already been nourished by the mystical theology of St. John of the Cross[1]. It should not be forgotten that, before he began his doctoral studies at Lublin, Karol Wojtyla had already completed his doctorate in theology at Rome. The topic of his dissertation, *Faith According to Saint John of the Cross*, written under the direction of Réginald Garrigou-Lagrange, is significant[2]. His work on John of the Cross under Garrigou-Lagrange enabled the young priest to link his own religious experience both to the speculative tradition of the Carmelite Thomists of the Second Scholasticism and to the more recent synthesis of spirituality and culture which he found in the theology of Garrigou-Lagrange, the Thomistic synthesis by which Jacques Maritain's *The Degrees of Knowledge* had already been influenced[3].

Years later, after his elevation to the episcopate, he was to take a leading part in the theological discussions at the Second Vatican Council. *Sources of Renewal*, the exposition and inter- pretation of the Council's teaching which he wrote for his own archdiocese some years after his return, is a work of theological

---

[1] John PAUL II, *Be Not Afraid!* [Interviews with André Frossard] (Garden City, N.Y.: Doubleday-Image, 1985), pp. 16-18.

[2] Karol WOJTYLA, *Faith According to Saint John of the Cross* (San Francis- co: Ignatius Press, 1981).

[3] Jacque Maritain, *The Degress of Knowledge* (New York: Scribner's, 1959).

significance in its own right[4]. The view of the Council which we find in it appears again in John Paul II's major encyclicals, *Redemptor Hominis* and *Laborem Exercens*[5]. Both his personal experience and his academic training had accustomed him to think about his world in the transcendent context of theology and prayer. The metaphysics of St. Thomas and the spirituality of St. John of the Cross had unified his experience as a young priest as, centuries before, they had unified the experience of Carmelite and Dominican theologians in the Thomist tradition of Salamanca. His involvement in Vatican II would notably expand his theological horizon. Scheler's phenomenology of values would increase the importance given to self-awareness in his metaphysics of the acting person[6]. Despite its development, however, the metaphysics which he would use to integrate the teaching of Vatican II into his own experience of prayer and culture would remain, in its essentials, the metaphysics of St. Thomas. Although Vatican II became the great source of his later theology, John Paul II would remain a consistent Thomist theologian.

In that case, it should not surprise us that the theological writing in *Sources of Renewal*, the pastoral teaching of the encyclicals, and the metaphysical reflection of philosophical works, like *The Acting Person*, are linked to each other by an intrinsic connection[7]. From the time of his first discovery of

---

[4] Karol WOJTYLA, *Sources of Renewal: The Implementation of the Second Vatican Council*, tr. P. Falla (San Francisco: Harper and Row, 1980).

[5] *The Redeemer of Man* [*Redemptor Hominis*] (Boston, St. Paul Editions, n.d.); *On Human Work* [*Laborem Exercens*] (Boston: St. Paul Editions, n.d.).

[6] Anna-Teresa TYMIENIECKA, "The Origins of the Philosophy of John Paul II", *Proceedings of the American Catholic Philosophical Association* 53 (1979), pp. 16-27. Dr. Tymieniecka is a leading Polish phenomenologist who is well acquainted with the thought of John Paul II. She co-operated with him in preparing the revised test of *The Acting Person* for its publication in Holland and in the United States.

[7] *The Acting Person* (Boston: Reidel, 1979).

metaphysics as a factory worker and underground seminarian, Wojtyla realized that the intellectual framework which he needed to unify his personal experience of the world and God had to be an inclusive and coherent philosophy of being[8]. That was the reason why, both in his personal life and in his later pastoral activity, philosophy became a matter of supreme importance to him. But, since the goal of his philosophy was to make sense out of his own experience and to guide his human action, it had to be a genuinely living one. That sort of living philosophy moreover would have to be worked out by serious reflection on his own inner life and on the experience of the men and women who shared the life and culture of the community which formed him. Living philosophy for Wojtyla was the fruit of metaphysical reflection on personal and communal life and not just an account of academic systems. Even in the classroom he preferred to "do philosophy himself" rather than lecture upon its history. Over the years then, to use his own terminology, a metaphysics of man and being, born of his own reflection, became the unifying form of his conscious personal action[9].

In his own life this philosophy of being and action was used to reflect on the pastoral experience of a priest and bishop who had trained professionally as a theologian. It was used to integrate that pastoral experience with the spiritual life of a man of prayer formed through the spirituality of St. John of the Cross. Willy-nilly then, when John Paul II was forced to think and pray his way through Vatican II, he was bound to work out his own synthetic view of its theological message. That synthesis would reveal itself when, after the Council, he found himself compelled to implement the Council's teachings, first in his own archdiocese, and then in the Universal Church. Naturally enough, in the working out of his own theological synthesis, the development of his philosophy and the evolution of his theology would influence

---

[8] *Be Not Afraid!*, p. 17.
[9] *Be Not Afraid!*, p. 17.

each other. For, after all, the experience of Wojtyla, the metaphysician, whose Thomism would become a personalism under the influence of Scheler, of Wojtyla, the theologian profoundly influenced by his work at the Council, and of Wojtyla, the reflective pastor presenting the Council's teachings to a modern word closed to the values of freedom, spirit, and transcendence, was the integrated experience of the same acting person.

Wojtyla's First Dissertation

Wojtyla's Thomism evolved considerably in the years between the completion of his first dissertation and the publication of *Sources of Renewal*. In *Faith According to Saint John of the Cross* he studied the role of faith in the Carmelite mystic's experience of God in the context of St. Thomas' metaphysics of faculty, act, habit, and virtue. The living faith of St. John of the Cross, he explained, was the supernatural virtue perfecting the intellect of a soul elevated by grace and drawn to God by charity[10]. In the process of its growing purification, the mind's living faith gradually purged it of the discursive conceptual *species* which it had acquired by the abstraction of their content from sense experience[11]. And so, through the active and passive purification of its knowledge, the adherence of the believing intellect to God's revelation came to depend less on its natural operation as a mind and more on the infused light which it owed to its supernatural participation in God's own divine knowledge[12].

However, since the mind's infused supernatural knowledge came from the supernatural light of faith, its object could be nothing other than the revealed truth to which the assent of faith

---

[10] *Faith According to Saint John of the Cross*, pp. 237-38; 255.

[11] *Faith According to Saint John of the Cross*, pp. 241-43; 252-53.

[12] *Faith According to Saint John of the Cross*, pp. 255-57.

was given. Even in the mystical encounter with God of a mind purged of conceptual knowledge, the adherence of the intellect must still be given to the "substance" of the truths which it had already learned through historical revelation[13]. Furthermore, the ontological union of the mind with God, effected by the theological virtue of faith, was not sufficient of itself alone to account for the soul's encounter with God on the higher levels of contemplative prayer. In addition to faith, the infused theological virtue of charity had its own important role to play in the soul's ascent to God. For, as John of the Cross pointed out in *The Ascent of Mount Carmel*, the Holy Spirit sent His light into the prayerful soul through the inner working of His gifts; and the gifts of the Holy Spirit, formed into unity through charity, were the means through which the Third Person of the Blessed Trinity brought the habit of charity from potency to act[14]. It was the charity operative in living faith which gave the soul the strength it needed to adhere firmly to the "substance" of revealed truths in its interior life of prayer.

Thus the soul's elevation by grace and the infused theological virtues was the necessary condition for the ontological union between the mind and God on which its supernatural life of prayer depended. That ontological union with God however could not overcome the innate imperfection of knowledge through faith on the psychological level. Psychological imperfection in its knowledge of God inevitably accompanied the operation of a discursive intellect dependent for its knowledge on conceptual *species* abstracted from sense experience. Growth in faith therefore could never be equated with increasing clarity in the mind's conceptual knowledge of God. On the contrary, the growing firmness with which the faith, vivified by charity, adhered to God must be attributed to the increasing ability of the mind to dispense with conceptual knowledge of God derived

---

[13] *Faith According to Saint John of the Cross*, pp. 245-46; 259-61.
[14] *Faith According to Saint John of the Cross*, pp. 249-50; 257-58.

from abstracted *species* in its ascent through the stages of its active and passive purification[15]. That was why the mind, in its journey from the world to God, rose above the conceptual science of theology in order to adhere more firmly to the "substance" of revelation in the non-conceptual wisdom of prayerful contemplation. Contemplative wisdom therefore still remained a wisdom whose source was faith. For no knowledge of God's own inner being available to the human mind could be more direct or immediate than the knowledge given by God Himself in revelation and accepted by man through faith. Mystical knowledge therefore could never rise above historical revelation, and the faith, vivified by charity, through which the mind adhered to the "substance" of God's revealed mysteries, could never yield its place as the highest form of knowledge of God in the power of any human soul united to its body[16].

Thomists who were familiar with the theology of Garrigou-Lagrange would have found little difficulty in seeing its reflection in Wojtyla's dissertation. Wojtyla's analyses of faith in terms of nature, faculty, act, and virtue followed the general lines of the analyses of faith by Garrigou-Lagrange's own master, Ambroise Gardeil, and of other Dominicans in his tradition[17]. The distinction drawn by Wojtyla between St. Thomas' conceptual science of theology and the non-conceptual mystical wisdom of St. John of the Cross would have been familiar to readers both of Garrigou-Lagrange and of Jacques Maritain's *The Degrees of Knowledge*[18]. It would not be unfair then to say that, in its main lines at least, the theology of Wojtyla's first dissertation was close to the Dominican Thomism of Garrigou-Lagrange for which Jacques Maritain and the Toulouse Dominicans won quite a few adherents in the first half of this century.

---

[15] *Faith According to Saint John of the Cross*, pp. 251-61.

[16] *Faith According to Saint John of the Cross*, pp. 257-61.

[17] For Gardeil's theology of faith see Roger Aubert, *Le Problème de l'Acte de Foi* (Louvain: Warny, 1961), pp. 395-450.

[18] MARITAIN, *The Degrees of Knowledge*, pp. 310-83.

There is little reason, I would think, to argue that John Paul II would no longer stand behind his first dissertation today. On the contrary, my feeling is that he could still claim that, although his account of John of the Cross' theology was given through the categories of traditional Thomism, it remains substantially correct. Nevertheless, Wojtyla's way of "theologizing as a Thomist" when he wrote his first dissertation as a young priest was markedly different from his way of "theologizing as a Thomist" when he published his own theology of the Council as Archbishop of Krakow. Using the language of his own later Thomism, we might say that the theology of his first dissertation was built upon a metaphysics of universal "nature" rather than upon a metaphysics of the conscious concrete person. Its source, in other words, was the universal structure of man as such formulated in the universal concept. The closest that a metaphysics of that sort could come to man, Wojtyla would later say, would be a metaphysics of the "supposit", an individual subsistent endowed with a rational nature; and in a metaphysics of the "rational supposit" the unique inner experience of the acting person, by the very nature of the case, must be seriously downplayed. Conscious experience could not receive its due[19].

A metaphysics of "nature" or of the "supposit", Wojtyla would later claim, could no longer structure the theology required to deal with our experience of the modern world. The metaphysics used to underpin an effective theology today must be a metaphysics whose starting point was man as a unique free subject[20]. Its main focus must be fixed on man's experience of himself in his moral action as an agent aware of his own responsibility for the human acts through which he achieves his own self-fulfilment. Modern man's experience of his world calls

---

[19] See Karol Wojtyla, "The Person: Subject and Community", *Review of Metaphysics* 33 (1979), 273-308, esp. 274-76.

[20] Karol Wojtyla, "The Task of Christian Philosophy Today", *Proceedings of the American Catholic Philosophical Association* 53 (1979), 3-4.

for a metaphysics of concrete subjectivity which nonetheless remains unquestionably a metaphysics of being. For the experience on which his reflection is based is man's awareness of himself as an existing being, a subsisting agent whose own reality as a person manifests itself through the self-determining activity in which man must engage in order to possess and fulfil himself. By reflecting on his inner experience of responsible action, modern man became aware of his unique and inalienable dignity as a personal subject whose self-fulfilment demanded the self-giving love through which he was able to participate in the lives of other free persons[21]. For the responsible, self-giving love, rooted in the dignity of every personal agent, formed the bond of authentic *communio*, the genuine community of human beings. Through their failure to recognize his dignity as a personal agent, the practical and theoretical materialism of classical liberal capitalism and Marxist Communism had dehumanized man by making him either the servant or the product of impersonal economic forces lower on the scale of being than man himself.

Wojtyla's later Thomism therefore was a philosophy of conscious subjectivity and the concrete person. Its personalism however insured that it would be as hostile to an idealism of pure consciousness as it would be to the sensism or logicism of contemporary empiricism. The major flaw in the procedure of modern philosophy, Wojtyla believed, was its methical decision to isolate, abstract, and then reify a partial element of human experience[22]. In idealism, the reified element was pure consciousness; in empiricism and Marxism, it was either sense experience or the patterns of linguistic or economic relations.

---

[21] These ideas are systematically developed in Wojtyla's article, "The Subject: Person and Community". They are more extensively worked out in *The Acting Person*. For a brief summary and discussion of Wojtyla's personalism, see Anselm Min, "John Paul II's Anthropology of Concrete Totality", *Proceedings of the American Catholic Philosophical Association* 58 (1984), 120-29.

[22] Min, "John Paul II's Anthropology". See also Wojtyla, "The Subject: Person and Community", 278-79.

But in all these instances of methodical abstraction and reifica-
tion, the concrete reality and the personal dignity of man, the
responsible, self-determining agent was lost. Inevitably therefore
the concrete intelligibility of man himself had to be reduced to
the abstract intelligibility of something less than man. It follows
then that Wojtyla's subjectivity is not to be equated with the pure
consciousness of idealistic phenomenology. Subjectivity for Wojtyla meant man's awareness of his own subsistent being revealed
in its activity through what St. Thomas would call an immediate
act of *intellectus*. Through that act of intellectual self-awareness,
the concrete intelligibility of man revealed itself. Man was seen
to be a concrete agent, an existent who determined his own being
by acting upon himself and others, and who brought his own
perfection from potency to act as he did so[23]. Wojtyla's personalism then was an experientially grounded metaphysics of act and
potency, immanent and transient action, nature, finality, person,
matter, spirit, and the analogous grades of being. It was, in short,
a reflectively grounded and expanded form of Thomism[24]. The
distinctive mark which, in Wojtyla's mind, set it off from older
forms of Thomism, such as the Thomism of his former mentor,
Garrigou-Lagrange, was that the concrete intelligibility of the
consciously acting person, manifested through St. Thomas' act of
intellectus, had not been "pared down" to make it fit inside the
limits of man's general "nature" represented in the abstract
concept. On the contrary, the intelligibility of man's human
nature had been given its proper place in the structure of the
concrete intelligibility of the conscious, acting person. In the full
sense of the word then, Wojtyla's later Thomism had become a
philosophy centered upon the dignity of the conscious self-
determining agent and, through the self-giving love made possi-

---

[23] WOJTYLA, "The Subject: Person and Community", 280-84.

[24] For a comparatively brief account of Wojtyla's personalist Thomism, see
Andrew N. Woznicki, *Karol Wojtyla's Existentialist Personalism* (New Britain,
Ct.: Mariel Publications, 1980).

ble by that dignity, on the community formed by man's participation in the lives of other persons. The older Thomisms, as Wojtyla saw it, could no longer meet the needs of modern man because they could not do full justice to these vital elements of human experience.

Wojtyla's Thomistic personalism was the metaphysics which he later used to underpin his own theology of the Council in *Sources of Renewal*. He had worked it out gradually in the course of his own intellectual evolution over a period of years. During his graduate studies at Lublin, he had been attracted, as were a number of Catholic thinkers at that time, to Scheler's phenomenology of the person and of the hierarchy of values manifested in the world of personal consciousness. One sign of that attraction was Wojtyla's second doctoral dissertation, published at Lublin in 1959, *Evaluation of the Possibility of a Christian Ethics Upon the Assumptions of Max Scheler's Philosophy*. A number of the distinctive characteristics of Wojtyla's Thomist personalism could be attributed to the abiding influence of Scheler. Among these would be its hostility to Kantian formalism in ethics, the importance which it gave to self-giving love in its philosophy of community, and the role which it still assigned to intentionality in the grasp of ethical values[25].

Despite his attraction to Scheler however the idealism implicit in the latter's philosophy of consciousness its consequent failure to do justice to the role of will and man's power of self-determination in his ethical action made it impossible for Wojtyla to make Scheler's phenomenology of values the foundation for his own Christian ethics. That became clear in 1969 when the Polish edition of *The Acting Person* was brought out at Lublin under the title *Osaba i Czyn*. Western readers had to wait another decade to become familiar with Wojtyla's major work when its second revised edition was published in 1979. Nothing

---

[25] TYMIENIESCKA, "The Origins of the Philosophy of John Paul the Second", 18-21.

essentially new was added in that edition, however, and Wojty-la's personalism had been worked out in its main lines by the time that the Polish edition of *The Acting Person* appeared.

Wojtyla's work at the Council took place in the decade between the completion of his study on Scheler and his system-atic exposition of his own philosophical anthropology in 1969. From 1962 to 1965, as a bishop and then as an archbishop, he took an active part in the shaping of the Council's documents on Christian Revelation, the Church, the Place of the Church in the Modern World, the Liturgy, and Religious Freedom[26]. The Council's focus on Christology, the Church, history, and reli-gious liberty reinforced the concern for the person and commun-ity which he had shown in his own speculative thought; and the combined influence of both Wojtyla's involvement with the Council and his own decade-long intellectual development on his theology was seen in *Sources of Renewal*, Wojtyla's theology of the Council, published in 1972, six years before he exchanged the See of Krakow for the See of Rome. In the structuring of his theology in that book, Wojtyla's personalist metaphysics was coherently employed.

SOURCES OF RENEWAL

Reflecting Wojtyla's involvement with the Council's *Dogmatic Constitution on the Church* [*Lumen Gentium*] and its *Pastoral Constitution on the Church in the Modern World* [*Gaudium et Spes*], *Source of Renewal* centered its attention on Vatican II's theology of the Church. The progress of Wojtyla's thought in his account of the Council was guided by a number of the leading ideas with which our consideration of his early works has made us familiar. Among these were faith, consciousness, self-determination, and the free agent's participation in the lives

---

[26] Basil HUME, "Foreword to the British Edition", in Karol Wojtyla, *Sign of Contradiction*, 1979), p. x.

of other persons through the authentic *communio* brought into being by self-giving interpersonal love. The Church's aim in the Council, Wojtyla explained, was to link her faith-given consciousness of herself with the consciousness of every man and woman alive today. Guided by her awareness of herself as a supernatural *communio*, a community of free agents, whose mission was to preserve and foster the personal dignity of each one of them, the Church felt a special urgency to speak to the men and women of the modern age[27]. For, in our times, millions of human beings felt themselves deprived of their personal dignity and alienated from the society in which they lived through the harsh and impersonal pattern of its social and economic life[28].

Every Christian therefore was urged to enrich the supernatural faith through which he was able to participate, as an individual member, in the ecclesial faith of the Church herself[29]. Faith was the source of the Church's conscious awareness both of her own nature and of the relation which linked her to the Triune God from whom she came[30]. The God who united Himself to every man and woman through His Church was the Father who had created the material and the spiritual universe. He was the Son whom the Father had sent to redeem the world after it had fallen from grace through sin. He was the Holy Spirit, sent by the Father through the Son to vivify individual souls and to form the *communio* which was able to become the People of God because first, through the crucified Incarnate Word and the Holy Spirit, it had been joined to Christ as the Mystical Body of which he was the Head. The Church therefore was the gift of the Triune God to every man through the redeeming death of Christ[31].

---

[27] *Sources of Renewal*, pp. 19-34, 114-121.
[28] *Sources of Renewal*, pp. 48-52, 264-69.
[29] *Sources of Renewal*, pp. 15-25.
[30] *Sources of Renewal*, pp. 35-41.
[31] *Sources of Renewal*, pp. 45-65, 86-97.

In Christ's Mystical Body then every responsible agent had his own God-given place and his own irreplaceable work had been assigned to him[32]. For, as the People of God, the Church had to carry on God's creative and redemptive work through the whole extent of human history until the end of time[33]. As one of the People of God therefore each individual Christian had his own proper vocation to arrive at his personal fulfilment through the temporal work allotted to him. The Church's members were not interchangeable parts in the *communio* of faith and love, as modern men often felt themselves to be in the impersonal collectivity which passed for society in the liberal West or the Communist east. Christians could never be interchangeable parts of an impersonal whole, since every one of them was called, in the measure of his own distinct vocation, to participate in the three-fold office of the redeeming Christ[34]. As prophet, each Christian was called to share, in his own way, in Christ's personal mission of salvific witness[35]. As priest, he was called to share as well in Christ's personal and sacramental life of prayer[36]. And as king, he was asked to share in a two-fold task. The first "regal" task assigned him was the achievement of personal self-mastery by consciously "determining himself" to follow the path of moral virtue in his own life. The second "regal" task assigned him was obedience to the command which God had given to man in *Genesis*. He was to "subdue the earth", and, by doing so, to arrive at the fulness of his personal dignity by making the earth fruitful through the work of his mind and hands[37]. In Wojtyla's theology of the Council, manual and intellectual labor was much more than a punishment imposed on man because of sin. As a participation in God's creative work, labor was a good with a

---

[32] *Sources of Renewal*, pp. 114-121.
[33] *Sources of Renewal*, pp. 182-87.
[34] *Sources of Renewal*, pp. 120-21, 133-36.
[35] *Sources of Renewal*, pp. 243-50.
[36] *Sources of Renewal*, pp. 221-30.
[37] *Sources of Renewal*, pp. 261-69.

positive value of its own. But, like the earth which it rendered fruitful, work could never be an end unto itself. Man was the only creature in the material world which God loved for its own sake[38]. Labor then, like the rest of material creation, must be subordinated to the dignity of the rational agent who performed it and for whose good it was intended. Consequently man's human dignity could never be subordinated to the interests of productive work itself[39].

Faith, in Wojtyla's theology of the Council, was not simply a faith of profession. It had to be more than the assent of the Christian's intellect to the revealed truth which the Church proclaimed about herself. It had to be a faith of vocation as well[40]. By faith of vocation Wojtyla understood the conscious commitment of each individual Christian to live out his own vocation in the modern world in the light of his supernatural faith. Enriching that supernatural faith of vocation in the Christians of his own archdiocese was the goal which had moved Wojtyla to write his *Sources of Renewal.* But, if that goal were to be achieved, Wojtyla believed, he must foster in the Christians for whom his book was written the fundamental conscious attitudes toward God and the world which their vocation to live in a *communio* of faith and love required of them. Wojtyla's convinction of the important place of fundamental moral attitudes in Christian living is one more indication of the abiding influence of Scheler on his thought. The same concern was often expressed by Dietrich von Hildebrand, Scheler's friend and colleague, with whose *Christian Ethics* Wojtyla was also familiar[41].

---

[38] *Sources of Renewal*, pp. 62

[39] These points are brought out forcefully in John Paul II's encyclical, *On Human Work* [*Laborem Exercens*], pp. 11-19.

[40] *Sources of Renewal*, pp. 58

[41] *Sources of Renewal*, pp. 203-04, 367-68, 421. Wojtyla refers to von Hildebrand in "The Subject: Person and Community". Von Hildebrand was a friend and colleague of Max Scheler. Through Joseph de Finance, S.J., a colleague of Bernard J.F. Lonergan during his years on the faculty of the

In *Sources of Renewal*, however, the proper structuring of the conscious fundamental attitudes required for an authentic life of faith was linked by Wojtyla to the proper ordering of revealed truths demanded by the logic of the Church's faith. In the Creed, he pointed out, the Church's confession of her own divine origin followed upon her confession of the prior truths on which her knowledge of her own nature rested. In proper order, these prior truths were the creation, the incarnation and redemption, and finally the sending of the Holy Spirit[42].

The logic of faith through which revealed truths were ordered was most important, according to Wojtyla, for a proper understanding of the Church's consciousness. In the logical order of faith, the origin of the Church was subsequent to the Father's mission of His Son, and of His Holy Spirit, through His Son, to perform the work of divine redemption[43]. In that case, the redemptive work of Christ had to be at the center of the consciousness which the Church possessed of her own origin and nature. Wojtyla's theology of the Church therefore was built upon a prior theology of the Trinity and the Incarnation[44]. For it was through the work of the redeeming Christ that His Spirit came to dwell in the Church which was His Body; and it was because the *communio* of faith and love had been formed into Christ's Body that every one of the People of God was sent in turn by Christ and the Holy Spirit on his own mission of salvation to the world.

That was why, for Wojtyla, the vertical dimension of the Church's consciousness had necessarily to be the primary dimension. For it was the vertical dimension of the Church's consciousness which made her aware that she had come from God, and

---

Gregorian University at Rome, von Hildebrand's philosophy of values was taken over and modified by Lonergan in the latter's *Method in Theology* (New York: Herder and Herder, 1972), pp. 30-31.

[42] *Sources of Renewal*, pp. 35-41
[43] *Sources of Renewal*, pp. 53-65, 206-07.
[44] *Sources of Renewal*, pp. 57-59, 66-100.

that she had been sent by the Father, through the Incarnate Word and the Holy Spirit, on her own horizontal mission to the world that God first created and then redeemed[45]. In the order of grace, as in the order of nature, everything came from God and was destined to return to him. There might be a temptation to over-emphasize the horizontal dimension of the Church's consciousness today, due to Christians' new concern for dialogue with the modern world. But to yield to that temptation, he was convinced, would seriously harm the Church. For unless the vertical dimension of her consciousness was clearly seen to be the primary dimension, the vision of the Church which formed the attitude of Christians in their apostolic outreach to the world could become distorted[46].

WOJTYLA'S LATER THEOLOGY

In *Sources of Renewal* Wojtyla gave the most complete and systematic presentation of his own theology. It was, as we have seen, a synthesis which received its inspiration from the documents of Vatican II and which took its structure from Wojtyla's personalist metaphysics. Person and community, consciousness, freedom, and responsible love were among the categories called upon most frequently in Wojtyla's theology of man's relationship to God and to his fellow men in the redemptive *communio* of Christ's Mystical Body. Man, Wojtyla claimed, should not be called the image of the Trinity simply because his mind could know the world and the God who had created it. Nor did man deserve to be called God's image because his human will, guided by his intellect, had the power to perform good actions freely. Wojtyla's theology of man therefore would carry him beyond the classic Thomist metaphysics of man's faculties in justifying man's claim to be called the image of the Trinity, just as his philosophy

---

[45] *Sources of Renewal*, pp. 36-41, 397-408.
[46] *Sources of Renewal*, pp. 267-271.

of man had carried him beyond the classic Thomist metaphysics of universal "nature" in its account of man as a conscious acting person. Like his philosophical anthropology, Wojtyla's theology of the image of God in man also bore the mark of his personalism.

The Triune God, from whom both the order of creation and the order of redemption came, Wojtyla explained, was an infinite *communio* constituted by the self-donation which each divine person made of himself to the others. In the Trinity then, to be a person meant to give oneself completely to other persons. And for that reason the Triune God was a *communio* of loving circumincession. As a participated image of the Trinity, each responsible agent was called as well to achieve the perfection of his own personhood by entering into the *communio* which personal agents brought into being by their free donation of themselves to one another[47]. Thus, in the order of creation, finite acting persons were moved to give themselves to other persons in the *communiones* formed by marriage, the family, and the more extensive societies of their human world. So too, in the order of grace, in which alone, the fulness of man's perfection as God's image could be reached, every human person was called to join himself to God by freely entering the *communio* of the Church and forming his conscious attitudes toward God, the world, and his fellow men by participating in the Church's own faith-given consciousness.

For man to do that, however, he had to be able to love the world's Creator more than he loved himself. But such ordered love of God was a love of which, before his redemption by Christ, no man was capable. Therefore, in order to be able to meet the demands of his own personhood, every man had first to turn to his Redeemer through an inner conversion of his mind and will. The cross of Christ, from which flowed the grace

---

[47] *Sources of Renewal*, pp. 61-62, 133-138.

required for that conversion, was therefore both the sign of man's salvation and the source of his human hope.

Yet, as Wojtyla said in his *Sign of Contradiction*, the retreat which he preached to the Papal Curia in 1976, Christ's self-revelation through His death on the cross would always remain a provocation to a sinful world. For the incarnation and the death of Christ confronted men who would like to be self-sufficient with a self-giving love to which their own pride and concupiscence were radically opposed[48]. Thus, in the successive meditations of Wojtyla's *Sign of Contradiction* the self-revelation of the incarnate and suffering Christ was presented to his hearers as a challenge to commit themselves to its truth with the living faith which sprang from personal conversion[49].

The God who revealed Himself in Wojtyla's *Sign of Contradiction* was the God of infinite majesty who had promised redemption to man in the convenant made with our race after its fall[50]. He was the Father who had then manifested His own self-giving love through the redeeming death of His incarnate Son[51]. Revealing Himself to man through the life and death of His own Son, God had also revealed to man the meaning of man's own reality and man no longer remained a mystery to himself[52]. God had enabled him to recognize his own dignity as a moral agent and to learn of the supernatural dignity which Christ, as a sacrifical priest, had conferred on every human being by giving him the power to commit himself in love to God and to his fellow men[53].

Thus the spirituality of Wojtyla's *Sign of Contradiction* flowed from the Christology and the anthropology which Wojtyla had proposed in his *Sources of Renewal*. Through the sequence

---

[48] *Sign of Contradiction*, pp. 28-32, 163-165.
[49] *Sign of Contradiction*, pp. 81-90.
[50] *Sign of Contradiction*, pp. 9-26.
[51] *Sign of Contradiction*, pp. 25-26, 150-51.
[52] *Sign of Contradiction*, pp. 101-02.
[53] *Sign of Contradiction*, pp. 130-41.

of its meditations Wojtyla was trying once again to enrich the
faith of vocation in his listeners by reminding them that living
faith had always to be the fruit of a struggle against the resistence
to it still operative in unconverted men. In a world which had
fallen from grace through sin, the counter-claim of human
self-sufficiency could always be expected to raise its voice in
contradiction to Christ's call from the cross to conversion and
redemption. And, in the will of fallen man, a counter-attitude of
resolute self-seeking could be expected to resist the attitude of
self-giving love revealed to the world through the sign of Christ's
redemptive death.

The *communio* formed by the love of responsible persons
for one another was made the basis as well of Wojtyla's defense
of the Church's sexual morality. This was evident in a number of
his publications, such as the article, "The Person: Subject and
Community", written for the *Review of Metaphysics* in 1976 and
his address, "Fruitful and Responsible Love" given to a Congress
on *Humanae Vitae* at Milan on the tenth anniversary of Pius VI's
encyclical[54]. Responsible love, Wojtyla argued, like every responsible human act, must be conformed to the truth made
known by the mind's conformity to reality. No moral agent could
possess himself through an act of responsible self-determination
unless that act respected the essential structure of his own human
person. Responsible love between man and woman formed the
"we" which structured the *communio* of marriage and the family.
As responsible agents then, both man and woman must respect
the intentionality of the act through which that "we" is formed.
Each of them was responsible both for the love which they gave
their partner and for the love given back to them in return[55]. The
respect demanded of them for that two-fold love in marriage
required the exclusiveness, the permanence and the fruitfulness
of their marital *communio*. Wojtyla's reasoning, it is true, ran

[54] *Fruitful and Responsible Love* (New York: Crossroads, 1979).
[55] "The Subject: Person and Community", 292-99.

along the lines of traditional natural law morality, but here once more in his personalist theology a metaphysics of "nature" had been expanded into a metaphysics of the responsible acting person[56].

Those of us who are familiar with John Paul II's first encyclical, *Redemptor Hominis*, will recognize in it the Christology, anthropology, and metaphysics of *communio* which we have found at work in Wojtyla's *Sources of Renewal* and *Sign of Contradiction*. The same personalism also permeated John Paul's encyclical on Human Work, *Laborem Exercens*. God had given man the command to "subdue the earth" in *Genesis* and man's intellectual and manual labor was his own finite participation in God's creative work[57]. But, work, like the earth, was ordered to man as its goal. Man's increase in personal dignity was the end to be achieved by it[58]. The materialism of liberal capitalism and Socialist collectivism erected a false opposition between capital and labor in the nineteenth century[59]. In reality however no such opposition could be found. For the concrete ground required for the existence of both capital and labor was the human person, through whose labor capital was produced[60]. The Socialism of the nineteenth century had indeed fostered an admirable solidarity among the workers exploited by the entrepreneurs who employed them; but the materialist collectivism of Communist society today could sustain no such solidarity[61]. For, in Marxist materialism, man himself becomes no more than the product of his own work[62]. The only true solidarity between capital and labor will be found in a society whose economic relations are governed by a proper understanding of man's

---

[56] *Fruitful and Responsible Love*, pp. 16-26.
[57] *On Human Work* [*Laborem Exercens*], pp. 11-15.
[58] *On Human Work* [*Laborem Exercens*], pp. 15-17, 22-24.
[59] *On Human Work* [*Laborem Exercens*], pp. 31-37.
[60] *On Human Work* [*Laborem Exercens*], pp. 29-31, 37-38.
[61] *On Human Work* [*Laborem Exercens*], pp. 19-21.
[62] *On Human Work* [*Laborem Exercens*], p. 33.

dignity as a free person. The value of labor ultimately rests on the dignity of man who produced capital by "subduing the earth" and "making it fruitful" at God's command.

WOJTYLA'S PLACE IN CATHOLIC THEOLOGY

As we have seen, Wojtyla's theology, in its main lines at least, is an exposition and practical application of Vatican II's theology of the Church. For Wojtyla therefore the Church is a *communio* of free persons whose origin is due to the Father's sending of His Son and His Holy Spirit so that, through her, their salvific mission might be carried on through time. The Church in which the vivifying Spirit lives then becomes, for Wojtyla, the Body of the redeeming Christ. *Lumen Gentium* had tied its theology of the Church to its theology of the Trinity and the Redemption and so, for that reason, like many other post-Conciliar theologies, does the theology of John Paul II. *Gaudium and Spes* presented its theology of the Church to the modern man who must grapple with the problems of contemporary society, and the same anthropological focus is characteristic of the theology of Wojtyla. The theology of *Lumen Gentium* and of *Gaudium et Spes* was then, as we have seen, very much in harmony with Wojtyla's own metaphysics of the subject whose personal self-development required a responsible commitment to the communities in which he lived.

The Council's link of its Trinitarian theology and Christology to its theological anthropology may well provide the explanation for a number of similarities which can be observed between the theology of Karol Wojtyla and the theology of Karl Rahner. For, as far as I can see, Rahner had no direct influence upon Wojtyla. Nevertheless, in both of their theologies, a metaphysics based upon the experience of the free self-conscious person links the Church to the Trinity and the Incarnation and grounds an intrinsic continuity between the orders of creation and redemption. In both theologies as well, great importance is placed upon the positive value of human work as a participation in God's creative activity, and the goal of human work is to bring creation to its fulfilment at the eschaton. Both theologies therefore are theologies of the person, community, and both promote the value of productive work and highlight Christ's second coming as the goal of human history.

Both *Lumen Gentium* and *Gaudium et Spes* had been influenced by the reflection upon the personal and communal value of productive work made prior to the Council by theologians, such as Henri de Lubac, who were endeavoring to respond to the challenge of contemporary Marxism. Both of these Constitutions had also been influenced by the strong current of personalist thought which made itself felt in Catholic philosophy and theology during the nineteen forties and the nineteen fifties. The effects of this Catholic personalism could be seen in Catholic thinkers as diverse as Henri de Lubac, Dietrich von Hildebrand, Jacques Maritain, and Gabriel Marcel. It was, in all probability, this personalist current of thought which lay behind Wojtyla's attempt to assimilate the value philosophy of Scheler into his own Thomism. For, a few years earlier, it had already moved the Jesuit Thomist, Joseph de Finance, to make the same attempt, and, by doing so, to introduce the value philosophy of Scheler into the ethics of his colleague at the Gregorian, Bernard Lonergan, in the latter's *Method in Theology*.

Despite this fact, however, and despite the prominent place assigned to *intellectus* in *The Acting Person*, there is little evidence that Wojtyla was directly influenced by any of the Transcendental Thomists. Nor is it likely that he would have been. The principal sources of the Polish Thomism in which he had been formed were the Thomism of Louvain, and the Thomisms of Maritain and Gilson. Not even the Polish Jesuits were likely to have turned for inspiration to either Maréchal or Rousselot, as their Frence confrères had done in the years between the wars. Jesuit Neo-Scholasticism in Poland had been formed in the tradition of the Jesuit faculties of Austria and Germany; and, until after World War II, that tradition was still firmly Suarezian.

But, although Wojtyla himself has not done so, there are aspects of his thought which could be developed by drawing upon the contributions made by the Transcendental Thomists. One of these might be Wojtyla's theology of faith as a participation in the consciousness of the Church. Karl Rahner addressed himself to the same topic in his earlier writings on the development of doctrine; and in his account of the relationship between the abiding non-conceptual consciousness of the Church and the historical series of the Church's conceptually structured dogmatic statements, Rahner made effective use of his celebrated distinction between transcendental and categorical revelation. That distinction, as we recall, rested, in its turn, on St. Thomas' earlier distinction between *intellectus* and *ratio* — a distinction which has been exploited with considerable success by Bernard Lonergan in his *Method in Theology*. Through his own development of that distinction — drawing upon St. Thomas' account of the role of insight in the abstraction of the concept — Lonergan has been able to make a persuasive case for a genuine identity of meaning even when, in diverse historical periods, that meaning has been expressed through a succession of logically discontinuous conceptual frameworks. Wojtyla then might well look to Lonergan for help in his own effort to explain how the Church's communal faith could remain the same, as he claims that it must, through its successive expressions in the series of her ecumenical councils. In this way, the theologies of Rahner and Lonergan, which continue and expand the Thomism of Maréchal and Rousselot, could support and extend Wojtyla's theology of the Church's communal faith, which he claims remains the same, through its development in history. For it is virtually the same metaphysics of *intellectus* and the judgement, which Transcendental Thomism has developed, which we find in *The Acting Person*.

Furthermore, as we have seen in our discussion of Wojtyla's transformation of the metaphysics of man as the image of the Trinity into a metaphysics of person and community, Wojtyla can be numbered among the late twentieth century Thomists who, like William Norris Clarke in our own country, have made it their aim to expand and, if need be, revise Thomistic metaphysics by centering it on the knowledge of the individual conscious subject derived from philosophical reflection on interpersonal activity. In its general outline therefore, Wojtyla's thought belongs to the stream of personalist Thomism, whose origin can be traced to the nineteen forties and nineteen fifties. This was a stream of Thomism which, as we have seen, left its mark upon the documents of the Council itself, and which, in the hands of later representatives, such as Wojtyla, continues to influence the theology of the post-Conciliar Church.

THE THEOLOGY OF JOHN PAUL II

A Response

John M. McDermott, S.J.

Since Fr. McCool was my professor of metaphysics, who more than any other taught me to think systematically, it is difficult for me to criticize him, especially after his very fine presentation of John Paul II's thought. Nonetheless, some comments rendering more precise some of the tensions in the Pope's thought might help to locate him in twentieth century Catholic thought. As Fr. McCool noted, the young Wojtyla's metaphysics presupposed universal natures while his later thought started with the individual, conscious, free person[1]. In the world of Garrigou-Lagrange being, i.e., all reality, was conceptualizable. As a result propositional truths of faith, calling for an intellectual assent, were expressed in concepts. These truths, as supernatural, exceeded the direct grasp of human intelligence and had to be accepted on the authoritative testimony of Christ and His Church; the witnesses' veracity was assured by miracles and the fulfilment of prophecies, both culminating in the resurrection. Since revelation closed with the death of the last apostle, there was little room for the development of dogmas except by way of conceptual precision and

---

[1] That Wojtyla was aware of the change is clear in *The Acting Person*, tr. A. Potocki (Dordrecht: D. Reidel, 1979), p. 77.

logical deduction or by appeal to ecclesial authority[2]. Yet in *Sources of Renewal* the archbishop of Cracow asserted that "faith is not merely the response of mind to an abstract truth". Rather it involves self-abandonment in "man's whole personal structure and spiritual dynamism". Because it involves a personal relation to the God revealing Himself (not just abstract propositions), faith can grow in a double manner, objectively and subjectively: the Church can understand better the content of faith, growing to the fullness of truth, and individuals can dedicate themselves to faith in an ever deeper, existential commitment. Indeed, the Church existentially lives her faith as a single whole while it is gradually enriched through history in her self-realization[3].

[2] A good view of this is found in A. Gardeil, O.P., *La credibilité et l'apologétique* (Paris: Galbada, 1908), pp. 1-30. In his *De Revelatione*, I (Roma: Ferrari, 1955), pp. 504f., R. Garrigou-Lagrange followed Gardeil's analysis of 1908, even though he praised the greatly changed edition of 1912 and claimed to follow it (pp. 398, n. 1, 503, n. 4). K. Wojtyla apparently followd Garrigou-Lagrange's position in *La Fe segun San Juan de la Cruz*, tr. A. Huerga (Madrid: BAC, 1979), pp. 33-36, 83f., 107f., 245, 254-257, for the clear distinction of natural and supernatural orders and the notion of propositional faith; moreover the clear distinction of intellect and will as separate faculties is found throughout. For an overview of the different understandings of faith that have divided Catholic theology in the twentieth century, cf. J. McDermott, S.J., "Faithful and Critical Reason in Theology", *Excellence in Seminary Education*, ed. S. Minkiel, etc. (Erie: Gannon U. Press, 1988), pp. 68-92 (reprinted in *Analecta 2* (1988), 9-24). For a brief overview of the Scholastic understandings of development of dogma cf. O. Chadwick, *From Bossuet to Newman* (Cambridge: University Press, 1957), pp. 21-28, 70-73 (baroque Scholasticism) and R. Schillebeeckx, O.P., *Revelation and Theology*, tr. N. Smith (New York: Sheed and Ward, 1967), pp. 63-68, 71f. (modern times).

[3] K. WOJTYLA, *The Sources of Renewal*, tr. P. Falla (London: Collins, 1980), pp. 20, 15, 18, 39-41. Cf. also A. Frossard, *"N'avez pas peur!": Dialogue avec Jean-Paul II* (Paris: Laffont, 1982), pp. 90-96. Many elements of this personal faith resemble the living faith, i.e., the faith formed by charity, that Wojtyla studied in John of the Cross. Its more than rational reference, its dynamic element, its juncture with charity, and the similarity between God intended by intellect and will and the soul itself all fit in well with a personalist understanding of faith. As we shall see, Wojtyla allows in *Person* for a personalist dynamism going beyond the dynamism of nature toward the personal

This change from propositional to personal faith involved major intellectual shifts of emphasis in Wojtyla's world view. From the days of Chalcedon the Church has remained faithful to the formula of "two natures, one person" while struggling to understand it. Theology has oscillated in its emphases between person and nature as between two poles that mutually condition each other. High medieval Scholasticism stressed the intelligibility of natures while maintaining Boethius' definition of person as an individual substance of a rational nature. Although at first reading that definition might hardly signify more than an individual rational nature, whose individuality in man might be attributed to "matter signed by quantity", Wojtyla, rejecting such a minimalist view, followed the Scholastics in ascribing to person, or subsistence, an incommunicability which prevented it from being possessed by anyone else[4]. How this personhood was more positively defined varied widely. Garrigou-Lagrange saw "person" as a substantial mode terminating an essence, as a point terminates a line, and rendering it completely ready to receive its act of existence. After F. Pelster proved the authenticity of St. Thomas' *De Unione Verbi Incarnati*, in which two acts of existence, a divine *esse* and a subordinate, human *esse*, were ascribed to Christ's ontological constitution, Maritain abandoned Garrigou-Lagrange's position to understand person, or subsist-

---

God. This is much like the "natural desire for the beatific vision" at the basis of much of transcendental Thomism. Nonetheless in *Fe* the starting point was not man's experience of himself as moral agent, but the faith in revealed truths obtained from hearing. Since the reality announced by the words is ultimately intended, there is an inherent tension between the words coming from without and the reality loved and experienced concretely in the theological virtues. But the clear natural-supernatural distinction in *Fe* would prevent anyone from identifying Wojtyla's later personal faith with John of the Cross's mystical experience through faith and charity.

[4] K. WOJTYLA, *Amore e Responsibilità*, 2nd ed., tr. A. Milanoli (Torino: Marietti, 1978), pp. 12, 14, 86, 113; ----, *Person*, p. 83; ----, "The Person: Subject and Community", *Review of Metaphysics* 33 (1979), 279, 288f. St. Thomas sometimes substituted "subsistence" for Boethius' "substance" in the definition.

ence, as that which possesses and exercises an act of existence[5]. Karol Wojtyla apparently presupposed something like Maritain's more existential understanding of person as the ontological basis of his phenomenological investigation, but his rethinking of person and freedom, perhaps the most profound in modern philosophy, goes beyond Maritain. Whereas the traditional conceptualist interpretation allowed for self-knowledge only through reflection upon a intellectual act already accomplished, Wojtyla noted an immediate, personal self-consciousness, or intuition of self, accompanying acts of knowing and willing[6]. The late Gardeil already raised hackles in the Cajetanian tradition by affirming the soul's habitual, non-thematic self-consciousness, and Maritain wrote of the soul's immediate knowledge of its act of existence[7]. But by stressing the person as moral agent Wojtyla placed freedom at the center of personhood. For him the person's incommunicability was attributable to the will as self-governing, and in this case the will had to be considered not a blind drive, but a faculty subordinate to the person[8].

The emphasis on person and freedom as opposed to nature with its necessary, inherent development gave rise to a whole series of tensions[9]. For just as little as personal intuition obviated

---

[5] R. GARRIGOU-LAGRANGE, O.P., *De Christo Salvatore* (Torino: Marietti, 1949), pp. 115-124; F. Pelster, S.J., "La Quaestio Disputata de Saint Thomas 'De Unione Verbi Incarnati'", *Archives de Philosophie*, 3 (1925), 198-245; J. Maritain, *Degrees of Knowledge*, tr. G. Phelan et alii (New York: Scribner's, 1959), pp. 430-444.

[6] WOJTYLA, *Person*, pp. 16f., 37, 42f., 47, 181, 261.

[7] A. GARDEIL, O.P., *La Structure de l'ame et l'expérience mystique*, 2nd ed. (Paris: Gabalda, 1927), II, pp. 91f., 94-121, 239-264; Maritain, *Degrees*, pp. 445-450; ----, *Quatre essais sur l'esprit dans sa condition charnelle* (Paris: Desclée de Brouwer, 1939), pp. 148-155. On this point cf. J. McDermott, S.J., "Maritain on Two Infinities: God and Matter", *International Philosophical Quarterly* 28 (1988), 259-261.

[8] WOJTYLA, *Person*, pp. 107, 121f., 135, 266f.; ----, *Amore*, pp. 14, 113; ----, "Person", 281-283; ----, *Laborem Exercens* 6.

[9] For "nature" as "necessary" and as "what happens in man" cf. Wojtyla, *Person*, pp. 117, 182f., 189, 210, 215-217; ----, *Amore*, pp. 41, 242. Cf. also

the need for conceptual formulations of objective natures, personal freedom did not destroy man's tie to nature, as occurs in Sartre's absurd world[10]. For both Thomas and Wojtyla, operation follows being[11]. Indeed the personal God created the nature which the finite person possessed[12]. While natures known objectively through concepts in traditional Thomism do not suffice to plumb the mystery of personal subjectivity, persons cannot exist without natures. Person and nature mutually condition each other[13]. For ultimately personal freedom is bound to objective truth; the moral subject must be constituted in truth[14]. Holding the just balance between person and nature demands that emphases be shifted when necessary. Sometimes Wojtyla argues from natural instincts that reveal values, e.g., the preservation and perpetuation of human life, whose truth personal freedom is obliged to acknowledge. Norms regarding the indissolubility of marriage and the prohibition of artificial birth control could be applied universally on the basis of the natural law[15]. In these cases surely the person is not subjugated to the necessity of nature but is called to integrate the natural dynamisms into his own personal dynamism[16]. Yet also in the person creatively forming himself are grounded inalienable rights which others

---

"Person", 277 for the "must" whereby the metaphysical person is bound to manifest his personal subjectivity. Hence, paradoxically "man is a person 'by nature'". Cf. also *Person*, pp. 122, 272f.

[10] WOJTYLA, *Person*, pp. 44, 84f., 182f., 208, 211, 216f.; ----, *Amore*, pp. 107f.

[11] WOJTYLA, *Person*, pp. 73, 82, 91, 113, 153f., 265; ----, "Person", 275, 284.

[12] WOJTYLA, *Amore*, pp. 44-47, 210f., 218, 233, 236f.

[13] WOJTYLA, *Person*, pp. 77, 181f., 44, 84, 85, 182f., 208, 211, 216f.; ----, *Amore*, pp. 52f., 214f., 217f., 284; ----, "Person", 277.

[14] WOJTYLA, *Person*, pp. 155, 162f., 165f., 172f., 235, 288; ----, *Amore*, pp. 103, 105f., 227; ----, "Person", 285.

[15] WOJTYLA, *Person*, pp. 215-218, 251, 258; ----, *Amore*, 38-44, 57-59, 87-89, 197-225, 246f., 272f. (cf. also pp. 165-168, for the sense of shame and the resulting norms of modesty).

[16] WOJTYLA, *Person*, pp. 111, 191, 195, 199, 202, 212, 255f.; ----, *Amore*, p. 235.

should acknowledge as natural rights in their personal relationships and thereby contribute to the participatory constitution of society, sharing in the common good. For man is by nature social and the person has an obligation to fulfill himself. Though man's transcendence and self-determination are previous to and condition ethical values, no opposition exists between ethical and personal norms and values[17]. Personal love is truly beyond justice, but it presupposes justice and does not destroy it. Liberty is for love and no laws can restrain love, yet the right to freedom is grounded in truth; thus freedom is subordinate to moral truth[18]. In this movement that grounds obligations and rights in both natures and persons it is clear that the uniqueness of the personal does not absolve man from the universality of the natural, moral law. Indeed, person allows man to accept the law more readily because the truth speaking to personal conscience makes the norm obligatory and the law can be seen as representing the will of the personal God addressing man's freedom[19].

A similar tension between person and nature is observed in Wojtyla's rational psychology. While intellect and will are recognized as separate faculties defined by their formal objects, the true, which one receives intentionally, and the good, to which one tends[20] — a view consistent with the Cajetanian tradition — the person not only knows himself immediately through the intellect but also actualizes the will in individual, free choices[21]. As nature and person mutually condition each other, so will and person manifest themselves mutually. The person may be said in

---

[17] WOJTYLA, *Person*, pp. 109f., 165, 228-231, 264, 266f., 270, 272f., 275f., 280, 296; ----, *Amore*, pp. 32-34, 57f., 171f.; ----, *Redemptor Hominis* 36.

[18] WOJTYLA, *Person*, pp. 154-156; ----, *Amore*, pp. 32f., 232-237.

[19] WOJTYLA, *Person*, pp. 162f., 165; ----, *Amore*, pp. 233-237.

[20] WOJTYLA, *Person*, pp. 126-128, 132, 144, 158, 168, 235f.; ----, "Person", 300. *Person* does not employ the actual words "formal object", but they are implied; *Amore*, p. 122, says explicitly that the good attracts the will.

[21] WOJTYLA, *Person*, pp. 105f., 121f., 266f.; cf. supra n. 6 for the intuition of self in knowing.

turn to depend on the dynamism of his nature and to dynamize himself[22]. The person, or ego, seems to be the individual, spiritual unity of knowing and willing previous to, or above, or underlying, the natural distinction of faculties[23]. Thus, although Wojtyla upholds the validity of basic principles for rational arguments, he recognizes that usually the beginning of the reasoning process and man's final synthetic grasp of meaning must be intuitively grounded[24]. (This raises the question whether the true, which ultimately frees man from subjectivity in the act of freedom, is conceptually formulated or may be open to the personal God who is Truth and Love Himself[25].) Analogously man's spirituality can be defended in terms of the soul that is formally opposed to matter and known by abstraction, not intuition, or the concretely experienced and intuited transcendence of freedom that is tied to a body as a unity in diversity[26]. Indeed, because of this unity in diversity of spirit and matter moral freedom has repercussions for man's body and for his habitual ways of acting[27]. Man's freedom does not consist merely of individually placed acts, choices of good or evil, but also

---

[22] *Ibid.*, pp. 117-120, 167.
[23] *Ibid.*, pp. 71, 107, 121f., 142, 158, 266f., 272f. This recalls the analysis of St. Thomas' text about the emanation of the faculties from the essence of the soul in J. Maritain, *Creative Intuition in Art and Poetry* (1954; rpt. New York: New American Library, 1974), pp. 66-108.
[24] *Ibid.*, pp. 181f., 147f.
[25] So in *Person* Wojtyla speaks of a dynamism to truth, which must involve some juncture of intellect and will going beyond concepts (137, 159); judgment also grasps truth previous to (conceptual) expression and is intuitive (145, 147); God is love (167). There is obviously a type of knowledge beyond concepts. As was noted above, there are no rules in the "field" of love (*Amore*, p. 119). God is personal Truth in *Redemptor Hominis* 19. In *The Whole Truth about Man*, ed. J. Schall (Boston: St. Paul, 1981), pp. 220, 255f., 273, 276, the Pope speaks about the God who is creative Love and the union of love and knowledge in the intellect's desire for truth, which is finally revealed in Christ, Truth made man. Cf. also n. 3 supra for the notion of personal faith.
[26] WOJTYLA, *Person*, pp. 181, 186, 255-258.
[27] *Ibid.*, pp. 201f., 206, 211f., 216, 219, 220-223.

creates the human subject himself in all his dimensions. For in choosing any object, man, who enjoys immediate self-knowledge, simultaneously chooses himself, creating himself through his free choices[28]. Hence, while the person does dominate himself in freedom, he also must dynamically win that freedom over the diversity in unity that is his body, which in turn grounds him in the world of natures[29].

Besides the shifts between person and nature, certain paradoxes can be identified in both person and nature. Both are sources of activity: the person of free determinations; the nature of spontaneous, instinctual reactions to stimuli, what "happens" dynamically in man — apparently another way of expressing the more traditional notion of a source of activity developing according to inherent, necessary laws[30]. In both nature and person there exist tensions between static and dynamic moments: the Aristotelian nature is known through abstract concepts in its formal cause for what it is, yet it is an internal principle of development propelling itself to fulfillment in its final cause; similarly the person, who already possesses and determines himself in transcendence, contains a tendency, or dynamism, toward further self-development, i.e., integration and transcendence. Though integration and transcendence are not the same, they are complementary. Integration looks toward the increasing unity of man's somatic and psychic elements, his whole emotional life. This ultimately is accomplished by the person. Transcendence is essentially the operation of the person, for it intends man's growth in moral responsibility and effective freedom, rooting the deepest meaning of his spiritual powers in moral truth[31].

---

[28] *Ibid.*, pp. 109, 118, 121, 191, 195, 199, 202, 212, 228-231, 255f.

[29] *Ibid.*, p. 208; ----, *Amore*, pp. 35-40.

[30] WOJTYLA, *Person*, pp. 72, 78f., 210, 215, 220, 225; for the link of nature and necessity cf. supra n. 9.

[31] WOJTYLA, *Person*, pp. 138, 146, 153-155, 184, 191, 195, 199, 202, 212, 225, 233, 249f., 255f., 258, 272; ----, *Amore*, pp. 110f., 179-182; ----, "Person", 282-287, 296.

This dynamic transcendence of the person explains how man is open to a personal God, made for personal relations with God, and ultimately intelligible only in Christ, in the supernatural order[32]. "Desire for truth is transfigured into a natural desire for God and finds its clarification only in the light of Christ, Truth made Man[33]". A similar claim is made that every love of a person must find its fulfillment and ground in the love of God, the infinite Good[34]. Yet the Pope's strong Christocentrism is never grounded in a necessity of nature. Like Christ, the truth of faith comes directly from God to man; it does not rise from creation[35]. The underlying Thomistic paradox of the natural desire for the supernatural is adequately explained neither by the "velleity" of Garrigou-Lagrange and Maritain nor by transcendental Thomism's natural dynamism, which ultimately leads to the postulation of a fundamental paradox[36]. For Wojtyla the abstractly

---

[32] WOJTYLA, *Amore*, pp. 13, 74, 124-126, 232-234, 238, 244; ----, *Sources*, pp. 73-75, 80f.,; *Redemptor Hominis* 1, 8-10, 13, 18, 21; ----, *Dives in Misericordia* 1f., 11; ----, *Salvifici Doloris*, 18, 31; ----, *Whole Truth*, pp. 223f., 273.

[33] WOJTYLA, *Whole Truth*, p. 273. Cf. also *Redemptor Hominis*, 18, where the "need" of the spiritual is predicated of those outside the Church.

[34] WOJTYLA, *Amore*, pp. 124f.

[35] WOJTYLA, *Whole Truth*, p. 271; ----, *Sources*, pp. 66-68 (and pp. 36-38 for the primacy of the vertical dimension of the Church); Frossard, pp. 61f.

[36] GARRIGOU-LAGRANGE, *De Revelatione*, pp. 359-376; Maritain, *Degrees*, pp. 283-291; but cf. the much stronger language of *Approaches to God*, tr. P. O'Reilly (New York: Harper and Brothers, 1954), pp. 109-114. For the admitted paradoxical quality of the natural desire for the supernatural cf. on Rousselot J. McDermott, S.J., *Love and Understanding* (Rome: Gregorian U., 1983), pp. 76-86, 154-160; J. Maréchal, S.J., "A propos du sentiment de présence chez les profanes at les mystiques", *Revue des Questions scientifiques* 15 (1909), 238-249, 405, 424-426; B. Lonergan, S.J., "The Natural Desire to See God", *Collection*, ed. F. Crowe (New York: Herder and Herder, 1967), 87, 90, 91; "Insight: Preface to a Discussion" ibid., 157; ----, "Christ as Subject: A Reply", ibid., 190f.; ----, *Insight* (1958; rpt. New York: Harper and Row, 1978), pp. 369, 721-729; ----, "The Subject", *A Second Collection*, ed. W. Ryan and B. Tyrrell (Philadelphia: Westminster, 1974), pp. 79-84; ----, *Method in Theology* (New York: Herder and Herder, 1972), pp. 106f., 122f., 235, 243, 278, 340, 342;

known natures can apparently guarantee the distinction of natural and supernatural but man's personal transcendence demands the God of grace revealed in Christ. That may be called a "natural desire for God", but in *The Acting Person* man's transcendental dynamism is always described in personal terms. Insofar as nature and person condition each other, St. Thomas' language may be employed, but Wojtyla prefers to speak of a personal dynamism and openness to God rather than of a natural dynamism and openness.

Clearly Karol Wojtyla has stretched the Cajetanian tradition to its limits and perhaps beyond them. Although his phenomenological analysis, opening up non-conceptualizable aspects of experience, did not bring him to transcendental Thomism, he was open, as Fr. McCool noted, to many of its insights: transcendental dynamism, basic unities of body and soul, intellect and will, natural and supernatural, Church as primordial sacrament, tradition as Church-consciousness, etc. Yet a comparison of Wojtyla's thought with transcendental Thomism reveals a tremendously complex scheme of similarities and dissimilarities. Surely Wojtyla would reject Rahner's equation of being and consciousness, however much conscious action reveals the being of the self and constitues the self[37]. Moreover, the starting points

---

J. Alfaro, S.J., "Transcendencia e inmanencia de lo sobrenatural", *Gregorianum* 38 (1957), esp. 39-42; H. de Lubac, S.J., *Surnaturel* (Paris: Aubier, 1946), pp. 484, 490-494; H.U. von Balthasar, *Theodramatik* (Einsiedeln: Johannes, 1973-1983), II/1, pp. 276f., 284-289, 377f.; II/2, pp. 236, 383f., 441-443, 473, 480-483; III, pp. 127-132, 151f.; J. Mouroux, *The Meaning of Man*, tr. A. Downes (1948; rpt. Garden City: Doubleday, 1961), pp. 113-136, 141-147, 164-170, 187-194, 210-226, 231-241, speaks of paradox almost everywhere. K. Rahner usually avoids the language of paradox, although he did speak of the "paradox" of supernatural love in "Über das Verhältnis von Natur und Gnade", *Schriften zur Theologie*, I (Einsiedeln: Benziger, 1954), 338, n. 1; cf. 336f.; but his basic notion of analogy is really paradoxical, consisting in a constant oscillation between polar opposites and maintaining that the analogous is previous to the univocal: *Grundkurs des Glaubens* (Freiburg: Herder, 1976), pp. 79-81; *Geist in Welt* (Innsbruck: Rauch, 1939), pp. 291-294.

[37] WOJTYLA, *Person*, pp. 278, 282f.; Rahner, *Geist*, pp. 41-46, 49, etc.

of Wojtyla and transcendental Thomism are different: Wojtyla begins with the self-possessing, self-determining subject who only secondarily, i.e., "accidentally", puts himself into relation with other men and the world[38], while transcendental Thomism starts with the dynamic relation to the world that aims at the subject-nature's full self-possession and self-donation in the beatific vision. Wojtyla's starting point is more in accord with Garrigou-Lagrange's, but even here great caution is demanded in the face of Wojtyla's flexible method. In *The Acting Person* the moral consciousness of the free agent has a fundamentally intersubjective character; in the community to which man is morally called for his ultimate fulfillment the reference to one's neighbor is primary. Though this seems in conflict with the very essence of a person as "incommunicable", Wojtyla spoke of the need and the appropriateness of the "paradox" of leaving one's self-possession to give oneself to another person; for in this "ecstacy" man grows in his being, which leads to his self-fulfillment[39]. In his theology Wojtyla starts from the living faith-experience of the Church — a point very much in keeping with a phenomenological method intent on observing concrete realities, which *de facto* exist in relation to each other. Inversely, the transcendental Thomists do not immediately relativize all earthly realities. They generally insist upon the judgment of truth that man can realize in this world short of the beatific vision, even though the judgment's ultimate grounding is discovered in God alone; and the best of them consistently maintained the significance and necessity of the natural-supernatural distinction,

---

[38] WOJTYLA, *Person*, p. 289.

[39] WOJTYLA, *Person*, pp. 162-164; cf. 173f., 263, 268, 272f., 275, 285, 291, 297; ----, *Amore*, pp. 86f., 113, 118f.; ----, "Person", 305f., 288, 291, 295. In traditional Catholic theology there was a similar tension between the notion of person as relation in Trinitarian doctrine and its notion as incommunicability in Christology. One suspects that both are aspects of the reality; it remains to work out how both aspects coalesce.

however paradoxical it appeared. Finally, it should be noted that not all transcendental Thomists insisted on the equation of being and knowing. Lonergan, for example, was content to relativize the old conceptualism by recognizing a concomitant, intuitive self-awareness of the knowing subject in every act of knowledge, even while admitting that the soul did not possess an immediate grasp of its essence[40] — a position very close to Wojtyla's notion of personal self-intuition. Yet when all is said and done, Wojtyla is not a transcendental Thomist. Despite his adaptive openness to so many insights of transcendental Thomism, the Pope enjoys a certain advantage from not joining the more dominant current of post-conciliar Catholic theology. For by not accepting as fundamental to ontology the natural dynamism for the beatific vision he avoids the dangers of conceptual relativization and experiential interiorization at the expense of history and objective truth which have marred the theologies of less careful followers of Rousselot, Maréchal, Rahner, and Lonergan.

Despite the amazing balance, width, depth, and flexibility of Wojtyla's thought, not all the tensions in his system have been clarified or resolved. Between his phenomenological method, describing the concrete, and his scientific, metaphysical analysis, concerned with abstract pattern, a synthesis must be realized. He himself admitted that many points in his phenomenology remain to be metaphysically grounded or supplemented[41]. Some spring immediately to mind. How can the necessities of nature be subsumed into personal freedom without being rendered non-necessary[42]? Surely without some necessary intellectual parameters freedom lapses into pure arbitrariness. As Wojtyla saw,

---

[40] B. LONERGAN, S.J., *Verbum: Word and Idea in Aquinas* (London: Longman, Darton, and Todd, 1968), pp. 75-92; for its basis in the metaphysical-psychological structures of knowing cf. also pp. 105f., 117, 123f., 126-128, 134, 138-140, 152, 161, 166.

[41] WOJTYLA, *Person*, pp. 186, 258.

[42] Cf. ibid., pp. 124f.; ----, *Amore*, p. 124, for an apparent awareness of the problem.

truth alone liberates man from such meaninglessness and the consequent enslavement of freedom[43]. Then again how are conceptual formulations and intuitions joined without totally relativizing the former or reducing the latter to a rational straightjacket? Furthermore, how can the person be described in terms of a dynamism without reducing freedom to the apparent necessity of a potency-act, desire-fulfillment schema[44]? Free will is not just an appetite; to will is to strive toward an end even while deciding, and a person surely distances himself from the will's dynamism which he uses in his transcendence[45]. But then how does this static moment, in which the man dynamizes his own subject, let itself be united to the personal dynamism[46]? In addition, how is the duality in unity of soul and body reconciled with the personal unity in duality of soma and psyche[47]? Finally in our list of sample questions, how is person related to existence[48]?

Despite all these questions the magnificent accomplishment of Wojtyla's thought should not be dismissed. His claim that his theology, or "a synthesis of my personal faith", was formed at Vatican II manifests the centrality of his thought in the development of twentieth century Catholic theology[49]. At the Council

---

[43] WOJTYLA, *Person*, pp. 137f., 144, 154f.

[44] WOJTYLA, *Person*, pp. 33, 59, 179, 63f., 112.

[45] WOJTYLA, *Person*, pp. 124f., 69, 121f., 266f.

[46] *Ibid.*, pp. 120f. Maritain, *Creative Intuition*, pp. 85-108, was also forced by experience to postulate a combination of activity and passivity at the essence of the soul, which is close to identifying his notion of person.

[47] Cf. WOJTYLA, *Person*, pp. 255f. Like K. RAHNER in *Geist in Welt* Wojtyla in *Person*'s phenomenological descriptions habitually uses "spirit" instead of "soul", probably to express better the greater unity with the body over the emotions. Yet, going beyond Rahner, Wojtyla, p. 223, was very much aware of a distinction between psyche and spirit. Psyche is not the moment of personal freedom; there is a spiritual element in man that is more natural than personal.

[48] Cf., e.g., Wojtyla, *Person*, pp. 68, 77, 282; ----, *Amore*, pp. 42, 72, for some texts showing a relation between person and nature, but not fully elaborated.

[49] Frossard, p. 102; cf. also p. 35 and countless encyclicals and talks in

the conceptual and transcendental currents of Thomism met and compromised. Whereas conceptualism tends to absolutize the finite structures of reality, transcendental thought tends to relativize them, emptying them of inherent consistency. The best thinkers of both schools were aware of the dangers and took steps to counteract them[50]. For basic to Catholic thought is its sacramental vision whereby finite realities serve as effective signs of God's presence in the world through which He appeals for the response of human freedom to His loving self-communication. Hence the worldly signs must possess a finite intelligibility lest they be incapable of signifying; yet their intelligibility cannot be absolute lest there be no need of referring to any reality beyond the world. On the merely intellectual level this balance of God and world, Infinite and finite, represents the philosophical notion of analogy, which allows man to have some knowledge of God and so remain free before the offer of revelation and grace. Karol Wojtyla stressed the necessity of the analogy of being, but more than that, he noted that the choice of personal freedom joins transcendence and limitation in response to moral obligation[51]. He has remained faithful to and deepened our appreciation of the traditional Catholic theological vision. His mastery of phenomenology helped him to remain close to the concrete without denying conceptual validity in order that the unique human supposit might remain free before the offer of grace given as gift with the objectivity of truth.

---

which the Pope confesses his commitment to Vatican II.

[50] For a brief overview cf. J. McDermott, S.J., "Sheehan, Rousselot, and Theological Method", *Gregorianum* 69 (1987), 714-717; for more detail cf. J. McDermott, S.J., *Love and Understanding;* ----, "Maritain on Two Infinities: God and Matter", *International Philosophical Quarterly* 28 (1988), 257-269; ----, "Karl Rahner on Two Infinities: God and Matter", ibid., 439-457.

[51] Wojtyla, *Person*, pp. 169f.; ----, *Whole Truth*, pp. 220f. Cf. also J. McDermott, S.J., "A New Approach to God's Existence", *The Thomist* 44 (1980), 219-250, and its correction and abbreviation as "Proof for Existence of God", in *The New Dictionary of Theology*, ed. J. Komonchak et alii (Dublin: Gill and Macmillan, 1987), 804-808.

"A VISION OF WHOLENESS": A REFLECTION ON THE USE OF SCRIPTURE IN A CROSS-SECTION OF PAPAL WRITINGS

TERRENCE PRENDERGAST, S.J.

INTRODUCTION

From the beginning of his pontificate and the vast literary output that has characterized his pastoral ministry to the church and world of our time, John Paul II's writings have intrigued, puzzled and challenged me. The way he reads and tries to actualize biblical texts fascinates me.

For example, I had often studied, read and taught the parable of the Prodigal Son, but I had never discovered the personalist dimensions in it, especially in decision-making, uncovered by John Paul in *Dives in Misericordia*, paragraphs 5-6:

> At the center of the prodigal son's consciousness, the sense of lost dignity is emerging, the sense of dignity that springs from the relationship of the son with the father. And it is with this decision that he sets out[1].

And in my theological studies, I had tried to reflect upon and articulate the way in which justice, mercy and love interrelate.

---

[1] JOHN PAUL II, *Encyclical Letter Dives in Misericordia*, "On the Mercy of God" (Boston: St. Paul Editions, 1980), p. 20. Henceforth, this encyclical is abbreviated DIM.

But I had never considered whether the very fact that mercy can be offered to another demeans that person and what this might mean for the modern man or woman in need of God's mercy. John Paul describes what is involved as follows:

> At times... we see in mercy above all a relationship of inequality between the one offering it and the one receiving it. And, in consequence, we are quick to deduce that mercy belittles the receiver, that it offends the dignity of man[2].

The pope's interpretation of the parable of the prodigal son is then shown to reveal the true nature of mercy and to support the dignity of the human person so much valued today. This emphasis on the dignity of the human person in the pope's thought explains, in part, the great stress he puts on *Genesis* 1:26-28 in all his writings, for it is there that the notion that the human person is created in the image and likeness of God is so powerfully expressed.

Not only did reading his encyclicals, apostolic letters and other writings stir reactions of both interest and puzzlement in me, so, too, did the reactions of others to his writings. Some years ago, I began to note the kinds of observations made about the writings of Pope John Paul II on the occasion of their publication. Besides amazement at his daringly radical critique of the ills afflicting contemporary society (for example, his pointing out the devastating social consequences flowing from the policies of both unbridled capitalism and atheistic communism in *Sollicitudo Rei Socialis*[3]), these reactions touched, *inter alia*, on the uses he made of the Scriptures in his writings. Generally, there was admiration for the Holy Father's exemplary and wide-ranging citation of the Scriptures, both the Old and New

---

[2] JOHN PAUL II, DIM, p. 22.

[3] JOHN PAUL II, *Encyclical Letter Sollicitudo Rei Socialis*, "On Social Concern" [hereafter SRS], (Washington: United States Catholic Conference, 1987), pp. 32-36 [par. 22].

Testaments. This was especially the case with regard to the much-admired encyclical DIM. Still, there were demurrals as well. Some remarked that John Paul did not make use of the Scriptures in the same way that contemporary scriptural scholarship does, vaguely intimating that perhaps his hermeneutics were somehow deficient.

At this point, perhaps, I should acknowledge that in my own reading of papal writings (chiefly the encyclicals, but also the occasional apostolic letter, post-Synodal reflection and miscellaneous writings), I admired the pope's bold creativity in his citation and interpretation of Scripture. But I also have to confess that I did not understand the principles underlying the interpretation he gave and I admit, as well, that there was something about the criticism of his use of Scripture that found a resonance in my reading of the pope's writings (after all, as a member of the biblical guild, I have been schooled in and favour certain academic approaches to the study of Scripture over other types of readings).

This set me to the task of looking more closely at all the sources grounding John Paul's teaching, in the hope that this might indicate whether and how these might form a pattern related to the way in which his scriptural sources are used. A cursory analysis of the footnotes listed in the encyclicals dealing with the three divine persons: *Redemptor Hominis* ("On the Redeemer of Man")[4], *Dives in Misericordia* ("On the Mercy of God") and *Dominum et Vivificantem* ("On the Holy Spirit in the Life of the Church and the World")[5] showed that the vast majority of the more than one hundred citations in each were biblical in origin (147 out of 205 or 71.7% for RH, 129 out of 140 or 92.1% for DIM and 226 out of 297 or 76% for DEV).

[4] JOHN PAUL II, *Encyclical Letter Redemptor Hominis*, "The Redeemer of Man" [henceforth RH] (Boston: St. Paul Editions, 1979).

[5] JOHN PAUL II, *Encyclical Letter Dominum et Vivificantem*, "On the Holy Spirit in the Life of the Church and the World" [hereafter DEV] (Sherbrooke, QC: Editions Paulines, 1986).

The remaining sources that Pope John Paul refers to are, ranked by the approximate overall frequency of their appearances, the documents of the Second Vatican Council (chiefly *Lumen Gentium* [hereafter LG], the Dogmatic Constitution on the Church, and *Gaudium et Spes* [GS], the Pastoral Constitution on the Church in the Modern World); close behind the Council documents are the teachings of his predecessor popes (especially John XXIII and Paul VI), then patristic and medieval sources (often St. Augustine and St. Thomas Aquinas, but some other ancient writers feature prominently) and, lastly, confessional or liturgical sources (for example, quotes from the Holy Saturday *Exsultet*, the creeds, hymns, etc.). Surprisingly few of the citations derive from previous ecumenical councils, although there are some notable appeals to the early ecumenical councils in *Redemptoris Mater*[6], but, curiously, none in DEV. Conspicuously absent from the encyclicals are references to contemporary authors or extra-ecclesial sources, although summaries of biblical scholarship are occasionally given in general ways to elaborate on the teaching being presented (for example, the Hebraic background to the concept of mercy in DIM) but not to the scholarly authors or the research that stand behind it[7].

Such a degree of restraint with regard to outside sources is not shown in other papal teaching presentations below the encyclical level. For example, in John Paul's apostolic letter *Augustinum Hipponensem*[8] there is, in footnote 65, a reference

---

[6] Cf. footnotes 9, 80 and 84 in John Paul II, *Encyclical Letter Redemptoris Mater*, "Mother of the Redeemer" (Sherbrooke, QC: Editions Paulines, 1987).

[7] For examples of summaries of scriptural research, cf. DIM footnotes 52, 60, 61. An exception to the principle of not quoting extra-ecclesial sources may be seen in SRS footnotes 36 and 47, which quote United Nations documentation (but no specific author or economic theory) on the world economic situation. The many historical references in John Paul II, *Encyclical Letter Slavorum Apostoli, On the Evangelizing Work of Saints Cyril and Methodius* (Boston: St. Paul Editions, 1985) may readily be understood as church sources.

[8] *On the Occasion of the Sixteenth Centenary of the Conversion of Saint Augustine* (Boston: St. Paul Editions, 1986).

to the 1967 work of L. Verheijen which argues the great impact
St. Augustine had and continues to have on the history of
western religious life. Also, in the letter to the young people of
the world on the occasion of the United Nations International
Year of Youth, the pope refers to Confucius, Gandhi, Buddhism
and other writers or traditions, which often find echoes in the
idealism of the young and young-at-heart[9]. Further, in the series
of Wednesday afternoon catecheses on the goodness and fruitfulness of creation, human sexuality and marriage, there are
numerous references to philosophers and schools of thought[10].

Framing an Approach to John Paul's Use of Scripture

Having noted the frequency with which recent papal writings lavishly have quoted both the Old and New Testaments, I
imagined it would be a fairly straightforward matter to list a few
of the conventionally accepted views of scholars today and, upon
examination, verify whether these conventional understandings
are present or absent in John Paul's formal writings. In random
fashion, I noted down several of the positions commonly agreed
on by biblical scholarship today, surmising that it might prove
illuminating to discover which, if any, of these ideas find a place
in the papal writings. I chose two positions from the field of the
Old Testament interpretation and two from the field of New
Testament interpretation, along with what we night designate an
overall principle regarding biblical writings in general. These
touch upon: a) Pentateuchal sources; b) the distinction between
Isaiah of Jerusalem and his later successor or successors
(Deutero-Isaiah and Trito-Isaiah); c) the three levels of the Jesus
tradition generally recognized within the Gospels; d) the distinction between the authentic letters of Paul and the post-Pauline

---

[9] Cf. JOHN PAUL II, *Apostolic Letter*, *"To the Youth of the World"*
(Sherbrooke, QC: Editions Paulines, 1985), paragraphs 7-8, pp. 22 [footnote 41]
and 26.
[10] Cf. below, pp. 76f.

tradition attributed to him; and e) the predilection today for emphasizing the distinctive characteristics of each biblical writer or a stream of biblical tradition. Allow me to describe briefly each of these positions before moving on to an examination of how John Paul's writings relate to each and all of them.

a) Although they disagree about the exact extent of the sources to be found in the Pentateuch, the majority of Roman Catholic scholars today acknowledge the different theologies that are designated as reflecting the Yahwist, the Elohist, the Deuteronomist and the Priestly Writer[11].

b) So, too, is there general recognition of more than one author at work in the canonical text of Isaiah (although there are disagreements about whether in it we need postulate one or two heirs to Isaiah of Jerusalem)[12].

c) New Testament scholars regularly invoke a distinction regarding the several levels of tradition found in gospel narratives. The first concerns the circumstances in the life and ministry of Jesus which might have occasioned a particular word or deed of Jesus (what the Germans refer to as the *Sitz-im-Leben Jesu*). A second level seeks to uncover the use which the church made of such words or deeds of Jesus for guiding its own life and practices (the *Sitz-im-Leben Kirche*). The third level seeks to discern the specific import such words or deeds of Jesus had for the evangelist's audience (*Sitz-im-Leben Evangelist*).

---

[11] Cf. RAYMOND E. BROWN, et al., *The New Jerome Biblical Commentary* [NJBC] (Englewood-Cliffs, NJ: Prentice Hall, 1990) on "The Pentateuch" and each of the five books of the Torah, pp. 3-109. This compendium of scholarly research, a re-working of the 1968 *Jerome Biblical Commentary* [JBC], does not depart from the earlier work regarding pentateuchal sources. Rather, both volumes testify to the accepted and settled nature of the scholarly consensus on the issue of sources in the five books of Moses.

[12] Cf. the division between "Isaiah 1-39" (pp. 229-248) and "Deutero-Isaiah and Trito-Isaiah" (pp. 329-348) in NJBC. The JBC article on Deutero-Isaiah had held out the view that chapters 56-65 had a different tone and provenance from the earlier work (cc. 40-55), but the entire article was then titled "Deutero-Isaiah".

The second and third levels of the gospel tradition seem to be explicitly recognized by the Second Vatican Council in the section dealing with the historicity of the Gospels in *Dei Verbum* [DV], its Decree on Divine Revelation (n. 19):

> The sacred authors, in writing the four Gospels, selected certain of the many elements which had been handed on, either orally or already in written form, others they synthesized or explained with an eye to the situation of the churches, the while sustaining the form of preaching, but always in such a fashion that they told us the honest truth about Jesus[13].

d) In recent years, New Testament scholars have increasingly postulated a distinction between the epistles which may be held to be authentically Pauline and those which need to be recognized as likely the pseudonymous work of Paul's successors. Sometimes these are denominated as the Deutero-Paulines (*Colossians, Ephesians* and, though somewhat controverted, *Second Thessalonians*). In the case of the Pastorals (*First* and *Second Timothy* and *Titus*), their author is sometimes called the Paulinist.

e) The last category refers to the increasing concern by scholars to distinguish the theology of a particular writer from that of his fellow sacred authors. Thus, reference is made to the anthropology of the Yahwist, the theology of the Second Isaiah, the Marcan concept of discipleship, the several ecclesiologies of Paul, of *Ephesians* and of Paulinist, etc.

---

[13] This understanding of the three levels of the gospel tradition regarding Jesus is found elaborated in the Pontifical Biblical Commission's 1964 instruction *Sacra Mater Ecclesia*, "On the Historical Truth of the Gospels" [SMS]. For a translation and elaboration of this pivotal document, cf. Joseph A. Fitzmyer, *A Christological Catechism* (Mahwah, NJ: Paulist Press, 1982), pp. 104-142. *Dei Verbum*, the constitution "On Divine Revelation" of Vatican II [DV], which refers to SMS in footnote 4 (paragraph 19) may be taken to support this triple level of tradition, at least implicitly. The three levels of the gospel tradition are everywhere presumed in contemporary scholarship on the Gospels, as may be seen throughout the JBC and the NJBC.

Overall one notes that these various theories tend to separate, distinguish, even atomize and multiply the message(s) of the Word of God. As we shall see, the direction of John Paul II, as he interprets Scripture, moves in the opposite direction.

Testing the Hypothesis

My primary frame of reference in considering these five notions derived from biblical scholarship will be the three main encyclicals RH, DIM and DEV, but I shall refer to a cross-section of other papal writings inasmuch as these qualify the findings.

a) The Various Sources in the Pentateuch

The first chapter of *Genesis* is by far the most widely cited Old Testament text in the writings of John Paul II. In RH, there are eleven references to the Old Testament, two each from *Isaiah* and the Psalms, while the remaining nine are from *Genesis* and all but one of these are from chapter 1. In DEV, there are forty-four Old Testament texts cited; sixteen [or slightly more than a third] of these are from *Genesis*, and eight [a half] of these are from the first chapter of *Genesis*. The exception to this predilection for *Genesis* 1 is found in DIM, where only two of the seventy-six Old Testament texts are from *Genesis*; nonetheless, they are both from the first chapter.

The key issue at stake in the pope's invocation of *Genesis* 1 lies in the conviction affirmed in *Genesis* that the human person is part of God's creation, all of which God saw to be good. Men and women are, as John Paul never tires of noting, created "in the image and likeness of God" and have been given responsibility for joining with God in the on-going task of making something of our world, of being in effect co-creators with God.

Nowhere in these three encyclicals does the pope refer to the underlying sources that constitute this first book of the Pentateuch. Yet, in the series of catechetical allocutions that were delivered over several years of presentations at the

Wednesday afternoon audiences, he dealt regularly and consistently on the themes of *Genesis*: creation, the power and challenges in human sexuality, the vocation that is marriage and other, kindred topics. In these, he showed himself to be aware of the presence of sources in *Genesis* 1-3. First of all, he several times alluded to the Yahwist, a writer so designated, the pope says, because he prefers to call God by the name Yahweh (Hebrew YHWH). Secondly, he intimates that the account in Genesis 1 was, in its composition, chronologically later than the Yahwist's account[14].

Here, I shall leave it to others to point out the importance of *Genesis* 1 for grounding John Paul's vision of the human person as subject. The significance of *Genesis* 1 in shaping that vision may be deduced from its recurring appearance in John Paul's writing. We note that, though John Paul alludes to pentateuchal sources in the shaping of *Genesis*, he does not do so in his encyclicals (the highest level of magisterial teaching), but does so freely in his addresses to audiences, a less elevated type of pronouncement. I suggest here that a conclusion worth considering is the recognition that the higher the authoritative level of the teaching given, the less likely the pope will be to allude to scriptural theories.

b) Diversity of Sources in Isaiah

In DIM, when he is describing in general terms the biblical witness to God's mercy, the pope alludes to the "consoling assurances" given by Isaiah (DIM, 4). The footnote (n. 34) refers the reader to two texts from *Isaiah* (1:18 and 51:4-16). The first of these scripture scholars would attribute to Isaiah of Jerusalem, while today many exegetes would argue that the latter text belongs to the vision of a successor of Isaiah, one who is

---

[14] Cf. JOHN PAUL II, *Uomo e Donna Lo Creò: Catechesi sull'Amore Umano* (ed. C. Caffarra, et al.; Rome: Città Nuova Editrice/Libreria Editrice Vaticana, 1985), pp. 33, 36.

generally known as Deutero-Isaiah or "the Second Isaiah".
Similarly, in the text of DEV, the pope regularly speaks of Isaiah
"the Prophet" and of the *Book of Isaiah*, no matter what part of
the writing is under study; the scriptural references are to
footnotes 52-60, which quote texts from *Isaiah* 11 and from
chapters 42-61 (what scholars would designate as of Deutero-
Isaiah and Trito-Isaiah).

Though Pope John Paul does not allude in these encyclicals
to scholarly positions on the composition of canonical, biblical
works, nonetheless he does make use of scholarly findings to
support the exposition of his teaching. Thus, one lengthy footnote in DIM (no. 52) describes the different shades of meaning in
the Hebrew terms for mercy (*hesed* and *rahamim*), explains the
problem the Septuagint authors had in translating the richness of
the Hebrew into Greek terminology and suggests the psychology
of the biblical world-view, which can enlighten our present
understanding of the text, since we share a different set of
conceptual categories today. In footnotes 60 and 61, also, John
Paul notes that the Hebrew concept of *hesed* underlies *Luke*
1:49-54 and 1:72 respectively, showing the unity of the biblical
witness in the two testaments. In none of these expositions,
however, is there any citation of a scholarly authority or source.

c) Levels in the Gospel Tradition

Scholarly writing about the Gospels today considers it a
commonplace to note the different tendencies of the synoptic
and Johannine traditions. Specialists have noted the symbolic
nature of a great deal of the Fourth Gospel, and the degree of
historical reliability to be found in *John* has been the object of
wide disagreement.

There can be no doubt, however, that Pope John Paul shows
a marked preference for the *Gospel of John*. In RH there are 189
references to New Testament texts; 54 (or 28.5%) of them are to
John's Gospel, which is three times the total number of references (18) to the three synoptics combined. In DEV, the overall
percentage of references to *John* is even higher than in RH: 98

(or 34.8%) out of the 281 New Testament citations and more than twice as many as the references to the three synoptics. The matter is slightly different in DIM, where two of the three synoptics outpace the number of citations from *John* (*Matthew* 19, *Mark* 2, *Luke* 27, *John* 9). This is explained in part by the pope's choice of the Lucan parable of the Prodigal Son as the New Testament example par excellence of God's mercy.

For John Paul, the mystery of the Incarnation is central to the Christian self-understanding, and he knows that this finds its clearest articulation in John's Gospel. But in his view, this focus on the incarnate Word of God must not be seen in isolation from the accomplishment of the redemption, the paschal mystery. In fact, the pope is at pains to keep the two aspects of salvation history inextricably connected, as may be seen in the movement from paragraph 8 of RH (in which he treats of the incarnation) to paragraph 9 (in which he focuses on the redemption). The incarnation is the starting-point because, as *Gaudium et Spes* had noted, "by his incarnation, he, the Son of God, in a certain way united himself with each man"[15].

We may grasp something of John Paul's methodology in quoting Scripture from the letter which he wrote on Palm Sunday in 1985 for the United Nations International Year of Youth ("To the Youth of the World")[16]. There, he provides an extended reflection on the encounter of the "rich young man" with Jesus (*Mark* 10:17-22 and parallels). The pope moves through the various aspects of the Marcan text, filling out the synoptic details with data from *John* and giving the whole episode an existential interpretation. Only when he has finished with *Mark*, does he move on to the Matthean account and what he considers to be its preservation of the "concluding phase" of the encounter and its suggestion about Jesus' call to perfection with which Matthew's

---

[15] Cf WALTER M. ABBOTT, ed., *The Documents of Vatican II* (New York: Doubleday, 1966); GS, par. 22, quoted in John Paul II, RH, par. 8.

[16] Cf. above, footnote 9.

account alone deals. The idealism of youth is challenged by the way the pope sees Jesus' dealing with the rich youth as a model of how he addresses every young person today; and references to Confucius, Gandhi and Buddhism fill out his appeal to heed the call from Christ to a particular vocation in life. All of this, John Paul locates within the teaching of the Council, observing that before Vatican II, the concept of "vocation" was applied first of all to the priesthood and religious life. The Council, he notes, has broadened this way of looking at things, seeing every Christian to have a vocation in life. The underlying message here is that the Council has simply extended, not changed, the Church's consistent tradition regarding a vocation. This is important for the pope's unifying vision of Church life.

From the call to every person, John Paul moves to a whole range of issues, locating them all in Scripture, the decrees of the Council (especially LG and GS) and the *Confessions* of St. Augustine.

But what of the scholar's distinction between the various levels of the gospel tradition about Jesus? So far as I can tell, there seem to be no allusions in his writings to the first two levels, what a saying or deed of Jesus meant in his own ministry and how the church made use of these to nurture its own life of faith in the period of the oral tradition, that is, before the Gospels themselves came into existence. In his recent apostolic letter on St. Joseph[17], the pope carries on a sustained analysis of the gospel accounts which feature Joseph, all of them found in the infancy accounts of *Matthew* 1-2 and *Luke* 1-2.

John Paul shows himself here to be aware of the author of each text, referring now and then to "the evangelist" when he wishes to denote the peculiarities of Matthew's or Luke's account. What a student schooled in modern scriptural methodology would find unusual is his easy movement between one or

---

[17] JOHN PAUL II, *Apostolic Letter Redemptoris Custos*, "The Guardian of the Redeemer" (Montreal, QC: Editions Paulines, 1989).

other Gospel. A graduate student in biblical studies today would be expected to do a thorough inventory now of all of the Matthean infancy account, then of the entire Lucan account and, only afterwards, draw them together to illustrate points of agreement or disagreement on one or other aspect.

My own hunch is that this is based on an intuition of John Paul's that only by acting thus can he uphold the historicity of the gospel witness to Jesus. At this point, I note that there is an on-going problematic for those who teach the Scriptures. It concerns the way in which people understand the contribution of the evangelist to the historical truth of the gospel narratives and, remember, this was one of the concerns of the Conciliar constitution on revelation. For many, even very bright, students, it is very difficult to conceive of the term "redactional" (the evangelist's emphases) in any other way than to mean "un-historical" and, therefore, in commonsense understanding the equivalent of "fictional" and "untrue". John Paul avoids all of this problematical point of hermeneutics by simultaneously noting that he is aware of the contribution of the evangelist but treating freely the episodes in each Gospel as historical without the slightest qualification.

d) Distinction Between Paul and the Post-Pauline Tradition

Up until fairly recently, it was quite common to attribute to Paul's authorship fourteen epistles: the seven uncontested epistles (*Romans, 1-2 Corinthians, Galatians, Philippians, 1 Thessalonians* and *Philemon*), those increasingly treated as Deutero-Pauline (*2 Thessalonians, Colossians, Ephesians*), the Pastorals (*1-2 Timothy* and *Titus*) and *Hebrews*. Today, there is a decline in the degree of "authenticity" attributed to these fourteen works as one moves from the uncontested epistles through *Hebrews*. In fact, there is a certain state of flux in the scholarly "consensus" on this issue, though, in recent years and with exceptions in the case of each of the epistles under debate, a certain agreement seems to be shaping up. This, in my view, is not merely a case of stubborn people coming on side to keep up with the rest, but rather a question of scholars who have "held out" on one epistle or the other (*Second Thessalonians* or *Colossians*, for example) being convinced by the evidence presented by peers.

Though I have not found any reference in John Paul's writings that reckons *Hebrews* to be Pauline, all of the others are treated as authentic, that is written by Paul himself or dictated to a fellow-apostle or scribe in such a way that Paul is himself the author (although, to my knowledge, the pope nowhere says this).

The establishment of a difference between Paul and his successors has, at times, implied and heightened a preference for the genuine Pauline doctrine and a corresponding denigration of the worth of the later heirs of the tradition begun by Paul. This is not a necessary corollary to these scholarly conclusions about authorship, but it may explain in part papal reluctance to make such a distinction. Having said this, it is worth observing that in his citation of the Pauline literature, John Paul's preference (at least in terms of the frequency of his citations of them) is for the category designated uncontested, then for the Deutero-Paulines, the Pastorals and *Hebrews*.

e) Recognition of the Integrity of a Writing

As I mentioned earlier with regard to John Paul's treatment of the infancy stories of Jesus, he adverts to the evangelist as an author. Likewise, in the letter to youth, which emphasises the Marcan account of the rich young man, or in DIM, which focuses on Luke as the evangelist of divine mercy, he can elaborate upon one Gospel for a sustained period, then turn to the contributions of the other gospel writers, either to one of the other synoptics or to John. So, too, in his treatment of *Genesis*, he can allude to the Yahwist's account of creation and the later (priestly) account which precedes it.

John Paul's conviction about how each person must determine his own creative contribution in answer to a divine call may underlie his attention to the specific biblical authors. Still, he does not draw out the distinctive theology of each as belonging to or typifying that author. Instead, it seems that he wishes to hold together the unity of the biblical witness so that, in practice, he does not draw conclusions about the distinctive viewpoints of the sacred writers, preferring instead to see all as part of the one Word of God that summons all people in every time and place.

Preliminary Conclusion

It may seem that we have uncovered very little harmony between John Paul's scriptural interpretative methods and modern scholarship. After all, except for an awareness of sources in the Pentateuch in catechetical sessions and a consciousness of the writer of a biblical document in a generalized sense, there is not a great deal that formally links John Paul and modern biblical scholarship. However, we have observed that there seems to be a degree of coherence between the level of the teaching in question and the degree of contact with scholarly positions. One issue may simply be caution regarding matters that are in flux and therefore can continue to change as scholarship evolves. The second, likely more pressing issue, may be a pastoral attempt to sustain a unitary vision of the one God who speaks equally powerfully through every biblical witness.

A Second or Phenomenological Approach to John Paul's Writings

Our investigation of the impact of current biblical conventions on the scriptural sources for Pope John Paul II's teaching has turned up largely negative conclusions. The data of scriptural research seem to find a very narrow ambit within these writings. Is there another approach that might offer greater insight into the matter? The phenomenological approach of David Kelsey suggests another way of approaching the issue.

In his 1975 work *The Uses of Scripture in Recent Theology*[18],

---

[18] D. KELSEY, *The Uses of Scripture in Recent Theology* (Philadelphia: Fortress, 1975).

Kelsey studied the writings of seven Protestant theologians, all of whom agreed that Christian theology must be done "in accord with Scripture". He began by asking what aspects of Scripture each theologian took to be authoritative and whether in their interpretation of the Scriptures they operated according to these principles.

Kelsey found that, for B.B. Warfield, Scripture was authoritative in its "doctrines" on account of the Scripture's intrinsic property of inerrancy, whereas for H.W. Bartsch it was biblical "concepts" which were authoritative and this because of their "distinctiveness".

Kelsey's five other theologians found biblical authority to reside not in a property of Scripture but in its function. G.E. Wright located the authority of a biblical text in its narrative function, one which suggests a dynamic rather than a static notion of God. Karl Barth's view of Scripture as narrative cohered with Wright's, except that his exegesis was Christological and the biblical narrative, when used in preaching and worship, "renders an agent" or makes the narrative come alive for those present. With various nuances about how this comes about in practice, L.S. Thornton, Rudolf Bultmann and Paul Tillich all similarly understood Scripture to speak with authority when "it expresses the occurrence of a revelatory event in the past and occasions its occurrence for someone in the present"[19].

The conclusion of Kelsey's research intimates that there is no such thing as a presuppositionless theology and that it is particularly important to delineate the authority or role Scripture is to play in the shaping of one's theology. Kelsey understands each theologian to begin his work with an act of the imagination in which he or she attempts to visualize in a single metaphorical judgment the full range of God's presence in the church's life. This imaginative act, then, acts as a norm (Barth would call it a "discrimen" — a term Kelsey makes his own) in the interpreta-

---

[19] Kelsey, *Uses of Scripture*, p. 83.

tion of theology. Scientific biblical criticism and the tradition will both act to limit the metaphor's range.

The merit in Kelsey's phenomenological approach is that it intends simply to investigate where the authority of Scripture lies for an author. To be useful in examining the works of John Paul, the Protestant approach to Scripture discussed by Kelsey would need to be qualified within a Roman Catholic perspective, with weight being given to those other aspects of the tradition which have authority, alongside the Scriptures, within the believing community. As we have seen, in the writings of Pope John Paul these sources would include conciliar documents, especially those of Vatican II, the magisterial pronouncements of earlier popes, citations from traditional theological authors, notably Augustine and Aquinas, and liturgical and spiritual sources. If there is an overarching "discrimen" or "imaginative act" that links all of these and which might serve as a touchstone for us in examining the writings of John Paul II, our investigation of the scriptural categories from modern scholarship would suggest that "wholeness" or completeness (over against "separation" or even distinction) might be that category.

I would like to turn now and give a brief overview of the three encyclicals that have been our chief focus, mentioning briefly some indications of the way in which Scripture relates to the other sources within them to serve as a base for the teachings of John Paul and examining how the category of wholeness might be verified as the "discrimen" or "imaginative act" in his literary output at the level of magisterium.

a) *Redemptor Hominis*

The structure of RH suggests that a wholeness exists between Scripture and tradition, between Christ and, not only the Christian, but every person living on the face of the earth, between the Church willed and constituted by Christ and the Church which speaks to the world of today. John Paul begins the encyclical by situating himself in continuity with his predecessors and especially with their ministry which was concretized in the

Council and its implementation. He also sets his eyes on the future, specifically the year 2000, the second millennium of both the incarnation and the redemption which was its culmination.

The second section begins with a proclamation of Jesus Christ as one who is in solidarity with every man and woman who has ever lived or is alive today. Here we see that, though the Scriptures are quoted quite extensively, the fundamental truth about Jesus Christ is located in the unity of his incarnation and paschal mystery and that these two integral aspects of the one saving mystery serve to link Christ with every person, man, woman or child.

The third section speaks of redeemed humanity in the modern world and how much the world needs the mystery of redemption; this constitutes an overview of those issues of justice, human rights, anxiety about the future and the consumerism and false sets of relationships to which it leads -- all of which intimate how the church lives as one with the world and not apart from it. The last section shows how, in practice, the church addresses these issues through the *aggiornamento* called for by the Council.

However, and this truth John Paul is at pains to emphasize, the renewal of the church is not to be carried out in discontinuity from but rather in continuity with what had preceded, Christian life through the ages. This fourth or concluding section of RH is a veritable web of scriptural citations, allusions to the Council, papal pronouncements, etc., all of which argue a case for seeing continuity between the Church of today and of the eras which preceded our own.

b) *Dives in Misericordia*

If RH establishes a unity between the Christ of the Scriptures and the Christ at work in the Church today, DIM presents the unity of the vision of God as "rich in mercy" in both Old and New Testaments. In effect, DIM presents a biblical theology which shows that the God who had been revealed in the Old Testament is the one who frees peoples and cultures not simply from the oppression of Egypt and Pharaoh but, through the proclamation of the prophets, from the bondage of sin. This genuine liberation, which touches human life in this world and the inner dynamic of relationships between individuals and their God and neighbor both, is continued in the preaching and saving death of Jesus. For in his resurrection Jesus experienced "the love of the Father which is more powerful than death" (par. 8). Again, picking up a leitmotif from RH, the mercy of God is to be handed on "from generation to generation", and this is to take place through the Church. Here, too, the continuity of salvation history includes the triad God-Jesus-Church. The warrant for this, as in RH, may be verified by reading LG and GS, in harmony with earlier authors, whether these be popes, theologians or saints. The message is the same one through the ages, but especially as it is proclaimed by the Council in our time.

c) *Dominum et Vivificantem*

The encyclical on the Life-giving Spirit begins by noting that in every age the church has tried to reawaken the faith of believers and this has, inevitably, meant a rediscovery of the place of the Holy Spirit in the life and mission of the church. He locates the need to do this today in harmony with his two earlier encyclicals, RH and DIM, and sees the task as inspired, as they were, by the Council:

> For the Conciliar texts, thanks to their teaching on the Church in herself and the Church in the world, move us to penetrate ever deeper into the Trinitarian mystery of God himself, through the Gospels, the Fathers and the liturgy: to the Father, through Christ, and in the Holy Spirit[20].

This important emphasis on the Council shows us that, for John Paul, the Holy Spirit at work today in church and world is *the*

---

[20] DEV, par. 2.

principle of continuity throughout the Church's history, no
matter what the era:

> The Holy Spirit, in his mysterious bond of divine communion
> with the Redeemer of man, is the one who brings about the
> continuity of his work: he takes from Christ and transmits to all,
> unceasingly entering into the history of the world through the
> heart of man[21].

The constant series of references to John's Gospel and the
Epistles to the Romans and *Galatians* should, in this perspective,
be seen as the foundation on which all of the other historical
attempts at discerning the Spirit are based. A more detailed
inquiry showing these connections would no doubt be fruitful,
but its scope is too great for the task we have set ourselves here.

While not wishing to exaggerate the importance of this for
understanding the use of Scripture in the writings of Pope John
Paul, the cursory overview of three important encyclicals shows
that the "discrimen" of wholeness and continuity between the
original revelation in the Bible, the church through the ages and
the Council has some validity as an interpretative principle for
those writings. In DEV, John Paul himself links the Council with
the Gospels, the Fathers and the liturgy as a unified witness.

CONCLUSION

In a recent editorial that appeared in the *Canadian Catholic
Review* on the occasion of the publication of Pope John Paul's
apostolic letter on Saint Joseph, the Basilian Daniel Callam,
taking note of the sources which the pope referred to in it and
those to which he did not refer, wondered "whether theologians
have not been doing their work or whether the Holy Father has
chosen to ignore what they have to say". He went on to remark:

---

[21] *Ibid.*, par. 67.

I was struck also by the Holy Father's approach to the Infancy Gospels (the opening chapters of Matthew and Luke), which takes no account of the revolution in our understanding of these chapters effected by Catholic biblical scholarship. More than one exegete has pointed out the difficulty of symbolism in the narrative about the birth of Jesus. The symbolism is apparent: Jesus is the New David, the new Moses, a new Israel coming out of Egypt; although rejected by the leading Jews, he is accepted by outcasts (the shepherds) and gentiles (the magi); his herald, Elijah redivivus, prophesies from the womb (cf. Jer. 1:5); his mother is the virgin of Isaiah 7. But if one reads these chapters symbolically, to what extent can one treat them as if the events actually happened as described? The encyclical simply ignores the question. The Holy Father treats every dream, every vision, every incident as hard historical fact, no different, as history, than the parables of Jesus or his crucifixion[22].

The stance of Fr. Callam's editorial raises the issue we have been considering, but from another perspective. No longer now is it the wonderment of the scholar about John Paul's reluctance to incorporate academic conclusions about biblical writings into his pastoral ministry of teaching the meaning of God's revelation in Jesus Christ for the church and world of today, but rather here we find a critique of biblical scholarship, presumably out of a concern for the pastoral implications of the exegete's academic conclusions.

However, in our investigation of the uses of Scripture by Pope John Paul, we have noted that in all encyclicals (and in the apostolic letters to the extent that they share a high level of magisterial teaching authority), contemporary theologians are simply not quoted at all. It is not a case of John Paul having little or no respect for biblical interpreters or theologians. This is a case that cannot be argued from silence and, besides, there are many occasions on which the Holy Father has told theologians and exegetes of the importance of their work for the Church. Rather, for John Paul it just is not important to quote contempo-

---

[22] *Canadian Catholic Review* 8:3 (March 1990), 82-83.

rary theologians, from whom, after all, other theologians might, and generally do, differ. The parry and thrust of academics over controversial issues has its place in theological research, but not, apparently, in magisterial articulations of the present stance of our faith community's self-understanding. Yet, there is a role that scholarship can play in a general way, as we may infer from John Paul's occasional references to the fruits of research in the biblical field: the meaning of *hesed*, how the Septuagint translates the Massoretic Text here and there, what we can know of the biblical conception of the human personality, etc.

The implied criticism of biblical scholarship which Callam makes may have some foundation in regard to the effects of its conclusions on the faith life of the church or its pastoral consequences. That John Paul shares these would have to be a matter of conjecture, because he does not tell us this fact himself. If John Paul is consistent — and there seems to be no reason to think that he is not — the "discrimen" of wholeness would suggest that allowing scriptural scholarship to follow its proper methodology alongside the teaching authority of the magisterium is consistent with John Paul's vision of the guidance of the Council on the life of the Church today.

In conclusion, the role of the magisterium in the life of the church, as we see it in the writings of Pope John Paul II, is to point to the wholeness of the believing community's experience. In this perspective, there is no cleavage between the Christ of the synoptics and the Jesus of the Fourth Gospel, nor between the merciful and loving God of the Old Testament and the God revealed in Jesus and in our world today. Moreover, it is the one and same Holy Spirit who has been active in our world throughout the ages and is now manifest in the contemporary period, most evidently in the deliberations of the members of the Second Vatican Council and in the other processes of collaboration and consultation that have characterized the post-conciliar time (the synod of bishops, the work of episcopal conferences, the increasing role of the laity with the ordained ministers of the Church immediately come to mind as examples). Therefore, one is not to postulate a cleavage between the pre-Vatican II church and the church undergoing renewal through the thrust of the Council. The major liturgical, patristic, systematic, conciliar and magisterial documentation are witness to the integrity, the wholeness of the tradition. So too are the Scriptures which John Paul II loves to quote frequently and at length; these traditions are one with the Scriptures which they try to embody and actualize in each new set of circumstances of ecclesial life. And this reality is so even if, in his citation' of the Scriptures, John Paul does not preoccupy himself with representing the consensus of scholars on how to interpret those Scriptures in our day.

"A VISION OF WHOLENESS"

A Response

JAMES SWETNAM, S.J.

In order to illustrate John Paul's use or non-use of the results of modern biblical scholarship, Father Prendergast has chosen "several of the positions commonly agreed on by biblical scholarship today" These are: 1) Pentateuchal sources; 2) multiple authorship for the *Book of Isaiah*; 3) the three levels of the Jesus tradition within the Gospels; 4) the distinction between authentic and non-authentic Pauline letters; 5) distinctive traits of biblical writers and traditions[1]. The choice is instructive: four out of the five norms involve source criticism in some form or other. Only the fifth position is concerned primarily with the meaning of the text as it stands, and even here source criticism enters in.

Father Prendergast's choice of assured norms for judging the pope's use or non-use of modern biblical scholarship is a reminder that until fairly recently "literary criticism" in the world of biblical studies involved above all theorizing about sources. Only in the past twenty years has there been a major shift in emphasis to trying to discover above all what a biblical text means as it stands[2]. Commonly agreed-on results of modern

---

[1] T. Prendergast, "A Vision of Wholeness", pp. 73f.

[2] Scripture scholars have always been concerned about the meaning of the biblical text, of course. But granted the need for qualification in an area as vast

biblical scholarship in the realm of saying what a text means are
not as easy to come by as they are for source criticism. But the
meaning of the text as it stands is what John Paul seems to be
principally interested in. In an address to the members of the
Pontificial Biblical Commission on April 7, 1989, the pope
remarked that an exegete should not be content with secondary
aspects of biblical texts but should place in evidence their
principal message which is a religious message:

> Of late not a few Christians have been heard to complain that
> exegesis has become an exercise in subtlety with no relation to the
> life of God's People. Obviously such a complaint can be chal-
> lenged. In many cases it is not justified. Still, one must be on
> one's guard. Fidelity to the task of interpretation should lead an
> exegete not to be content with studying secondary aspects of
> biblical texts but to place in evidence their principal message
> which is a religious message, a call to conversion and good news
> of salvation, capable of transforming each person and human
> society as a whole by introducing it to communion with God[3].

By exhorting exegetes to emphasize the principal, religious
message of a text, the pope is joining his voice to those scholars
who feel that biblical scholarship is finally on track after decades
of over-emphasis on how the biblical text came to be.

Not only does John Paul seem to be unconvinced about the
commonly agreed-on results of source criticism as helpful for

---

and complicated and variegated as the history of exegesis, the generalization
seems valid.

[3] "Ces derniers temps on a entendu bien des chrétiens se plaindre de ce que
l'exégèse était devenue un art raffiné, sans rapport avec la vie du Peuple de
Dieu. Cette plainte peut évidemment être contestée; en bien des cas, elle n'est
pas justifiée. Il y a lieu, cependant, d'y être attentif. La fidélité même à sa tâche
d'interprétation exige de l'exégète qu'il ne se contente pas d'étudier des aspects
secondaires des textes bibliques, mais qu'il mette bien en valeur leur message
principal, qui est un message religieux, un appel à la conversion et un bonne
nouvelle de salut, capable de transformer chaque personne et la société
humaine, en l'introduisant dans la communion divine" (*AAS* 81 [1989] 1124).

illumining the meaning of the biblical text, he also seems to think that the results are not as assured as they should be to warrant drawing inferences from them[4]. In an address to the Biblical Commission in April, 1985, the pope stated that scholars should distinguish accurately the text of Scripture from conjectures however learned:

> Your ecclesial task should be to treat the Sacred Writings inspired by God with the utmost veneration and to distinguish accurately the text of Sacred Scripture from learned conjectures, both yours and others'. It is not unusual today with regard to this matter that a certain confusion be noted inasmuch as there are some who have more faith in views which are conjectures than in words which are divine[5].

Certainly the pope is not afraid to use modern scholarship when it seems to him to illumine the text: witness his use of philology in *Dives in Misericordia*[6]. And he does not hesitate to cite sources when they seem called for, as, for example, his references to Confucius, Gandhi, Buddhism, etc.[7] It is not sources as such which he fails to use, but sources which are uncertain and/or which fail to illumine the meaning of a biblical text.

All this does not mean, of course, that the pope's use of Scripture is always at odds with the meaning of the text. But if there are documents where his use of the biblical text is

---

[4] Cf. Prendergast's view (p. 77): "I suggest here that a conclusion worth considering is the recognition that the higher the authoritative level of the teaching given, the less likely the pope will be to allude to scriptural theories".

[5] "Vestrum ecclesiale munus efficere debet ut Sacras Litteras a Deo inspiratas maxima veneratione prosequamini, utque accurate secernatis textus Sacrae Scripturae a doctorum coniecturis, tum vestris tum aliorum. Non raro in hac re hodie quaedam confusio potest animadverti, quandoquidem quidam sunt qui recognitionibus maiorem fidem adiciant, quam quae verbis divinis debetur" (*AAS* 77 [1985] 972).

[6] Prendergast, pp. 72 and 78.

[7] *Ibid.*, pp. 72f.

impressive (*Dominum et Vivificantem*), there are others where such use is not always felicitous (*Redemptoris Mater*)[8].

John Paul's relative neglect of the conciliar document *Dei Verbum* may be an indication that he is not entirely at ease in the field of Scripture, as contrasted with philosophy and theology[9]. Could it be that this document of Vatican II, for all of its epoch-making significance, is not really adequate for giving detailed guidelines as to how Scripture should be fully restored to its place at the center of Catholic life and thought[10]? Father Prendergast's use of David Kelsey instead of some authoritative work of the magisterium seems to suggest as much[11].

Catholic scholarship should devote more attention to the elaboration of ways in which Scripture can find a purchase in contemporary Catholic life[12]. Father Prendergast suggest the category of "wholeness"[13]. While useful to remind Catholic scholars that they should work within not only the totality of Catholic tradition, but also within the global outreach of Christ and his Church, this seems too general to suffice. What is also needed is an agreed-on hermeneutics which will single out specific ways in which the Bible should enter into the life of Catholics.

In sum: unqualified negativity about John Paul's use of

---

[8] Mariology is an area in Scripture where contemporary biblical scholarship is bearing fruit. But much remains to be done.

[9] To judge from the non-biblical citations in the three encyclicals examined by Prendergast, the Vatican Council documents on the Church have pride of place in the thought of John Paul II. (Prendergast, p. 72.)

[10] The Church universal could benefit from a Synod of the Bishops centering on the pastoral use of the Bible. Such a synod could be the occasion for working out a preliminary official draft about the ways in which Scripture is "used" in the Church and thus act as a complement to "*Dei Verbum*".

[11] Cf. Prendergast, pp. 83-85.

[12] Cf. the remarks by R. Brown in his article on biblical interpretation in *The New Jerome Biblical Commentary*, ed. J.A. Fitzmyer, *et. al.*, (Englewood Cliffs: Prentice Hall, 1990), 1146-1160.

[13] Cf. Prendergast, pp. 85-88.

Scripture is not warranted; not infrequently it is insightful and inspiring. But when Father Prendergast's findings are viewed from the perspective of the pope's statements to the Pontifical Biblical Commission, the pope emerges as a wistful biblist. If he seems to be wistful, perhaps his wistfulness is caused by his vague suspicion that despite his willingness to learn from contemporary biblical scholarship he is still to some extent on the outside of the Bible looking in. And this can only be because, to a certain extent, contemporary biblical scholarship is in the same position.

THE SPIRITUALITY OF POPE JOHN PAUL II

Most Rev. John R. Sheets, S.J.

Part I. Introduction: pre-notes for understanding the spirituality of Pope John Paul II

Spirituality: Non-Christian, People of Israel, Christian

It is not easy to define the word "spirituality". It is often used today in a generic sense to describe what is common to all religions. One hears, for example, of the spirituality of Hinduism, of Buddhism, of Confucianism, as well as the spirituality of Judaism and Christianity. The same word, then, is used to describe the content of religions that are radically different in their perception of the divine, creation, history, and the meaning of the human person.

Used in this way, the word "spirituality" has a certain usefulness. It points to the fact that all religions touch in some way on the realm of the spirit. On the other hand, if it is left unexamined, it leads to great ambiguity. As applied to the People of God of the Old Testament, and even more particularly to the People of God of the New Testament, its sense is unique and cannot be used of other religions.

The word "spirituality" is also used to distinguish different patterns that the Holy Spirit creates to bring about a certain social concentration of some aspects of his gifts. For this reason, we speak, for example, of Dominican spirituality, Franciscan, Jesuit spirituality, lay, priestly, married spiritualities, etc. I shall comment on this again later in the paper.

Before attempting to describe the spirituality of Pope John Paul II, it is necessary to clarify the meaning of spirituality. I shall limit myself to the tradition of Judaism and Christianity. The spirituality of both the Old Testament and the New is sharply contrasted with that of all the ancient religions. In the interest of brevity, I shall limit myself to a few brief comments.

In the Old Testament, the Holy Spirit is the source of creation as well as the one who sustains creation (cf. Gen. 1; Ps. 104). The Spirit is both the creative as well as the differentiating Spirit. The first creation account in *Genesis* describes the work of the Spirit as source of all created reality. The description of the stages of creation as taking place within seven days, culminating in the Sabbath, is a way of describing the differentiating activity of the Spirit in creation. The creation account moves from non-living, to living, to man and woman, to the highest activity of man and woman symbolized in the Sabbath, the day of rest, where the human person finds his fulfillment in worship.

After the fall, the creative Spirit in *Genesis* becomes the *re-creative* Spirit. All of the activity of the Spirit in history, then, is to re-create, re-form, re-unite, re-orientate mankind to God. The intricate network of various re-creative acts turns around the covenant.

A new phenomenon comes into the world with the prophets of Israel. A new aspect of the presence of the re-creative Spirit comes into being. The Spirit unveils through human words the intentionality of God in his re-creative work.

In both the Old Testament and the New, the Spirit of God is seen both as the creative presence that grounds all created reality, and as the empowering presence who brings about the saving *events*. These events, then, take on another aspect of the Spirit as they are *sacramentalized*. The saving events are rendered present through the Spirit through sacred word and ritual.

In both the Old Testament and the New Testament, then, spirituality has to do with the way that a person's whole life is reoriented through God's entrance into history through saving deeds and saving words. Israel's way to God was through a faith-response to God who entered into their history. It was not primarily a response to God who was immanent within the world of nature.

It is important then, at the outset, to see the uniqueness of the work of the Spirit within the tradition of Israel. The Christian faith sees itself both in continuity with the spirituality of Israel, but also as the fulfillment of the promises of a new outpouring of the Spirit. "I shall give you a new heart, and put a new spirit within you" (Ezek. 36:25; cf. Jer. 31:31-34; Jl. 3:1-5; Acts 2:16-21). "When in former times God spoke to our forefathers, he spoke in fragmentary and varied fashion through the prophets. But in this final age he has spoken to us in the Son whom he has made heir to the whole universe..." (Heb. 1:1f.).

Coming to the New Testament, then, the fullness of the gift of the Spirit is inseparably linked to Christ. He is described as endowed with the gift of the Spirit without measure. "'He whom God sent utters the words of God, so measureless is God's gift of the Spirt'" (Jn. 3:34). "On the last and greatest day of the festival Jesus stood and cried aloud, 'If anyone is thirsty let him come to me; whoever believes in me, let him drink'. He was speaking of the Spirit which believers in him would receive later; for the Spirit had not yet been given, because Jesus had not yet been glorified" (Jn. 7:37-39).

Jesus' own spirituality then is a complete congruence of his inner self with the movement of the Spirit. All that he does has its origin in what he sees the Father doing. "'In truth, in very truth I tell you: the Son can do nothing of himself; he does only what he sees the Father doing'" (Jn. 5:19). This inner symmetry of Christ's mind, will, heart with the Father comes from the fullness of the presence of the Spirit.

Christ's spirituality is a re-creative, or a *redemptive spirituality*. "God so loved the world that he gave his only Son, that everyone who has faith in him many not die but have eternal life" (Jn. 3:16). The re-creative power of the Holy Spirit in Jesus empowers him to make a complete gift of himself. He is completely at the disposal of the Father's will. The Johannine emphases are found in the synoptics in the theme of the Suffering Servant and in the way that the Eucharist renders present Christ's self-gift for the world.

PART II. THE SPIRITUALITY OF POPE JOHN PAUL II

A. *The Pauline Character of Pope John Paul's Spirituality*

a) The Pneumatic Person

   The fullest expression of a redemptive spirituality is found in the letters of St. Paul. Naturally since he wrote in Greek, he makes use of the Greek word, *pneuma*, to translate the Hebrew word for spirit. Unfortunately the English words, spirit, spiritual, spirituality, do not carry the full weight of either the Greek or the Hebrew words for spirit. Paul uses the adjective, *pneumatikos*, to describe the person who has been transformed by the indwelling Spirit of God into the likeness of Christ.

   From now on, then, I shall make use of the words, *pneumatic person*, to help transmit the Pauline sense of the way that the Holy Spirit brings a whole new reality into existence, what he calls, "the New Creation". "When anyone is united to Christ, there is a new world. The old order has gone, and a new order has already begun" (2 Cor. 5:17).

   The Holy Spirit gives the baptized person a "paschal shape". He takes on the very image of Christ in his giving himself *for* us and *to* us in the paschal mystery.

   This pneumatic transformation affects every aspect of the baptized person. It pneumatizes his thoughts, affections, choices, attitudes, emotions. It works against all the anti-Spirit forces that remain: sin, sickness, the devil, and the inherent destiny to death, which belongs to all of us because of solidarity with the first Adam (cf. 1 Cor. 15:45).

   The spirituality of Pope John Paul II has a remarkably Pauline tone. It will be helpful, then, to sketch the main characteristics of Pauline soteriology to show the mutual similarities. Later on in the paper I shall attempt to bring out how the spirituality of Pope John Paul not only assimilates Pauline soteriology but has its own special emphases.

The spirituality of Pope John Paul II is inseparable from his theological thought. Both are remarkably Pauline. Going back a step further, the philosophical underpinnings of the Holy Father's thought form a kind of a foreshadowing on a rational level of the truths of revelation known through faith. In his thought there is found in an eminent way the compenetration of these two ways of knowing that are related but distinct, faith and reason.

His faith leads him to understand. And his understanding helps him see the divine "logic" within the truths of the faith. There is a remarkable consistency then between the philosophical thought and his theology.

The philosophical forshadowings are found in the way that he understands the human person, and the relationship of person to community. It is difficult to summarize his philosophical thought in a few statements. He sees the human person as a self whose unity comes from the unifying power of *self-possession*. The person, therefore, is "held together", sustained, and moved forward through his progressive self-possession. This self-possession involves a whole "field" of various activities. But most important are *consciousness* and *conscience*.

Self-possession, however, is not static. It is takes place through *self-realization*. Self-realization takes places through obedience to truth which is perceived through conscience. Self-realization is animated through love which energizes the person and draws the person upward and outward into various forms of *community*. The essence of community is com-munion, that is, oneness-with, a oneness that comes from a shared-existence.

Pope John Paul II's philosophical construct of the human person, then, has the following elements: a dynamic view of the person who is the center of various self-sustaining, self-realizing activities which draw the person into ever wider and deeper relationships with other persons and other things. The person, then, is sustained by act, realized by act, and finds fulfillment through act. However, act involves the other, that is, relationship, person. Person, relationship, community, consciousness, conscience — all of these are energized, held together, and directed through act.

There is a remarkable correspondence between the Holy Father's philosophical construct of the human person and what characterizes Pauline thought. It is something like the relationship between the geometrical forms which an artist draws to guide his expression in another medium, namely, the realm of art. Geometry and art are completely different modes of expression. But they are related when it comes to art. In fact, there is a certain continuity between them.

What are some of the factors that contributed to this remarkable symmetry between his philosophical thought and Pauline theology and spirituality? The principle influence in philosophy was, of course, St. Thomas Aquinas. John Paul's work on Max Scheler gave his thought a certain phenomenological turn. This was more through a certain methodological tuning rather than through influence on the content of his thought.

But there were other conscious and unconscious influences at work to form the particular constellation of elements that constitute his philosophy. In the Russian-dominated Poland in which he worked, all publications had to be submitted to censorship by state officials. Nothing could be published without the government's permission. Permission was often denied on the pretext that there was no paper. It was against the law to attack Marxism directly. Polish intellectuals took another approach. They raised the question: what does it mean to be human? They approached the answer to the question philosophically, but through a philosophy shaped by Christian humanism.

In this way they could avoid government censure. At the same time they could achieve a double objective: indirectly attack the Marxist system in its notion of man; at the same time present the Christian view from a philosophical perspective. This approach indirectly pointed to the basis of man's dignity as rooted in his relationship to God the creator and Christ the redeemer.

b) Symmetry Between Pope John Paul II's Philosophical Thought and Faith

After this little detour on the philosophical underpinnings and background of Pope John Paul II's thought, I want to return to Pauline thought and point out more explicity the symmetry between his philosophy and Pauline spirituality.

The following elements are key points in Pauline thought. It will be clear how the truths of faith find a certain symmetry or echo with the philosophical thought of Pope John Paul.

In the first place, there is the notion of *vocation*. It is the Father's call, in Christ, through the Holy Spirit, which initiates, sustains the whole process of salvation. Christian existence is always *response* to the call of the Father. Through revelation we know we are sustained from above, by God as creator and Christ as redeemer. The call to join into the new form of com-munion with Christ and the Father is *vocation*. This finds in Pope John Paul II's thought a counterpart in the inner dynamism of the personal subject to respond to the call to further and further humanization. The life of the acting person, if he is faithful to the demands of truth and love, forms a kind of spiral moving upward, toward the one who is calling.

Secondly, there is the centrality of *self-realization* through openness to com-munion with others. In Pauline thought nothing is more central than the way the person finds himself through entering into com-munion. This primary com-munion is with Christ. But this mode of com-munion draws a person into the ecclesial Christ, the Church.

The following thoughts are borrowed from Joseph Fitzmyer's book, *Paul and His Theology*[1]. He points out the central-

[1] J. FITZMYER, S.J., *Paul and His Theology*, 2nd ed. (Englewood Cliffs: Prentice-Hall, 1987).

ity of the notion of com-munion in Pauline thought. One way Paul expresses this com-munion is through the use of prepositions implying an intense intimacy with Christ. The Greek preposi- tions which are translated into English as "in", "through", "into", "with" become a way of expressing the most profound aspects of the identity of the Christian as com-munion.

The word "in", as "in Christ, in the Lord", occurs 165 times. It is a shorthand way of describing all the aspects of the identity of the Christian as a new person coming from his incorporation into Christ.

Paul often creates new words to express the transformation in the person as "acting-person". The one who is taken up into com-munion with Christ takes on the identity of the "Acting- Person" of Christ. He is "with-formed" with Jesus, "with-heir", "with-suffering", "with-crucified", "with-dying", "with-buried", "with-raised", "with-glorified".

The Church in Pauline thought becomes the *matrix* (Latin for "womb") which brings the person into com-munion with Christ and at the same time into com-munion with others united with Christ.

In John Paul II's philosophy of the acting-person, we find a certain philosophical silhouette of the fuller reality to which the acting-person is called. The human acting-person finds his fulfill- ment in being taken up into the Acting-Person of Christ. This is simply another way of re-stating the various ways that St. Paul describes the new identity of the Christian. "Baptized into union with him, you have clothed yourself with him. There is no such thing as Jew and Greek, slave and freeman, male and female; for you are all one person in Christ Jesus" (Gal. 3: 27f.). "Your mind must be renewed by a spiritual revolution, so that you may put on the new self that has been created in God's way, in the goodness and holiness of truth" (Eph. 4:23f.). "You have stripped off your old behavior with your old self, and you have put on a new self which will progress towards true knowledge the more it is renewed in the image of its creator" (Col. 3:9f.).

c) Relationship

The centrality of relationship in Pauline thought as well as in that of Pope John Paul is clear. It is important to grasp the full meaning this term took on in the Christian faith.

In his book, *Introduction to Christianity*, Joseph Ratzinger describes how the notion of relationship changed when it was used to express the com-munion within the Trinity as well as the other aspects of com-munion which define Christian existence.

> With the perception that, seen as substance, God is one, but that there exists in him the phenomenon of dialogue, of differentiation and of relationship through speech, the category *relatio* gained a completely new significance for Christian thought. To Aristotle it was among the "accidents", the chance circumstances of being, which are separate from substance, the sole sustaining form of the real. The experience of the God who conducts a dialogue, of the God who is not only *logos* but also *dia-logos*, not only idea and meaning, but speech and word in the reciprocal exchange of conversation — this experience exploded the ancient division of reality into substance, the real thing, and accidents, the merely circumstantial. It now became clear that the dialogue, the *relatio*, stands beside the substance as an equally primordial form of being[2].

Relationship then brings about a new identity, a shared identity, a oneness with Christ, a share in Christ's relationship to the Father. It is a *new creation* brought about through *union*, that is, relationship, with Christ.

Paul stressed the change that takes place in the center of one's being, the self. "I live now, not I but Christ lives in me" (Gal. 2:20). Philosophically and psychologically the statement is absurd. How is it possible to have two "I's", two selves, without some kind of schizoid or hybrid person? The answer lies in a new reality that has come about through relationship.

---

[2] J. RATZINGER, *Introduction to Christianity*, tr. J. Foster (New York: Herder and Herder, 1970), p. 131.

d) Transposition

C.S. Lewis has a favorite term he uses to describe the "descents" of God into different levels of our existence and the corresponding way that different levels of our existence are taken up into God's being. He calls it "transposition". It is the mystery of how the "more" is put into the "less". It is a phenomenon that takes place every moment of our lives on a human level, but we are scarcely aware of it. For example, my thought is going from my mind to the keys of the word processor, to the screen, to the printer. Your eyes are picking up little black marks called letters and words on a sheet of paper. But in the "less" of those black marks you pick up the "more" of my meaning. Similarly a composer does the same with little marks on a sheet of paper. A musician reads them and recreates the music of the composer.

All of the mysteries of our faith are in some way the transposition into us of what belongs to God: the breathing of his life and image into us. His inter-trinitarian relationships are breathed into the "clay" of our natural existence. The most mysterious of all the transpositions is that of the transposition of the Word into our human flesh: "And the Word became flesh and came to dwell among us" (Jn. 1:14). Closely related to this "descent" is the transposition of the Christ's mission into the "clay" of the apostles. "'As the Father sent me, so I send you'. He breathed on them, saying, 'Receive the Holy Spirit...'" (Jn. 20:21f.).

Those events are made present to us through the transposition of the transforming power of the paschal mystery into *sacramental signs*, into water and word in baptism, into bread and wine in the Eucharist, to touch us with the transforming power of the paschal mystery.

The whole mystery of the New Creation is the mystery of the manifold way in which a gift mode of com-munion comes about through the transposition into us of what belongs to Christ. "The one united to Christ is one spirit with him" (1 Cor. 6:17). "God's love has flooded our inmost heart through the Holy Spirit he has given us" (Rom. 5:5). "For the Spirit explores everything, even the depths of God's own nature... This is the Spirit we have received from God..." (1 Cor. 2:10,12).

In the writings of Pope John Paul, he explores the mystery of transposition, though he does not use the word. When he is speaking philosophically, he explores as it were the underside of the transposition, as we see it from below, from reason. In his encyclicals, instructions, homilies, he views it from above, as the paschal mystery illumines our minds with a new way of knowing (faith), and irradiates our hearts through a new mode of loving (charity).

B. *The Uniqueness of the Spirituality of Pope John Paul II*

Above I commented briefly on some of the ways that the word "spirituality" is used. Frankly I am uncomfortable with the word. It corresponds in some way to the word "style" in relationship to the actual writing of an author. A literary critic might be able to describe the "style" of, e.g., Shakespeare, Byron, Keats, etc. But what the word "style" describes is an abstraction. Style exists really only in the actual words of an author.

Similarly, the word "spirituality" is an abstraction. In the existential order only the *pneumatic person* exists. The Holy Spirit can, however, create, so to speak, a certain *species* of pneumatic person, that is, those whose lives form a certain identical pattern because they are given the same gifts. In this way, then, we can speak of certain "spiritualities"; for example, the spirituality of the laity, of priesthood, of religious life, secular institutes, Benedictine, Franciscan, Jesuit, priestly spiritualities, etc.

Different "spiritualities" arise, then, because the Holy Spirit draws forth from the natural gifts of different individuals special pneumatic gifts. The different "spiritualities" arise from a certain convergence of gifts toward a common focus. Those called into special vocations are drawn into this convergence to form a community, as we saw above when speaking of particular spiritualities, such as laity, religious life, priestly, etc.

This convergence has several components. First it draws them into a common *vision* within the overall faith-vision. Secondly, it gives them certain basic *instinct-orientations* that move them toward common goals and means. Thirdly, it draws them into *collaborative and supportive activities*, marked by the common vision and shared "inspirited" instincts.

After these long pre-steps we finally come to the point of this paper: how can we describe the spirituality of Pope John Paul II?

Recalling what was said above, spirituality is not an abstraction, not a "style" of the spiritual life. It is a particular way in which the Holy Spirit orientates the pneumatic person. The Holy Spirit provides a vision, with a focus, with an inner orientation of the self to express the fullness of the Spirit within a certain concentration or focussing of the gifts of the Spirit.

The key both to Pope John Paul II's theology and spirituality is in the title of his first encyclical, *Redemptor Hominis*. Those two words have to be seen as two foci within an ellipse. They are distinct, but inseparably related. Together they form a whole "field" which fills the inner space of the ellipse.

Redemptor is a word which sums up the whole turning of God toward men throughout salvation history "to rescue them from death and feed them in time of famine" (Ps. 32:19). It comprises the *motive* behind the saving deeds, God's mercy; the *goal*, eternal life; the *means*, Christ, Church, sacraments.

Hominis, man, is the other pole of the ellipse. They are inseparably related. All of God's saving activity converges on man. Why? "What is man that you should care for him?" (Ps. 8:4) Around that question and answer revolves the theology and spirituality of Pope John Paul II.

All of his letters unfold some aspect of this relationship, God as redeemer, and man as redeemed. The encyclical *Redemptor Hominis* presents the axis around which all his thought and heart revolve. On the one hand, the theme of redeemer is a way of focussing the whole meaning of God in his saving acts. The word, man, meaning the human person, both individually and collectively, gets beneath all differences of culture, history, religion, ethnicity, to point to that dignity which belongs to every human person.

This vision and orientation provides Pope John Paul II with the theological basis out of which he addresses all peoples, Christian, non-Christian, Jewish, pagan, Muslim, etc. It is the basis of his sense of respect for all human persons.

His own heart, his own spirituality, is also a redemptive heart, and a redemptive spirituality. He carries out the mission of Christ the redeemer, to free mankind from sin, error, prejudice, and to minister the healing and saving word of the gospel.

He can meet all people at whatever stage they are in their relationship to God, atheist, non-believer, believer, as did Christ the redeemer. This accounts for the mysterious sense people of all different backgrounds, ages, states of life, have that somehow he meets them personally where they are.

His second encyclical, *Rich in Mercy*, describes redemptive love as mercy. Mercy, he says, is another name for love, as it enters into the misery of another.

At the heart of all his talks, journeys, writing, is redemptive love as mercy. But these do not remain merely words. They are embodied in his inner self. He never comes across as censorious, condescending, but as the embodiment of mercy.

His letter on Mary, *Mother of the Redeemer*, situates the meaning of Mary within God's redemptive love. God's own redemptive love is realized through Mary's *fiat*. She herself enters deeply into the redemptive role of Jesus.

In his apostolic exhortation on the nature of religious life, *Gift of Redemption*, he unfolds the theology and spirituality of religious life as rooted in a redemptive mode of life.

The apostolic letter, *On the Meaning of Human Suffering*, is a profound meditation on the way that human suffering is a special way of sharing Christ's redemptive mission.

The profound roots of the his theology and spirituality are

disclosed in the encyclical, *Lord and Giver of Life*. Here he gets
to the *Pneuma* (Spirit) behind all the pneumatic activity in time.
The Holy Spirit is both within the Trinitarian life and the
inspirer, orchestrator of all the redemptive activity in time and
history. Hence he comes also to a kind of spiritual metaphysics,
an absolute basis behind all spirituality: the nature of the person
as one who finds himself in making a gift of himself. The theme
of the Holy Spirit as uncreated love-gift, the energizing power
behind all gift-giving, whether in nature, or in salvation, is the
heart of Pope John Paul's spirituality. The giving of gift, and
receiving of gift is found primordially in the communion that
constitutes the Trinitarian life. "'He will take what is mine and
declare it to you'" (Jn 16:13). "This communion has its original
source in the Father" (DEV 22).

"He himself, as love, is the eternal uncreated gift. In him is
the source and the beginning of every giving of gifts to creatures"
(DEV 34). "...the Holy Spirit becomes present in the Paschal
Mystery *in all his divine subjectivity*: as the one who is now to
continue the salvific work rooted in the sacrifice of the cross"
(DEV 42).

The Spirit is person-love, uncreated gift, the eternal source
of every gift that comes from God, the direct principle and the
subject of God's self-communication in the order of grace. "The
mystery of the incarnation constitutes the climax of this giving, this
divine self-communication" (DEV 50). "...the Church unceasingly professes her faith that *there exists in our created world
a Spirit who is an uncreated gift*" (DEV 62).

CONCLUSION

The Spirit has created within the mind, heart, and faith of
Pope John Paul II a remarkable coherence of philosophy,
theology, spirituality. He keeps repeating in one way or another:
"The way of the Church is man". The Polish word for "way" is
also the word for "path", "road". What I think he is saying here
is that the full weight of God's redemptive love, with its source in

the Spirit who is uncreated gift, is to pour all the riches of the gift into man. This is also the way of the Church. It has to follow the way of Christ, who followed the way chosen by the Father.

Everything in Pope John Paul's personality, life experience, grace turned him to man. His esteem of man is in sharp contrast to his experience of man's inhumanity to man during the whole of his life, especially his youth. He lived through the Nazi occupation. He spent most of his later years under Russian occupation until he became Pope. The horrors of Auschwitz took place within a day's journey from his home. Another one of the concentration camps was a few miles away from Lublin, where Karol Wojtyla taught before he was made bishop of Krakow.

How could someone who had witnessed the fury of man's hatred of man find at the heart of his faith the dignity of man and make that the theme of all his thought and teaching? Personally I think it was a mystical grace. Cardinal Lustiger of Paris calls Pope John Paul II a mystic. I think he is right.

His life is of a single piece. It is something like a fugue that has its own sense of unity. There are few people in history whose lives are an unfolding of a basic orientation that remains throughout. Such were Pascal, Newman, Teilhard de Chardin. Such also is Karol Wojtyla.

The way of the Church is to continue until the end of time to pour God's mercy and love into the human heart. "God's love has flooded our inmost heart through the Holy Spirit he has given us" (Rom. 5:5). That sums up the spirituality of Pope John Paul II, a pneumatic person who gives as a gift what he has received as a gift.

APPENDIX

There are many ways that a person can apply the spirituality of Pope John Paul to the *Spiritual Exercises*. The second part of *Lord and Giver of Life* is particularly helpful for the First Week. It deals with the Holy Spirit converting the human heart. The letter, *Rich in Mercy*, is particularly helpful for the Second and

Third Weeks. *The Christian Meaning of Suffering* is especially appropriate for the Third Week. The encyclical on the Holy Spirit is particularly helpful for the Fourth Week. The theme of the Spirit as gift and source of all gifts can fill out and enrich the basic theme of love as response to God's gift-giving in the *Contemplatio ad Amorem*. And of course the social encyclicals see justice as inseparable from the respect for human dignity.

THE SPIRITUALITY OF POPE JOHN PAUL II

A Response

GARY GURTLER, S.J.

Philosophy, theology, and scriptural exegesis have been described in the papers presented here as ways of approaching and understanding John Paul's thought and mode of action. It seems to me that such understanding is necessary but not sufficient. What they lack is the integration and motivation provided by his spirituality. John Sheets has given us a fine introduction for this project, pointing out the Pope's Pauline and hence Christocentric spirituality and highlighting the relational character of his understanding of the human person, with the consequent tension between the individual and the community. Both dimensions are essential for the Pope, showing his Catholic sense of the prominence of the individual conscience and at the same time how that conscience emerges within and is informed by the community, especially the community of faith.

In our own time of transition with the gnostic currents that seem always to be associated with such periods, the Pope articulates the Catholic tradition in a remarkably clear and apt fashion. This is particularly true in terms of his spirituality, which provides us with the integrative key to his use of philosophical and theological methods and concepts. Following John Sheet's lead, our reflections will be based on the encyclical, *Dominum et Vivificantem*, as well as his exhortation to religious, *Redemptionis Donum*. It is in this realm if anywhere that we have a chance for appreciating his role as teacher and supreme pastor in the Church. Let me draw out a few ideas that John Sheets has touched upon to indicate what I mean.

For me, the center of John Paul's spirituality is precisely that intuitive grasp of the paschal mystery that we find indicated so clearly in his writings. This provides the paradoxical center of his reflection on human nature, caught between the death and resurrection of Christ. His use of the professional tools of philosopher and theologian are at the service of this primordial experience of the Christian in relation to the mystery of Christ as described in the Scriptures and as realized in our lives through the sacraments. It is a way in which our approach toward the truth of the gospel parallels the way in which our knowledge of the created order is at once both subjectively and objectively attained. John Paul uses all the resources of contemporary thought, but does so only insofar as they can illuminate this basic mystery at the heart of his own experience, as it is of any Christian. He uses these contemporary resources as he does the tradition, to understand the nature and implications of the Christian mystery in a holistic way, as we saw in Terrence Prendergast's paper on John Paul's use of Scripture.

As an example, the Pope's analysis of the specific nature of religious vocation in his exhortation, *Redemptionis Donum*, can serve to illustrate the integration of his personalist philosophy and scriptural exegesis with his reflection on the Christian life. He uses the passage from the synoptic Gospels on the call of the rich young man (Mt. 19:21; Mk. 10:21; Lk. 18:22) to get at "the interior structure of a vocation" (RD 3). In the analysis that follows, this structure is an ecounter of love, in which the psychological and spiritual center of the individual, the "I", is constituted in relation to the other, but always with the choice or free response that preserves the individual's autonomy, even when the other is God the Father loving each one in Christ.

It is, I think, counterproductive to sort out the various strands of this analysis as if to determine where the philosophy or scriptural exegesis ends and the personal experience or pastoral role of John Paul begins. The richness is precisely their integration in his own life, and the poverty is in the response of the reader who can only pick up the one or two aspects that conform to his own interest or limitations. This integration, furthermore, gives the Pope's writings a unique universality. He is articulating most profoundly the Christian tradition, but in such a thoroughly human way that those of other religious tradition as well as non-believers can find in them, or perhaps more accurately in him, something that touches their own human experience.

However much this sense of the tradition is an expression of his own personal development and character, it is of course a fundamental responsibility of his office as chief pastor in the Church, serving the unity of the Church not only in our present global context but precisely as historically continuous. Certain themes become prominent from this point of view. John Paul, for example, has a profound sense of the sacraments that sees them as tied to the historical Jesus precisely in the context of the apocalyptic expectation of his return. He thus constantly reaffirms the realism of the sacramental presence, especially in the Eucharist, but does so not so much by appeal to scholastic categories of substance and accidents but by reference to the resurrected Christ and the power of the Spirit.

This emphasis on the resurrection for understanding the sacraments also allows him to connect them, as we see especially in *Dominum et Vivificantem*, with the mystery of sin and the human conscience. The problem of conscience points up strikingly his conflation of philosophical categories and theological concepts both with his own spirituality and his public role in these final years of the second millennium. It is hard to single out one passage from this sustained meditation on sin and conscience in Part II of *Dominum et Vivificantem*, but let the following serve as representative and as an inducement to read and ponder this whole section.

The *Holy Spirit "convinces concerning sin"* in relation to the mystery of man's origins, showing the fact that man is a *created being*, and therefore in complete ontological and ethical dependence upon the Creator. The Holy Spirit remind us, at the same time, of the hereditary sinfulness of human nature. But the Holy Spirit the Counsellor "convinces concerning sin" *always in relation to the Cross of Christ*. In the context of this relationship Christianity rejects any "fatalism" regarding sin (DEV 44).

This brief passage functions as a synthesis of John Paul's vision, as a Christian and as a human being, for these final years of the twentieth century. It is grounded in an understanding of human nature that is both the product of philosophical reflection and biblical revelation, with clear ethical or moral implications that do not shy away from the specific problems, global and regional, that face the human community of our time. One might say that the single aspect that is peculiarly Christian is the optimism expressed in the rejection of fatalism. It is also a very Christian way of expressing optimism since it is not a facile avoidance of the seriousness of contemporary economic, social and political problems nor their quick and illusory solution.

In a word, it is an optimism rooted in the cross of Christ, not as an historical event remembered but as a present reality operative through the resurrection of Christ in the power of the Spirit. I find that John Paul's approach highlights an aspect of the resurrection appearances that has been part of my own meditation in celebrating the paschal mystery during the past several years. It slowly dawned on me that these appearances always involve the confrontation of the sin and fears of the apostles with the peace and grace of the risen Lord. This means that the mission of the apostles is exactly as the Pope describes it, extending this forgiveness to others and lasting until the second coming.

This vision is much different from the secularized versions of Christianity operative in the western world, whether in Marxism or capitalism, where sin and evil are seen as something that can be eliminated from the human condition or are defined solely by the cultural context. John Paul sees sin precisely in relation to the cross of Christ and thus defined always as the relationship between the transcendent and the human response to it, with even the personalist structure of his thought finding its ultimate source and meaning at the foot of the cross.

There is thus no gnostic escape from the reality of evil, and further this same vision does much to explain John Paul's understanding of the Church and his mode of governance within it. I can only hint here in a quick sketch how his spirituality informs his notion of the Church as a community of faith. First, it is not a society modeled on the state. The state has the practical, and thus subordinate, function of serving the common good. The Church, however, is concerned with the meaning of human existence in all its profundity, not in a theoretical mode but in the lived expression of the sacramental encounter with Christ and its extension precisely through the Church to the whole human community. The sacraments as it were define the dynamic of Christian life, with the resources of philosophy and theology seeking to clarify that dynamic ever more completely.

The section on conscience remains central in this articulation of the nature of the Church, since conscience is the focal point both for the dignity of the individual and the responsibility of the Church to proclaim the moral law. John Paul writes:

> This capacity to command what is good and to forbid evil, placed in man by the Creator, *is the main characteristic of the personal subject.* But at the same time, "in the depths of his conscience, man detects a law which he does not impose upon himself, but which holds him to obedience" (DEV 43).

From such passages, we can see that John Paul's personalism is clearly and definitively post-Cartesian. The individual is not an isolated subjectivity, but in dynamic relation to the other. John Sheets gives justifiable prominence to this category of relation in Christian thinking in general and the thought of the Pope in particular. It is within this relational context that the Catholic tradition concerning the inviolability of conscience can exist without falling into individualistic chaos, and its hierarchical structure in conserving that tradition both challenges and checks itself and the individual conscience.

The same kind of dynamic can be found in positive form in his analysis of religious vocation with which we began these reflections. John Paul sees religious consecration as a response rooted deeply in the call of the gospel to each religious.

> This consciousness of belonging to Christ *opens* your hearts, thoughts and actions, with the key of the mystery of redemption, to all the sufferings, all the necessities and all the hopes of the human community and of the world itself, in the midst of which your evangelical consecration has inserted you as a particular sign of the presence of God (RD 8).

As conscience is the locus of the inviolable worth of each human being, so the response to the call of God reveals the capacity of that same individual to take upon himself the deepest concerns of the other without limit. In the interplay of the two concepts, conscience and consecration, we find the dynamic that keeps both of them healthy and human. A conscience that closes the individual off from his fellows is somehow radically ill-formed and a consecration that receives gifts that are not shared forfeits those very gifts.

The governance that operates in this realm of personal relationship, however it may be described politically or socially, must also have this essentially personal character. Perhaps this explains the keen sense John Paul has of his role as the visible and personal center of unity in the Church, and the great importance he places on the pastoral visitations he makes. In addition, he clearly sees his responsibility as preserving and fostering the unity of the Church not only across the cultural and linguistic diversity of the present, but in deep continuity with the past. It is only in and through her past that the Church has continuous access to that fulness of time in Jesus Christ, a perspective clearly at odds with an idolization of the present with its peculiar myth of scientific and technological progress. His personal experience during and after World War II surely gives his opposition to the various formulations of that myth enduring credibility in the dual role as pastor within the Church and as its representative on the wider world scene.

HUMAN SOLIDARITY AND THE CHURCH IN THE THOUGHT OF JOHN PAUL II

JOSEPH MURPHY, S.J.

1. *Karol Wojtyla: From Nature to Person*

In assessing the thought of John Paul II on the solidarity of mankind it is worthwhile reviewing briefly his earlier philosophy as a backdrop to his theological work. Many Christian readers have at least some idea of Karol Wojtyla as a phenomenologist reliant upon the work of Max Scheler and the developments of a school of thought from Husserl onward. His familiarity with the French existentialists and personalists is quite prominent in his commentaries on freedom and subjectivity. Yet these avenues of thought are for Wojtyla also responsive to his earlier grounding in Thomism and Neo-Scholasticism. Two of our participants at this conference, Fr. John McDermott and Fr. Gerald McCool, have, in previous talks, accurately summarized Wojtyla's journey from philosophy into theology and made my rather limited investigation of his more difficult works both enjoyable and enlightening. I refer the reader to their papers for judging the accuracy of what immediately follows.

In his talk "The Theology of John Paul II", Gerald McCool notes that John Paul is a Thomist, updated by Scheler, who writes a metaphysics of man and being. Wojtyla's first dissertation, *Faith According to Saint John of the Cross*, demonstrates a faith purged of conceptual species but still attached to historical revelation[1]. Firmness in faith must be attributed to the ability of the mind to dispense with conceptual knowledge, and so the mind rises above the science of theology to adhere to the substance of revelation in the non-conceptual wisdom of contemplation. McCool claims, however, that today John Paul would reject this position, based as it was on a metaphysics of universal nature and not on the concrete conscious person. The closest such a metaphysics could come to man, Wojtyla would later say, would be a metaphysics of the supposit, an individual subsistent endowed with a rational nature; and in such a scheme the unique inner experience of the acting person would be seriously downplayed since conscious experience could not receive its due. To correct this, Wojtyla would later say that the metaphysics for a good theology must start with man as a unique, free, concrete subject, aware of his responsibility. In this way, responsible self-giving love would form the bond of *communio*.

Wojtyla's personalism, however, McCool notes, is not compatible with an idealism of pure consciousness or with the sensism of empiricism, in both of which the self-determining agent is surrendered to a partial experience. Subjectivity for Wojtyla is, then, man's awareness of his own subsistent being, revealed in its activity through what St. Thomas could name an immediate act of *intellectus*. In this way Wojtyla moves to an experientially grounded metaphysics of act, potency, immanent and transient action, nature, finality, person, and so on. This is a change from the older Thomism of Garrigou-Lagrange and others in that the acting person is not just an item cut to fit inside of an abstract general nature; rather, human nature is now placed inside the intelligibility of the conscious person.

John McDermott, in analyzing at length *The Acting Person* (1969), agrees with McCool's intepretation of Wojtyla's personalism and adds that theology after Chalcedon "wavered be-

[1] Karol WOJTYLA, *Faith According to Saint John of the Cross* (San Francisco: Ignatius Press, 1981).

tween person and nature", so to speak[2]. Wojtyla chose to reject the minimalist Boethian view when he agreed with Scholastics who had spoken of person as subsistent and incommunicable, and with Maritain who saw person as that which exercises an act of existence, a view unlike Garrigou-Lagrange's, which described person more like a point terminating a line. In *The Acting Person* Wojtyla allowed for self-knowledge not just through reflection after an intellectual act but through an intuition of self like that of Maritain's immediate knowledge of the soul's act of existence. Then Wojtyla placed freedom at the center of personhood and incommunicability, where the will exercises its self-governing.

McDermott notes that, for Wojtyla, person and nature mutually condition each other, operation follows being, personal freedom is bound to objective truth, and natural instincts reveal values which freedom must acknowledge. Thus, natural law, from which no one is absolved, must be personally integrated because objective truth speaks to conscience in revealing the will of a personal God.

In short the person dynamizes himself, the person which is the ego, the individual spiritual unity of knowing and willing previous to, above, or underlying the natural distinction of faculties. Man's spirituality is now described either in terms of a soul formally opposed to matter and known by abstraction or else by a freedom tied to a body as a unity in diversity, a freedom that must be won over this diversity which grounds man in the world of natures. Also, McDermott can find in Wojtyla an obvious tension between person and nature. On the one hand, person has free determinations while nature reacts to stimuli. Yet, nature is also dynamic with regard to final cause while person, though free, moves toward further development.

---

[2] John M. McDermott, "The Theology of John Paul II: A Response" John Paul II Conference, Loyola University, Chicago, 1990. Fr. McCool's talk was also presented at this meeting.

Both Fr. McCool and Fr. McDermott pursue the early theological consequences of Wojtyla's personalism. McCool says that in *Sources of Renewal* (1972) Cardinal Wojtyla, in commenting on the documents of Vatican II, moved to treat ecclesial faith as the Church's awareness of her own nature and her link to the Triune God[3]. Thus, faith is not mere assent but a vocation in the Church subsequent to the missions of the Trinity and with the Church herself the source of mission for all. McCool claims that, whereas in the order of creation persons gave themselves in self-donation within societies, in the order of grace each person joined himself to God by entering the *communio* of the Church by overcoming through Christ's Cross the selfishness of closure. The Church is now a *communio* of free persons caused by the Trinitarian missions. Finally, McCool would liken Wojtyla's metaphysics of a free self-conscious person to that of Rahner in that both men express an intrinsic continuity between the orders of creation and redemption once Church is linked to Trinity. McCool compares Wojtyla to the transcendental Thomists in so far as his theology of faith is a participation in the communal consciousness of the Church. Rahner, for example, had an abiding non-conceptual consciousness of Church in contrast to dogmatic statements of a categorical kind, paralleling the distinction in Thomism between *intellectus* and *ratio*, and in Lonergan between meaning and its cultural expression.

McDermott also looks to the nature-grace, creation-redemption relation in Wojtyla to observe his philosophy moving into a theology. He says Wojtyla overcame the argument, as in Garrigou-Lagrange or Maritain, of a natural dynamism for God by showing that, although abstractly known natures methodologically safeguard a distinction betwen the natural and the supernatural, man's personal transcendence demands the God of grace revealed in Christ. This "natural" dynamism is, as trans-

---

[3] Karol WOJTYLA, *Sources of Renewal: The Implementation of the Second Vatican Council* (San Francisco: Harper and Row, 1980).

cendental, really personal and not of nature. Hence, Wojtyla's Christocentrism is never grounded in the necessity of nature but is directly from God in faith.

McDermott finds only moderate agreement between Wojtyla and the transcendental Thomists. Whereas in earlier writings the self-determining, self-possessing subject only "accidentally" puts himself in relation with others, in *The Acting Person* Wojtyla portrays an intersubjective person, one in contrast to that familiar person of "incommunicability", yet one displaying the appropriate paradox of necessarily leaving self to be given to another.

Lastly, McDermott finds in Wojtyla that "balance" of God and the world, of infinite and finite, that philosophical analogy which gives man some knowledge of God but lets him be free before revelation. He says Wojtyla "joins transcendence and limitation in the human requirement to respond to moral obligation". His method kept him close to the concrete, as when faith-experience of the Church is a *de facto* reality, without denying conceptual validity, so that the unique human supposit might remain free before grace as gift with the objectivity of truth. Still, questions remain for McDermott: How can the necessities of nature be subsumed under person without being rendered non-necessary? Is not freedom then arbitrariness? How are conceptual formulations and intuitions joined? How can person be a dynamism without reducing freedom to a potency-act analysis?

Both McCool and McDermott, more fully than this summary indicates, in tracing the transition from Wojtyla's philosophy to a theology, leave us with further questions which, I believe, Wojtyla, as John Paul II, the eminent theologian, adequately answers. Let me describe the issues for which we seek a resolution in his theology.

One could wonder if the conflict between person and nature, freedom and determinism, nature and history, the universal and the particular, as in Scholastic controversy, or the one and the many, as in classical antiquity, is not a replay of a rationalism that sees truth as necessary rather than free. A sophisticated personalism of a merely philosophical sort provides the same dilemma as the abstract analysis of nature. To use person rather than nature as a starting point is to flip the coin over, like Lonergan's choice, for example, to begin philosophy with epistemology rather than metaphysics. "Person over nature" sounds like a return visit to an argument between radical existentialism and nature-oriented essentialism.

Yet, the effort to begin with person over nature is a plea for concreteness and historical rootedness. The danger, however, lies in exalting the personal subjectivity of freedom toward an unstructured autonomy such that there is in man no responsiveness to an exterior norm. Conversely, the other danger lurks in obedience to a law which, as deductive, seems inferior to man's dignity. The objections to *Humanae Vitae*, for example, critical of a so-called biologism or physicalism, display the anxiety of modern consciousness in the face of any fixed humanity which would threaten to stifle creativity. The solution of Josef Fuchs and others, that human nature *is* creative reason, still lacks an exterior objective norm without which morality is caught in its endless situational subjectivity. Even the personalist philosophy of Karol Wojtyla, at least as far as *The Acting Person*, leaves its readers still searching for that strange "balance" between person and community, between subject and object, freedom and necessity. His personalism remains, without his further theology, too limited to subjectivity. The only objectivity worthy of human "nature" is a personal objective Other which cannot be simply spatially opposed to the acting self or embraced by its functions but which must share a union with that self other than by accidental relation.

2. *John Paul II: From Person to Co-Person*

The effort of the philosopher Wojtyla to move beyond "nature-analysis" to a person-centered freedom and historicity is reminiscent of many personalist works, among them, in English-speaking philosophy, that of John Macmurray in his famous Gifford Lectures of 1953 and 1954[4]. Eschewing both an existential philosophy lacking in formal structure and an overly formal analytic-linguistic philosophy lacking in content, Macmurray held that the heritage of modern and contemporary thinking delivered to the philosophical world a person-less void. For him the mistake since Descartes onward was the naming of the thinking self as primary and the acting self as derivative. With great care Macmurray in *The Self as Agent* attempted to show that the unreal (derivative or secondary) self is the thinking self and the real (acting) self is primary. A human subject must be in act before exercising the derivative powers of thought, and so on. He thus rejects the Cartesian criterion of transcendental universal doubt as non-historical and he finds similar criticism for much of the idealist tradition.

The attempt by Wojtyla and other personalists to overcome the limits of abstract conceptualization with intuition and contemplation is clearly an attempt to begin cognitional analysis immersed in reality. The acting person of Wojtyla resembles the self-as-agent which Macmurray posits as the true person. Almost immediately, however, Macmurray found even this self hardly an improvement on that isolated self of thought. The person cannot act in a void and the only true or real self is the co-agent, the reactive, relational person. In *Persons in Relation*, the second set of Gifford lectures, Macmurray makes the sub-personal world derivative from a knowledge of the personal, from an immersion in immediate co-personal activity from earliest childhood whereby self-knowledge is first a knowledge of not being the already known and experienced Other — the mother, the more distant father, that tree. Macmurray finds the human cosmos known and

---

[4] John MACMURRAY, *The Self as Agent* (London: Faber and Faber, 1957); idem, *Persons in Relation* (London: Faber and Faber, 1961). These two volumes also bear the common title *The Form of the Personal*, Gifford Lectures in 1953 and 1954.

built, then, not by the dispassionate, distant "looking" activity of subject toward object, but by the clash of wills. Though he concludes to only a natural theology, his overcoming of both the limited primacy of derivative thought and the isolationism of separated subjective freedom leaves room for a Christian explanation of the personal cosmos in terms of the New Covenant in which Christ is the personal free formal cause of a personal humanity, a point to be dealt with later.

Before describing John Paul II's theology of humankind, richer than the term "personalism" signifies, I mention three further difficulties in the above philosophical descriptions. Firstly: there is not yet a clear explanation of the human person as embodied. Secondly: substance remains superior to relation, which is treated as accidental. Thirdly: "person" is treated as a category. We shall see how John Paul has given us a theology of the human person which is at once a Christocentric cosmology and eschatology and which conquers these difficulties.

John Paul II leaves no doubt in his early writings as pope that he has a way to advance his early personalism. He transcends reflection on the "person" of philosophy by defining Man, male and female, as in the image of God. The image is no longer the rational supposit or incommunicable subject but is a co-personal unity analogously reflective and re-presentative of the Trinitarian God. Hence, to be image is not merely to possess intelligence and will as an isolated subject, however dynamic, free, creative or intuitive one may be. Humans do not independently image the pure-spirit deity, the *Deus Unus* of natural theology, but rather the Father who sends the Son to give the Spirit. In the co-personal relation of the couple there exists the male, the female and the bond, a tri-relationality constitutive of human identity.

It can then be said that male and female share the same nature but differ as persons, with the advantage that the elusive "incommunicability" of the rational supposit now enjoys the visible complementarity of the sexual distinction. The mystery of what is incommunicable is replaced not with what is ordinary but with what is irreducible, both in its inexhaustible connection with the transcendence of spirit and in its dynamic relationality as a being-for-another. This means that sexuality for John Paul II has a primacy in the order of being and is not mere function. The quality of being male or female is an entitative habit, not a secondary difference like race, nationality, or language. By elevating the uniqueness of personal incommunicability, better called "unrepeatability", to the embodied condition of sexual otherness John Paul can speak of the human community, here the couple, as effectively substantial. Since his personalism insisted on the priority of person over mere nature, particularly the lower nature of unfree supposits, and since personal being is, as the core of substantial freedom, primarily relational, then the true, more accurate substance will be the human species itself. His *Original Unity of Man and Woman* develops these very themes.

The definition of Man in *Genesis* 2 reveals his double solitude, that of being alone as different from things and animals and that of needing a partner. Solitude defines Man's subjectivity as it is constituted by self-knowledge[5] and by a unique relationship with the Creator, a solitude known from the body, which tells him he is among but different from the animals and a solitude with which he is also person[6]. In a sense corporality precedes sexuality in that Man's original solitude as difference precedes his sexual isolation; but the Man of *Genesis* 2 returns to sleep (non-being) in order to re-emerge as dual by the exclusive power of the Creator[7]. The fuller creation of Man as a unity in

---

[5] JOHN PAUL II, *The Original Unity of Man and Woman: Catechesis on the Book of Genesis* (Boston: St. Paul Editions, 1981), address of October 19, 1979. Citations from *Original Unity* and from *Marriage and Celibacy* (note 16 below) are referred to more helpfully by the date on which a talk was given since both collections were the pope's general Wednesday audiences in those years, 1979-1984.

[6] *Original Unity*, October 24, 1979.

[7] *Ibid.*, November 7, 1979.

duality displays the very identity of human nature. Man became the image of God not only through his own humanity but also through the communion of persons which man and woman form. Man is right from the beginning not only an image of God through spiritual reason and will, which reflect the solitary Person or Deity ruling the world, but also and essentially Man is an image of a divine communion of persons. In saying "flesh of my flesh" Adam identifies the essence of humanity. The sexual body reveals Man[8].

John Paul goes on to say that male and female are two incarnations of the same solitude, two ways of being a body, of being human, two complementary dimensions of self-consciousness and self-determination. That is, femininity finds itself in the presence of masculinity and masculinity is confirmed through femininity[9]. The shamelessness of body-consciousness or nakedness in *Genesis* 2 stands for an original depth inherent in the person, that which is visibly male and female, through which the personal intimacy of mutual communication is constituted. This exterior perception corresponds to the interior fullness of man's vision in God[10]. Nakedness signifies the good of God's vision before any rupture occurs between what is spiritual and sensible or between what is human and what is sexual[11].

The pope states that, in effect, the body expresses the person since man alone does not realize his full essence unless he is also with and for another. In this sense there is no human nature of only the isolated subject. The self-consciousness of Adam and Eve after the Fall, the destructive, non-immediate self-knowledge, a knowledge also of good and evil and naked-ness, first allows for "nature" to be limited to the isolated person or rational supposit. This later self-knowledge leads to self-

---

[8] *Ibid.*, November 14, 1979.
[9] *Ibid.*, November 21, 1979.
[10] *Ibid.*, December 19, 1979.
[11] *Ibid.*, January 2, 1980.

awareness in the sense of self-worship. But before the Fall Man comes into being with consciousness of the finality of his own masculinity-femininity, that is, of his own sexuality[12]. John Paul claims that the teaching of *Genesis* on the nuptial meaning of the body is the fundamental element of human existence in the world, a meaning that can only be understood in the context of the person. The body has a nuptial meaning because the man-person, as the Council says, is a creature that God willed for its own sake and that can fully discover itself only in a sincere self-giving[13].

The pope refers often to the male-female primacy of *Genesis* as primordially sacramental, revelatory of the hidden God. This sacrament is constituted with man as a body by means of his visible masculinity and femininity, for the body alone is capable of making visible what is invisible: the spiritual and the divine[14]. Sex decides not only the somatic individuality of man, but defines at the same time personal identity and concreteness. In this personal identity and concreteness, as an unrepeatable female or male self, Man is known. The "knowledge" about which *Genesis* 4 speaks arrives at the roots of identity and concreteness which man and woman owe to their sex, a concreteness that signifies the uniqueness and the unrepeatability of the person[15].

In a later work on the same theme, *Marriage and Celibacy*, the pope further ties the body's original innocence to the eschaton, noting that sexual characteristics, as primary, remain in spite of there being no marrying in the end time, as in *Luke* 20, *Matthew* 22 and *Mark* 12[16]. We need to think of the reality of the

---

[12] *Ibid.*, January 9, 1980.
[13] *Ibid.*, January 16, 1980.
[14] *Ibid.*, February 20, 1980.
[15] *Ibid.*, March 5, 1980.
[16] JOHN PAUL II, *The Theology of Marriage and Celibacy: Catechesis on Marriage and Celibacy in the Light of the Resurrection of the Body* (Boston: St. Paul Editions, 1986), address of December 2, 1981.

"other" world in the categories of the rediscovery of a new and
perfect subjectivity of everyone and at the same time of a new
perfect intersubjectivity of all such that eschatological reality will
become the source of the perfect realization of the trinitarian
order in the created world of persons[17]. The original significance
of being a body, as well as being male and female, relates to Man
created as person and called to life in a communion of persons.
Marriage and procreation in themselves did not determine
exhaustively the original meaning of being a body but gave it a
historical dimension. In the risen state the nuptial meaning of the
body will still be realized as personal and communitarian[18].

It is now possible for virginity and continence in this life to
be "sexual" states which anticipate the eschatological virginity of
the risen Man revealed in the absolute and eternal nuptial
meaning of the glorified body in union with God, glorified also
through the union of a perfect intersubjectivity[19]. And thus,
maleness and femaleness, proper to the very constitution of
humanity, along with their unity, remain "from the beginning",
that is, to their ontological depth, the work of God[20]. Christ's
words in *Matthew* 19 lead Man toward the call in which, in a new
way even though remaining dual by nature and directed as man
towards woman and as woman towards man, Man is capable of
discovering in his solitude, which never ceases to be a personal
dimension of everyone's dual nature, a new and even fuller form
of intersubjective communion with others through celibacy and
virginity[21].

Lest our treatment of a human nature in its entitative
duality, as opposed to the monistic individuality of a rational
supposit with only accidental relations, make one imagine that all
must marry in order to acquire human actuation, the pope's

---

[17] *Ibid.*, December 9, 1981.
[18] *Ibid.*, January 13, 1982.
[19] *Ibid.*, March 24, 1982.
[20] *Ibid.*, March 31, 1982.
[21] *Ibid.*, April 7, 1982.

doctrine on celibacy and solitude, as linked by Christ to sexual bodily duality in both the beginning and the eschaton, makes the co-personhood of the primordial covenant pluriform. The woman in *Canticles* 4, for example, is both sister and bride with "sister" expressing the union in mankind alongside her difference and her feminine originality, and not only regarding sex but in the very way of "being person", which, for John Paul, means both "being subject" and "being in relationship"[22].

John Paul always quotes the rich doctrinal and patristic traditions of the Church which refer to Christ as the Spouse of the Church and the Spouse of souls, given to both in Eucharistic mystery. For him the key to understanding the sacramentality of marriage, not to mention the nature of humanity, is the spousal love of Christ for the Church demonstrated in *Ephesians* 5. Christ is Head of the Church as Savior of His Body. The Church is exactly that Body which receives from Him all that through which it becomes and is His Body. As Head and Savior of the Church He is also Bridegroom of His Bride, as husband with this wife, as head with this body[23]. Furthermore this spousal analogy does not destroy all head-body talk even though it is clear that an organic (unfree) union is not at issue. As man and woman are two distinct subjects, the spousal union is described as "one flesh". The pope admits that Christ is a different subject from the Church but that in view of His relationship He is united with her *as in* an organic union; that is, the Church is so strongly herself in virtue of a union with Christ. The pope even sees each baptism as a kind of spousal love in which the Church is prepared for Christ[24]. As for the Church being a sacrament, the pope reminds us that Vatican II says it is *in the nature of* a sacrament, not that it is a sacrament, and that the use is only analogical to that of the seven sacraments.

---

[22] *Ibid.*, May 30, 1984.
[23] *Ibid.*, August 18, 1982.
[24] *Ibid.*, August 25, 1982.

On several occasions John Paul refers to marriage as a primordial sacrament, as from the beginning. It is not then surprising that, since the Christ-Church relation parallels that of marriage, and vice versa, that Christ is also always present in the beginning. Numerous references to *Colossians* and *Ephesians* point out the existence in his theology of a primordial Christ in whom we are chosen before the foundation of the world and in whom the eternal plan was hidden for ages and then revealed. Between *Genesis* and *Ephesians*, of course, the rich tradition of the prophets intervenes, as in *Isaiah* 54 where "your Maker is your husband", another reference to an inchoate spousal love transformed fully in *Ephesians* 5[25]. The pope states clearly that the biblical analogy serves more as an existential intuition in which the analogates are all but reciprocal in their causality. That is, the biblical analogy of spousal love not only explains the ineffable mystery of our foundation in Christ before the world but the mystery also defines and determines the understanding of the analogy so that the comparison of marriage to the Christ-Church relation decides the manner of understanding marriage itself. The visible sign of marriage in the beginning of time linked to the visible sign of Christ and the Church transfers the eternal plan of love into a historical dimension. *Ephesians* brings both of these signs together into one great mystery or great sacrament[26].

It would seem from John Paul's repeated emphasis on *Ephesians* that he treats the orders of creation and redemption as one, possibly favoring the Scotist view of the Incarnation which has a Christ present to the world not only *propter peccatum*. He says that before sin Man bore in his soul the fruit of eternal election in Christ by which election Man, male and female, was holy and blameless before God, a primordial innocence in the shamelessness of that original nakedness in *Genesis* 2. That is, the reality of man's creation was already due to the perennial

---

[25] *Ibid.*, September 22, 1982.
[26] *Ibid.*, September 29, 1982.

election in Christ. The later sin would turn this ever-present and faithful Christ into our Redeemer. Hence, the pope can call the original duality of the sinless couple of *Genesis* a testimony that marriage is a central part of what he calls the sacrament of creation and thus marriage is the primordial sacrament[27]. The same sign of marriage continues from creation across to redemption, showing that there is a single order of imaging the divine even before sin and that this imaging and its healing include the bi-subjectivity of the bodily.

One drawback to analogical language is that the hearer might approve of the beauty with which Christ and Church are called spouses but fail to see here more than a wonderful fitting metaphor, a kind of intentional extrinsic attribution which reduces the "one flesh" language to something purely spiritual. But John Paul insists that the sacramentality of marriage is not merely a model and figure of the sacrament of Christ and the Church but an essential part of the new heritage. Granting that it is a prototype and that all sacraments find their prototype in marriage, he adds that the comparison is not merely metaphorical but a renewal or re-creation of that which constituted the salvific content of the primordial sacrament of creation[28]. He does not wish to take away from the Christ-Church relation anything that marriage means or has in its sign value at creation. We can then suppose that the union of Christ with the Church is not less substantial than that between husband and wife. Secondly, if male and female are united by inclusive nature and not merely by relational accident but by a union as ontologically rich as any meaning that the term "substance" could confer, then we can describe the unity of humankind in the Church as co-personally substantial and the union of this Church with Christ as the same. This leads to the paradoxical notion of a free substantiality which we will treat below.

---

[27] *Ibid.*, October 6, 1982.
[28] *Ibid.*, October 20, 1982.

If we can now observe a progression from his philosophy to his theology, we can say that John Paul has taken his original personalism beyond the isolation of a free, intuitive, contemplative, existential subject who "reaches out" for another in accidental relation. To be human is to be in another and for another just as it is to be from another in creation. The "creation in Christ" of *Ephesians* 1, *Colossians* 1, and in the prologue of John's Gospel points to a humanity whose self-awareness is that of being irrevocably given, a being-created that is unerasable but one which has yet, paradoxically, to be accepted, a further actuation known as life in the Spirit. In *Genesis* 2 this proper self-awareness was one of definitive presence to God through the mediate presence to the creation, when Adam knew himself in depth through Eve without the "self-consciousness" of nakedness, the result of a flawed attempt at self-creation, of trying to "be like gods". This unfallen consciousness alone, however, as participated *intellectus* or as pure reason, did not account sufficiently for our subjectivity and our imaging of God because of the absence in it of reference to the body. But *Genesis* clearly says that only the embodied spirit knows the other and that the sexual differentiation accounts for the first instance of total human recognition.

We are perhaps too accustomed to distinguishing persons in God from persons on earth, in that we assign one substance to the former and one substance for one person to the latter. Our contention is that this is a cosmological heritage from a natural theology which originally concludes to a deity whose trinitarian relations are "accidentally" added to our knowledge of God by the gratuitous extra of revelation. A primordial Christocentrism, as John Paul uses it, improves on this. I am suggesting therefrom that the union of persons, prototypically in the marital bond, subsequently in the Church, salvifically in the New Covenant union of Christ and the Church, and eventually in the eschaton, is properly called substantial. Some of Aristotle's critics say he did not conclude for sure whether the human individual or the species was more properly the substance. Boethius settled on the rational supposit. But is not the mind's search for conceptual unity and for the supposit compatible with a richer metaphysics, respectful of relation, in which the union of two subsequent subjects is ontologically more profound than the comfortable unity of the supposit? One sometimes hears: "The marital bond: that's only a relation", or "Christ and the Church: but that's a beautiful metaphor", as if to say that the relation is functionally subsequent to a higher reality, and possibly perishable, and as if to say that the Christ-Church union is only spiritual. If so, union in the Holy Spirit, either before the Fall and minus the incarnation, or today across the many world religious, would be enough for salvation. But such is not the Catholic faith which lives by the sacraments as constitutive and not as mere memorials.

In order to transfer the unity of the couple, which John Paul insists is our very human self-understanding or identity, to a converted metaphysical model, I earlier spoke of a free substance. By this is meant the one flesh unity of the New Covenant which at times is clearer than the Head-members image of other Pauline material. I called Christ the formal cause of humanity, as if to invite Aristotle and Thomas to pronounce here. When Rahner tried to clarify the nature-grace dilemma and the discussion on obediential potency by speaking of a "quasi-formal" causality he used the term to avoid the necessity which ordinary formal causality found in substantial form implies, and yet he also wanted to avoid the extrinsicism of a merely exemplary cause, whereby Christ and his grace would be free with a kind of accidental optionality. How do we explain the intrinsic modification of grace without "adding" it to nature or necessitating it? It is not enough to say that man is a potential hearer of the word if God should happen to speak and then add quickly that, not to worry, God has spoken universally and from the beginning though He need not have. Rather, one must start with John Paul "in the beginning" with Christ and not with a natural theology. The only God we know there is the one revealed in Jesus of Nazareth who appears as Son of the Father to give us the Spirit.

Consequently, Christ, analogously to formal causes, if we

wish to speak this way, has the presence to the world of
constitutive being, He who makes the Church, humanity itself, to
be what it is, to be one with Him and therefore formed by Him
more than just exemplarily. But unlike other formal causes,
Christ's formality does not unfreely inform a cosmological supposit, as when form and matter combine in animals. Rather, this
intense formal presence, the offer of being, must also be
accepted in the Holy Spirit, a feature that makes Christ to be a
free formal cause, so to speak, and which is effectively an
intensification of contemporary personalism's free subjectivity to
the level of first act. If one should ask whether calling Christ a
formal cause verges on pantheism, as if Christ were equated with
the traditional *esse* of Thomist philosophy, we can reply that the
issue is in the end one of free union with God. Another approach
could explore the Christ as final cause of humanity. In translating
philosophical terms like "form" and "*esse*" into theological use
we are only trying to account for the meaning of creation in
Christ, whether formal, final or existential, but in any case free.
Thus, the presence of Christ to us can be labeled sufficient grace,
and our proper response to it in the Holy Spirit we label
efficacious grace, both on the level of substance. Conversely, the
reality of sin is, to borrow some of Tillich's language, that we
refuse to be. The paradox of sin is that, instead of suffering
annihilation we continue to be in Christ but without His Spirit,
an absurd contradiction much closer to the substantial disruption
of angelic sin. The claim that sin would only cause a slippage into
a "natural" state leads us perhaps to misunderstand the graced
order as only a condition *propter peccatum*, an accidental addition.

In this respect, the covenantal unity of man and woman as
two persons in one nature who in their self-donation finalize the
tri-relationality that images the Godhead provides us with a
model for a bodily indwelling that is both substantial and free.
We are not accustomed to thinking in this fashion because most
physical union for us is either, if free, extrinsic and optional, as in
aggregates, or if actual, organic according to a necessary struc-

ture. Some references to the Mystical Body of Christ can be poorly understood, "mystical" being a synonym for "spiritual" or "intentional" or at best "dynamic". What we have held, if we read the pope correctly, is that within humanity, and analogously to the Trinity, substance and relation are on equal footing in the order of being, an accomplishment begun in personalism's turning to freedom in escape from the oppressive nature of a fixed cosmos.

It seems that Joseph Ratzinger could agree here when, in his *Introduction to Christianity*, he calls the God of philosophy a God of pure thought, self-centered[29]. He shows that the move to a personal *logos* is an option for a personal creative meaning and for the primacy of the particular as against the universal, a primacy of freedom as against the primacy of cosmic necessity or natural law[30]. He notes that the person is more than the individual and oneness is not the unique and final reality; plurality too has its right[31]. If it seems bold to question the favoring of the human rational supposit as our clearest experienced substantiality, Ratzinger points out that some current physics describes the structure of even lower matter as parcels of waves, as a being that has no substance but is purely actual. And if the densest being — God — can subsist only in a multitude of relations and thereby form a perfect unity and the fullness of being, that is, if we are surrounded on both sides by "substances" equally and fully in relation, it should not be forbidding to extend substantial status, ordinarily ascribed to the rational supposit, to the human species, the Church and the Christ-Church relation[32]. It will, however, be a free substantiality of persons and not a simply organic one of form and matter. Ratzinger notes that, whereas for Aristotle relation was among the accidents, it

---

[29] Joseph RATZINGER, *Introduction to Christianity* (New York: Crossroads, 1985), p. 110.
[30] *Ibid.*, 111.
[31] *Ibid.*, 113.
[32] *Ibid.*, 125.

becomes clear in studying the Christian God that dialogue or relation stands beside substance as an equally primordial form of being[33]. As for our existence Ratzinger notes that Christian unity is first of all unity with Christ, which becomes possible where insistence on one's own individuality ceases and is replaced by pure, unreserved being "from" and "for"[34]. In sympathy with the efforts of personalism he notes that "the most individual element in us — the only thing that belongs to us in the last analysis — our own I, is at the same time the least individual element of all, for it is precisely our I that we have neither for ourselves nor from ourselves"[35].

Though not mentioning the human body in his exposition, Ratzinger does question the favored substantiality of the sub-personal world of atoms and objects and even goes so far as to say that traditional "objectifying thought" can be surmounted when one respects the primordial reality of relation. We now might ask whether the substance of a rational nature proposed by Boethius was really a cosmological product of this unsurmounted objectifying thought. To borrow an example from moral theology today, we are aware of the anxiety in the abortion controversies centered on the search for the person. Against the simplistic requirements of conscious performance and semi-adult development which empiricists, some of them Catholic, demand in ascribing personhood to a fetus, the Church has relied on her traditional statement that what will be human is already such. This claim is not only a statement about genetic uniqueness and directionality but is an invitation to define the human person as also in relation from the start. That is, the search for the objectified and conceptually clear and distinct person, in treating it as a category, is often a search for a cosmologically pure, inner-worldly reality available by rational inspection. The docu-

---

[33] *Ibid.*, 131.
[34] *Ibid.*, 132.
[35] *Ibid.*, 137.

ment against *in vitro* fertilization, *Donum vitae*, in refusing to define the child as a product, thereby also avoids defining the person as simply a pure object. That is, to be human is also to be received as human and not merely to be "gotten out there". Thus, the coming to be of the child is on a par with its very being as far as identity is concerned. Were it otherwise, the human person would be a distinct quantity and "more" would be better.

And if early life is intrinsically relational, this feature could apply to even its initial moments. Some Catholic theologians hold that the totipotentiality of the cells and the ability to twin are signs of non-personhood. It must at least be *one*, they say, before it can ever be a person. The unity they accept, however, is parallel to the form-matter organic confinement of living things. They await the moment of "one cell" when the pronuclei of sperm and ovum unite, a point called "syngamy" which occurs about twenty-two hours after penetration of the ovum wall by the sperm, which penetration had been the traditional moment of conception. The first twenty-two hours are then, they say, possibly a time of relationality, of lining up and ordering of one gamete to the other. For some, delayed contraception or early abortifacient activity is permissible until the nuclei have fused. Yet, though syngamy is a disputed moment and the processes before it are not so clearly identifiable, is it not the wrong question once again to demand cosmological organic unity as the proper notion of substance, being, and oneness? Is not the relational union of the cells between ovum penetration and syngamy, which is much more than their orientation to one another in their loose states, also possibly determinative and constitutive of a substantiality?

3. *Human Solidarity and the Church According to John Paul II*

We have noted heretofore in the writings of the current pope the progression from a person-centered philosophy to a co-personal theology based on the Scriptures. Only at the end of *The Acting Person* did Karol Wojtyla come to deal with intersubjectivity by participation. Though he insisted that when we are "together with others" the man-person remains the manifest subject of acting and being, he also said we can speak of a "quasi-subjectiveness" which is constituted by all the people existing and acting together. Yet the man-person is always the proper substantial subject because the community is a reality of the accidental order[36]. Being and acting with others, he said earlier, does not constitute a new subject but only introduces new relations. We can begin to see how much farther he went in his later commentaries on *Genesis* and the Letters. Also in *Person* he defines solidarity as the attitude of a community in which the common good properly conditions and initiates participation[37]. To this notion he adds that of "neighbor", the ability to participate in the humanness of every human being such that there can be a personal community at all. That is, "neighbor" regards man's humanness alone, which does not limit him to any community but which transcends all communities as their base[38].

One of Wojtyla's critics had suggested that the essential knowledge of man as person is the knowledge that emerges in his relations to other persons, a suggestion Wojtyla explicitly rejected[39] as practically impossible without a prior mastery of the categories of self-possession and self-governance. As to the suggestion that the community should be presupposed in any discussion of the acting person, he said that from the point of view "of method as well as of substance the correct solution seems to be the one that would recognize the priority of the conception of the person and the action"[40]. We, on the contrary, have claimed that his subsequent theology opens up the notion of

[36] KAROL WOJTYLA, *The Acting Person* (Dordrecht: D. Reidel, 1979), pp. 333-334.
[37] *Ibid.*, 334.
[38] *Ibid.*, 350.
[39] *Ibid.*, 316.
[40] *Ibid.*, 356.

community as prior and not merely as an aggregation of accidental relations since the human substance, male and female, is created in Christ.

The priority of the person at the end of his philosophy text would leave him still vulnerable for the positions of people like Maritain whose works he tried to transcend. Maritain spoke, in *The Person and the Common Good*, for example, of a human being caught "between two poles; a material pole which does not concern the true person but... what is called individuality, and a spiritual pole, which does concern true personality"[41]. Personality for Maritain signifies interiority to self; it is the subsistence, the "ultimate achievement by which the creative influx seals, within itself, a nature face to face with the whole order of existence so that the existence which it receives is its own perfection"[42]. The dignity of imaging God is proper to us, he says, because God is spirit and we have souls capable of knowing and loving. There is no adequate mention of Christ, the body, or the Trinity throughout his whole description of the common good, the human species, and the eschaton, where the soul's happiness is the vision of the deity. It is our contention and the pope's, it would seem, that such an absence of any theology of the body not only makes communitarian relations accidental but paves the way for the reality of the Church being reduced to a merely spiritual, extrinsic and intentional fellowship, alive in the Holy Spirit perhaps, but not as the Body of Christ.

At this point we can start pulling together John Paul's basic theological anthropology in its implications for his social doctrine and the unity of the human species.

a) Centrality and universality of Christ

The pope claims that the Word of God and the Jesus of history are inseparable, for Christ is the goal and center of

---

[41] Jacques MARITAIN, *The Person and the Common Good* (Notre Dame: Univ. of Notre Dame Press, 1972), p. 33.
[42] *Ibid.*, 41.

history with absolute and unique significance. Thus, God's gifts to other people are inseparable from Christ who is at the beginning of creation, as proclaimed by the Scriptures in Eph. 1; Rom. 3:24; Col. 1:12-14; Gal. 3:13; 2 Cor. 5:18-29; and elsewhere[43].

We can interpret this to mean that the pope is not relying on the older explanation of a creation-redemption, nature-grace scheme to begin his anthropology.

b) Eucharist as cause of the Church

The redeeming action of Christ is through the Eucharist which is the center and goal of all sacramental life that began with Baptism[44]. In the Eucharist we have a continual renewing of the sacrifice of the Cross. The truth of life is that the Eucharist builds the Church from this sacrifice which is a sacrifice-sacrament, a communion-sacrament, and a presence-sacrament[45]. The Lord unites us with Himself and with one another by a bond stronger than any natural union and, thus, united, sends us into the whole world. In the Eucharist the fruits of the earth are transformed mysteriously but substantially through the power of the Holy Spirit and the words of the minister into the Body and Blood of the Lord[46].

This means that the Eucharist as event (sacrifice) is the place of novelty within history and is the central act around which the world means. It is that by which the cosmos has significance, since the pope has effectively dismissed a "natural" order with its independent rhythms as purely a secular construct. The world lives only by the presence of Christ within it. The traditional

---

[43] JOHN PAUL II, *Redemptoris Missio* (1990), n. 6; idem, *Centesimus Annus* (1991), n. 62; idem, *Redemptoris Mater* (1987), n. 1; idem, *Redemptor Hominis* (1979), n. 1, 8. Encyclicals are cited hereafter by original Latin titles and numbers.

[44] JOHN PAUL II, *Dominicae Cenae* (1980), nn. 4, 7, 9.

[45] *Redemptor Hominis*, nn. 7, 20.

[46] JOHN PAUL II, *Sollicitudo Rei Socialis* (1987), n. 48.

divine concursus merits replacement by the creation in Christ which is really his constant presence, a presence we know as Eucharistic. All other presences refer back to it, and it is anticipated in the sacraments of initiation.

c) Church as Body and Bride of Christ

In the economy of salvation Bridegroom and Bride share the same life and gifts and yet remain distinct, as male and female are irreducibly distinct. All members also respond as bride to the gift of the love of Christ who is redeemer and bridegroom and they also present their bodies for sacrifice in a priestly role of witness, one combined with kingly and prophetic witness. These three express the organic unity of body and its relation to head[47]. The Eucharist is the sacrament of the bridegroom and the bride and makes present in a sacramental manner the redemptive act of Christ who creates the Church, His Body to which he is united. We can conclude that in instituting the Eucharist Christ wished to express the relationship between the feminine and the masculine[48]. In what is personal masculine and feminine differ yet explain and complete each other[49]. The Church is not merely a sociological deduction but is also Christ's Mystical Body, an ontological reality[50].

The issue here is the freedom of each Christian in the face of the truth of revelation. A totally organic unity resembles an imposition of order. The one-flesh relation protects, as did Mary's Annunciation and Immaculate Conception, the free reception in the Spirit of the very intrinsic being which creation in Christ is meant to bestow. Thus the gift is not only additional or extrinsic or merely spiritual but is the presence of wholeness and graced integrity which also contains the holiness of material-

---

[47] JOHN PAUL II, *Mulieris Dignitatem* (1988), n. 27.
[48] *Ibid.*, n. 25.
[49] *Ibid.*
[50] *Redemptor Hominis*, n. 21.

ity and freely unites the species. The "one flesh" language of freedom can better reveal what Pius XII envisioned in *Mystici Corporis* when he wrote that "in a natural body the principle of unity so unites the parts that each lacks its own individual subsistence; in the Mystical Body that mutual union, though intrinsic, links the members by a bond which leaves to each intact his own personality". To insist at this point on the traditional substantial sufficiency of the rational supposit would really reduce this Mystical Body language to the description of only a moral union.

d) Church as Mother and as feminine after the model of Mary

Mary as full of grace has been eternally present in the mystery of Christ and the Father of mercies willed that the consent of the predestined Mother should precede the Incarnation; thus she is present even before the creation of the world[51]. Mary accepted her election as Mother of God guided by a spousal love. Her consent to motherhood is a result of total self-giving to God in virginity[52]. The motherhood of Mary finds a continuation in the Church and through the Church, and she continues to be a permanent model in the Church, which is called virgin and mother also as it brings forth children in the Holy Spirit[53]. The Church is a virgin faithful to her spouse with a love that is marital in *Ephesians* 5 and celibate in *Matthew* 19 and *2 Corinthians* 11. The woman Mary, or "woman", is the archetype of the whole human race. The motherhood of every woman is not only of flesh and blood but is a listening to the word of God; the history of every human being passes through the threshold of woman's motherhood[54]. A consecrated woman, for example, finds her Spouse in every person and also has a

---

[51] *Redemptoris Mater*, nn. 7, 13, 19.
[52] *Ibid.*, n. 39.
[53] *Ibid.*, nn. 24, 42, 43.
[54] *Mulieris Dignitatem*, n. 19.

motherhood according to the spirit. Marriage, whether physical
or spiritual, signifies the sincere gift of the person[55].

This means that the one-flesh union of Jesus with His
. Mother is the prime analogate or antetype, historically speaking,
of the present Christ-Church relation, one begun in the Old
Testament between God and humanity. The Church is not only a
mother figuratively or metaphorically but actually, since it is the
source of ultimate meaning and actual being. It is the only place
where humanity comes to mean or actually to exist, provided
that we describe secular existence to be a cosmological, post-
lapsarian construct.

e) Solidarity of humankind is in Christ and the Church

Solidarity is the means for achieving a public life whose goal
is human development, which public life is the good of everyone
and of each person taken as a whole[56]. The dignity of the person
constitutes the foundation of the equality of all people among
themselves. What they are is more important than what they
have[57]. We are all really responsible for all and solidarity will
exist when we recognize that the goods of creation are meant for
all. This solidarity is inspired by a new model of unity of the race
and reflects the intimate life of the Trinity, a communion[58]. Real
historical man is the way for the Church to go because each man
has been redeemed by Christ. Her first concern is for the
individual[59]. The Church as body is the source of each person's
life[60]. Moreover, the self-awareness of the Church is formed in
dialogue directed to the "other"[61].

This means that the Church and Christ are not the private

---

[55] *Ibid.*, n. 21.
[56] JOHN PAUL II, *Christifideles Laici*, (1988), n. 42.
[57] *Ibid.*, n. 37.
[58] *Sollicitudo Rei Socialis*, nn. 38, 40.
[59] *Centesimus Annus*, n. 52; *Redemptor Hominis*, n. 14.
[60] *Redemptor Hominis*, n. 18.
[61] *Ibid.*, n. 11.

property of Christians nor are they peculiar items of religious devotion or belonging. The Church is immediately on mission because the human race is already essentially one in its creation in Christ.

f) The Spirit is in all the world but only as Spirit of Christ

The Spirit works in the human conscience throughout the world and comes in every conversion by virtue of Christ's departure[62]. The Spirit is also present in creation and the "let us make" of *Genesis* suggests already the Trinitarian mystery, for the Spirit goes back even before Christ[63]. The Council reminds us of the Spirit's activity outside the visible body of the Church in all those people of good will in whose hearts grace works unseen. Christ died for all and since the ultimate vocation of man is one and divine, we ought to believe that the Holy Spirit in a manner known only to God offers to every man the possibility of being associated with the Paschal mystery[64]. Salvation is available for some only mysteriously but it is still a grace of Christ, for the church found in unbelievers is incomplete unless it is related to the kingdom of God present in the Church[65]. The Spirit is universal and not limited by space and time. He is at the very source of man's existential and religious questioning occasioned by the very structures of man's being[66]. Every authentic prayer is prompted by the Holy Spirit who is mysteriously present in every human heart. He is not an alternative to Christ nor a filler between Christ and the Logos. He only prepares for the gospel and can only be understood in reference to Christ. Discernment of His presence is the responsibility of the Church[67].

[62] JOHN PAUL II, *Dominum et Vivificantem* (1986), n. 45.
[63] *Ibid.*, nn. 12, 53.
[64] *Ibid.*, n. 53.
[65] JOHN PAUL II, *Redemptoris Missio* (1990), nn. 10, 20.
[66] *Ibid.*, n. 28.
[67] *Ibid.*, n. 29.

This surely means that the *Filioque* is quite relevant to preaching the Christian faith. All salvation is centered on Jesus of Nazareth to whose salvific presence, Eucharistically, we continue to respond in the Spirit. Non-historical salvations continue to be gnostic in form.

g) Christian mission is to make the hidden Christ explicit

The Church says that all are called to catholic unity whether they be explicit Catholics or not and the Holy Spirit is the principal agent of this mission[68]. Proclaiming Christ does not violate freedom of conscience, for all people are impelled by nature and morally bound to seek and obey the truth[69]. Christ is the one savior and all other kinds of mediation cannot be complementary to or parallel to His but can only get their meaning from Him[70]. Even atheism depends on belief for its proclamation. How can it alone have rights if belief does not[71]? The Church cannot be secularized in an anthropocentric reductive manner. Baptism is not a mere external sign but the establishing of a bond with the Trinity and an entry into Christ's Body[72]. The Church proposes but does not impose at all and she honors the sanctuary of conscience, for religious freedom remains the guarantee of all freedoms that insure the common good. She and her missionaries are aware that they further human freedom by proclaiming Christ for there exists in everyone an expectation, even if unconscious, of knowing the truth about God and man[73]. We must seek the universal unity of all Christians without diminishing the treasure of truth in the Church. Ecumenism demands this. It is noble to seek to understand every person and to analyze every system for what is right,

---

[68] *Ibid.*, nn. 9, 21.
[69] *Ibid.*, n. 8.
[70] *Ibid.*, n. 5.
[71] *Redemptor Hominis*, n. 17.
[72] *Redemptoris Missio*, nn. 14, 47.
[73] *Ibid.*, nn. 39, 45, 46.

but this does not mean losing certitude about one's own faith or weakening one's morality[74].

Herein the pope has indicated what it means that the true Church of Christ subsists in the Catholic Church. If the world is truly redeemed, salvation will be visible in life and action and not merely intentional, ineffable, or eschatological.

h) Church relates freely to social and political orders

Every individual must respond first to God, and society cannot replace this. The kingdom of God is in the world, not of it, but it can give life to society. And so the Church responds to the autonomy of the democratic order with a vision of human dignity. Since it is not an ideology, the Christian faith does not presume to imprison changing sociopolitical realities in a rigid schema but always respects freedom[75]. Social groups have their own autonomy just as the family has its own. Higher orders should not interfere in lower orders[76] and no social group or political party has the right to usurp the role of sole leader[77].

Here the freedom with which the Church preaches the gospel without compromise but without imposing it extends to the political order. There are not two levels of humanity but only one humanity as yet not completely unified. Hence, the Church's doctrine is never private, but only free. As Christ is freely present to the Church, the Church is freely present to the world, never being meant as an option but unable to be imposed by force or necessity. As the Church responds to Christ in the Spirit, so must the world respond to the Church. In a limited way, then, the pope and other theologians and Councils have spoken analogously of the Church as sacrament.

---

[74] *Redemptor Hominis*, n. 6.
[75] *Centesimus Annus*, nn. 13, 25, 46, 47.
[76] *Ibid.*, nn. 13, 48.
[77] *Sollicitudo Rei Socialis*, n. 15.

i) Family, not State or production, is the center of society
    The family as a cell of society is the most effective means for
humanizing and personalizing society. It is also a society in its
own original right, and so society is gravely obliged to honor
subsidiarity here[78]. Since man and woman are one flesh and as
such the image of the unity of the Mystical Body, they are also
the image or model of a unity within society, which ought to be
the Church. Thus, the family has an evangelizing mission and the
Church exists in the family as it does in a particular church or
bishop[79]. Work constitutes a foundation for the family and is at
the heart of the social question. Women are to be supported in
the home and not made to work or act against their nature. Man
is the subject of work as a person and a rational ordering being.
His domination refers to his dignity and is not permission to
abuse the environment in subduing it[80]. The earth is given to the
whole human race without favor and the right to private property
is not absolute[81].

    The truism that the family is the center loses its vapidity
when one fails to find some other center in a social or political
program of a secular nature. Actually, the family is the cause of
society in its furthering of the human species and its imaging of
the New Covenant.

j) Roles in Church and society are distinct
    Baptismal dignity takes on a manner of life which sets a lay
person apart without bringing a total separation from the min-
isterial priesthood or the religious state. According to the
Council there is a special secular character for the laity even
though all members share in the Church's secular dimension in
different ways. The laity fulfill their Christian vocation in the

[78] JOHN PAUL II, *Familiaris Consortio* (1981), nn. 43, 45.
[79] *Ibid.*, nn. 19, 48, 54.
[80] JOHN PAUL II, *Laborem Exercens* (1981), nn. 6, 19.
[81] *Centesimus Annus*, nn. 30, 31.

world in an ecclesiological and theological way, not just sociologically[82]. Lay people may never relinquish their participation in public life in promoting the common good[83]. The different vocations are — laity, in witnessing to the significance of temporal realities; priests, in guaranteeing the sacramental presence of Christ; and religious, in witnessing to the eschatological nature of the Church[84]. The charism of the priest is different in degree and essence since Orders is not merely a functional office nor a mere performance[85]. The priest offers Mass *in persona Christi*; this means more than offering in the name of or in place of Christ. It means in specific sacramental identification with the eternal High Priest[86]. In Baptism and Confirmation a woman is made sharer in the threefold mission of Christ and is charged with the duty to evangelize according to her proper gifts. Her non-ordination is based on Christ as bridegroom and Church as bride, qualities not based on dignity or holiness. Her tasks include bringing full dignity to conjugal life and motherhood, assuring the moral dimension of culture and exercising sensitivity to what the human person is, a charge entrusted to her by God in a pre-eminent way[87].

Here the pope is repeating the basic structure of creation and redemption as based on the radical primacy of the sexual. His argument depends on the Church's self-understanding drawn from *Genesis* and *Ephesians* on the primordiality of marriage and virginity. Also dependent on this radical starting point for their consistent intelligibility would be other sexual questions today — homosexuality, *in vitro* fertilization, divorce, contraception, etc. One way to approach the pope's doctrine here is to presume the opposite thesis. If women could be ordained it would mean that

---

[82] *Christifideles Laici*, n. 15.
[83] *Ibid.*, n. 42.
[84] *Ibid.*, n. 55.
[85] *Ibid.*, nn. 22, 23.
[86] *Dominicae Cenae*, nn. 8, 9.
[87] *Christifideles Laici*, n. 51.

the central event of salvation, the ongoing presence of Christ to the Church, is not associated with any radical sexual symbolism that goes back to the "beginning" in *Genesis* and in *Matthew* 19. The reality of Christ's presence would then either be one in the Spirit alone, a presence by faith, or, if also corporeal, then a presence as divine *anthropos* alone, not as Son of the Father. Christ would not then significantly be present to humanity by the freedom of His Mother's acceptance but only as one human integer, one rational supposit among others. Human nature would be complete in the individual and the duality in human nature so frequently insisted on by the pope would then be largely functional. The sexual diversity would be like diversity in race or language.

4. *Concluding remarks*

In assembling this paper for a group of Jesuits I have been happy to use, as I said, the contributions of participants like Gerald McCool and John McDermott. Several of the themes I chose to find in John Paul's writings coincide with the work of two of my former colleagues. Fr. Donald Keefe in his recent masterful two-volume systematic *Covenantal Theology* develops a theological metaphysics of history based on the New Covenant and the Eucharist[88]. Fr. Earl Muller has comprehensively explored Trinity and marriage in Paul in his recent volume from Peter Lang Press[89]. These works present comprehensively what I have skipped over. Sister Susan Wood, another colleague, wrote a definitive dissertation on the Church in Henri de Lubac in which so many of my current topics — Church as Bride, People, Sacrament — were analyzed in the work of one of the finest theological minds of our time.

---

[88] Donald J. KEEFE, *Covenantal Theology. The Eucharistic Order of History* (Lanham, MD: University Press of America, 1991).

[89] Earl C. MULLER, *Trinity and Marriage in Paul. The Establishment of a Communitarian Analogy of the Trinity Grounded in the Theological Shape of Pauline Thought* (New York: Peter Lang Press, 1990).

Let me borrow from Fr. Avery Dulles, another participant in this conference, to highlight one major theme. I have contended throughout that John Paul would agree that the Eucharist is the cause of the Church. I even added "cause of the world" in an extension of Christ's formal causality to the divine concursus, presuming a conflation of the orders of grace and creation and the primordiality of Christ and His Mother in the order of existence. In *The Catholicity of the Church* (1985) Avery Dulles points out that Christ is truly present in the Church through the Holy Spirit, making the Church therefore a real representation of Christ[90]. He also says that in the history of theology authors, Moehler for example, have hesitated whether to trace the Church and its catholicity primarily to Christ or to the Holy Spirit. Vatican II insisted that the Church is vivified by the Holy Spirit. Avery adds that the immediate relationship of the Church to the Holy Spirit as its animating principle does not prevent the Church from being the Body of Christ, but on the contrary causes it to be His Body and the whole function of the Spirit is to mediate Christ's presence[91].

I contend that we need to separate very carefully the two presences of Christ and the Spirit in the current economy of salvation. Dulles does not fail to cite from *Colossians* and from *Ephesians* regarding the personal presence of Christ to His Body, as we have, and he investigates the presence of Christ to the world in theories like Teilhard's and Blondel's *vinculum substantiale*, which are really efforts to find a formal cause for the world. But in the Church today there seems to be a one-sided emphasis on the role of the Spirit, whether for ecumenical reasons or simply from the loss of sacramental realism. When Dulles says that Catholics hold for a sacramental presence which, while real in its own order, is effected by the faith of the Church and

---

[90] Avery DULLES, *The Catholicity of the Church* (Oxford: Clarendon Press, 1985), p. 168.
[91] *Ibid.*, pp. 44-45.

perceptible only in faith[92], not all hearers today have his appreciation of transubstantiation or Holy Orders to supplement that statement. I presume he does not mean that our faith causes the presence of Christ but rather that the Holy Spirit, working in us and the Church as He did in the heart of Mary, disposes us to receive the Christ in more than just mind or heart. The presence of Christ in the world is not merely commemorative or intentional or somehow so transcultural as to be transcendental.

I have also contended that the pope's theology corrects an understanding of Christ that would describe Him as only the generic *anthropos*. If His maleness is not symbolic, as His Mother's feminity was also symbolic and primordial, then we truly have a different economy at work. For one thing, all the talk of Body and Bride and Mother and even sacrament, when applied to the Church, would become pious metaphor. I have tried to say, on the other hand, not what roles the Church can play in its many models, but substantially what the Church is in itself most deeply.

The recent letter from the Congregation for the Doctrine of the Faith of May 28, 1992, reminds us that ecclesial communion has its root and center in the Holy Eucharist where the Church expresses herself permanently in most essential form[93]. Unity or communion between particular churches is rooted not only in the same faith and in the common baptism but above all in the Eucharist and the episcopate[94]. The letter goes on to link the Eucharist with the episcopate and with Petrine primacy in ways that will stir the ecumenical waters. But such concreteness of salvation is precisely the issue to face.

I could close with a more positive ecumenical observation. The primacy which John Paul gave to sexuality and the definition of human nature as a duality, a doctrine expanded to marriage,

---

[92] *Ibid.*, p. 117.

[93] Doctrinal Congregation for the Faith, "Some Aspects of the Church Understood as Communion", n. 5, in *Origins* 22:7 (June 25, 1992), 108-112.

[94] *Ibid.*, n. 11.

celibacy and Orders, caused him on several occasions to speak of marriage as the primordial sacrament. Is it not interesting that the Church so readily recognizes the marriages of non-Catholic Christians as sacraments and, more so, tolerates with some favor and much hope the union of a Catholic with an unbaptized person? Yet, given the seriousness of the Church's harder sayings on sexuality and her consistency in not recognizing irregular second marriages, one would think that the so-called non-sacramental marriage in the second instance might be judged the equivalent of fornication, a case of extra-marital sexual expression. At least one theologian has speculated on the possibility of the conferral of a sacramental bond in these cases after the manner in which the unbeliever, as a member of humanity, and therefore created in Christ, can validly baptize. The point is that marriage, the first sacrament chronologically and the central one ontologically in the spousal character of the Eucharist, becomes in another sense the last or widest sacrament, the instance of evangelization and mission and a means of initiation into the faith. It becomes the true praxis, the center-piece of society and the occasion for evangelization to the unbeliever, an evangelization mediated by his own will and freedom in the face of a Christian person whom he loves.

In this way, John Paul's early personalism, transformed by the nuptial metaphysics of the Christian faith, extends to the entire world not by some manner of institutional structure or proclamation but in a mission of love. The objectivity of "natural law" which John McDermott held up for preservation against the radical personalism of a philosophy of subjectivity is a personal objectivity. The spouses enter a reality objective to themselves and which is given by God but they do so by their own freedom and as an exercise of love, liberation and self-realization through another. A personalist metaphysics could wish for no further freedom nor could John Paul have a wider audience for it than the entire humanity to which he feels missioned in love.

HUMAN SOLIDARITY AND THE CHURCH IN THE THOUGHT OF JOHN PAUL II

A Response

BENJAMIN FIORE, S.J.

Joseph Murphy's paper builds on the contributions of John McDermott and Gerald McCool at the first conference on the thought of John Paul II in tracing the relation of the pope's personalist philosophy to his theology in order to highlight the pope's starting point in the person rather than in nature. He goes on to elaborate the pope's theological analyses of the two creation stories in *Genesis* where the pope finds mythical expressions of the truth of human existence as revealed by the body; e.g., the human's solitude among created reality, the human as image of God in a *communio* of persons in a loving gift to and for others, the subsequent revelation of human uniqueness in its concrete embodiment as sexually differentiated, the nuptial meaning of the human body manifested in sexual complementarity, the primordial character of the sacrament of marriage. From the pope's reference to the husband-wife/Christ-Church analogy in *Ephesians*, Murphy goes on to stress that Christ's presence in the world is constitutive of it, of the Church, and of humanity itself. This enlivening presence can be freely accepted or rejected and thus the covenantal unity of man and woman, which images the relationality of the godhead, provides Murphy with a model for a bodily indwelling that is both substantial and free. Consequently, he finds in the pope's thought that within humanity substance and relation are on equal footing in the order of being.

Fr. Murphy's paper thus ranges widely and with a perceptive eye across the writings of Pope John Paul II. As a result, he brings to light many aspects of that solidarity which reveals the reality of both the human person and the Church. While the readers of this paper cannot but be impressed with the author's grasp of the pope's insight and their metaphysical, anthropological and ecclesiological implications, they might also note that some of paper's conclusions could profit from further nuance.

To begin with, perhaps it is too much to say that the pope "in his later writing has taken his original personalism beyond the isolation of a free, intuitive, contemplative existential subject who 'reaches out' to another in accidental relation"[1]. Even in *Acting Person*, when speaking of the subject's basic perception of the moral responsibility by which he realizes himself, Wojtyla wrote:

> The relation between the efficacy and the responsibility of the person may serve as the framework for establishing the elementary fact on which rest the whole moral and legal order in its full interhuman and social dimensions. Nevertheless, this relation, like obligation, is in the first place an inner reality of the person, a reality that exists within the person. It is only owing to this interpersonal reality that we in turn can speak of the social significance of responsibility and lay down for it some principles in social life[2].

---

[1] J. MURPHY, S.J., "Human Solidarity and the Church in the Thought of John Paul II", *supra*, p. 138.

[2] K. WOJTYLA, *The Acting Person*, tr. A. Potocki (Boston: Reidel, 1979), p. 169; cf. also pp. 163f., 173f., 263, 275, 285, 290f., 297. The intersubjectivity of the person is strongly emphasized in Wojtyla's article "The Person: Subject and Community", *The Review of Metaphysics* 33 (1979), 273-308. In "Karl Rahner and Pope John Paul II: Anthropological Implications for Economics and the Social Order", in *Proceedings of the Catholic Theological Society of America*, 1985, ed. J. Gower, R. Modras paraphrased the thought of *The Acting Person* thus: "We exist and act together with others not only usually but universally so

Since the *Acting Person* is one of Wojtyla's early and complete expressions of his philosophical personalism, it is hard to give too much importance to a change of view from his early writing. When the ideas appear with greater force in the pope's philosophical/theological reflections on the creation stories, these early insights are not novel but are given flesh in a novel way.

Second, Murphy's explanation of Jesus as free formal cause of the human, to whom the offer of being is made and by whom it must be accepted in the Holy Spirit[3] surely leaves Jesus free in the offer, but where does it leave human freedom? Also, with what is the human persuaded to accept the free offer? Furthermore, if it is being in relation that is important in the creation of the human, then to what extent does the relation of contest and resistance, such as that to Jesus' offer of being, constitute the being of a person? In the event of a persistent human "no" to God's offer of being which images Himself, are God's formerly free hands tied so that He must always say "yes"? If God does say "no" in response, what are the implications for the substantial existence itself of the human? Is there a hell for the wicked; or, better, are there any wicked left around for hell? If Fr. Murphy is correct in seeing man "become the image of God not only through his own humanity but also through the communion of persons which man and women form"[4], then is the sovereign creativity of God held at bay until man decides for or against entering the communion of persons?

Third, the contrast drawn a number of times in the paper between a "pious metaphor" and a "symbol" would have to be elaborated on from the perspective of the kinds and uses of religious language. Symbol and metaphor are not in themselves opposites, nor is a religious symbol necessarily more valuable than a pious metaphor. Then, too, the realism that Murphy sees

---

that participation is a 'specific constituent' of the human person. We realize ourselves as persons by fulfillment of our obligations".

[3] *Murphy.*, pp. 139f.
[4] *Ibid.*, p. 132.

behind Wojtyla's discussion of the body and its nuptial meaning
in the context of the analysis of the creation stories has to be
judiciously discussed so that the symbolic is not lost in the focus
on the real or substantial. A substantial union of persons
mystically in the body of Christ as more than "spiritual" or
"intentional"[5] raises concerns about the distinction in essence
and existence between the human and the divine. The assertion
that the person of each human in this union remains intact[6] also
needs further exposition. Perhaps dissolving the ambiguity of the
symbolic in the direction of the real, as this paper does, loses the
distinction between God and man which religious symbolism
aims to protect. Perhaps, too, Wojtyla would not press his
philosophical analysis of the symbolic creation stories as far as
Murphy tends to pull it.

With the statement of these cautions about Fr. Murphy's
clarification of and further speculation about Wojtyla's philo-
sophical/theological analysis of the human and the primordial
human relationship, marriage, I shall now consider some of
Murphy's treatment of human solidarity and the Church in light
of ten themes that recur in the pope's major encyclicals.

The first theme that Murphy chooses is "Centrality and
Universality of Christ". He finds that the pope does not rely on
creation/redemption, nature/grace to begin his anthropology but
rather rests it on Jesus as creative Word and Jesus of history,
center and goal of history. Nonetheless, it is not insignificant that
when the pope describes the human as fundamentally a worker in
light of the command to dominate the earth, and confirmed as
such by the historical Jesus' work (*Laborem Exercens*) he links
the toil of work with Jesus' Paschal mystery. Humans are to
accept their toil as part of the cross of Christ and in the same
spirit of redemption in which Jesus accepted His cross for us.
And just as work is not to be separated from the cross of Christ,

---

[5] *Ibid.*, pp. 140f.
[6] *Ibid.*, pp. 140f.

so too the "new good" which work produces and which fore-shadows the new age, advancing the growth of the body of the new human family, reflects the resurrection.

Likewise in *Centesimus Annus* John Paul II notes that the recent transformation in central-eastern Europe would have been unthinkable without an immense trust in God and without the people's uniting their own sufferings for the sake of truth and freedom to the sufferings of Christ on the cross. The Messianic victory of the crucified Jesus has long established a pattern for human self-understanding and struggle in the Polish Christian consciousness, a pattern which is alluded to in the pope's writings.

Finally, Murphy himself later isolates the theme of the "Eucharist as Cause of the Church" in the pope's writings. The Eucharist, he notes, is "a continual renewal of the sacrifice of the Cross" which builds the Church. By the "sacrifice-sacrament" the Lord unites us with himself and with one another[7]. Further on he says that the world lives only by the presence of Christ within it, a creative, constant presence. Thus, the redemption/creation theology is not far from the pope's anthropological starting point.

To what Murphy says about "The Church as Body and Bride of Christ", i.e., that it is an ontological reality and not a mere sociological deduction or moral union, I would add the following. The pope in *Centesimus Annus* reminds us that Leo XIII claimed "citizenship status" for the Church whereby it validly promotes its vision of justice and witnesses to Christ among other organizations in society. In this activity, the Church has shown particular concern for the poor (the preferential option), which is a "special form of privacy in the exercise of Christian charity". This latter effort is based on the conviction that human dignity is a possession common to all, regardless of their personal convictions, in view of the fact that every individual bears the image of

---

[7] *Ibid.*, p. 146.

God and thereby deserves respect. This "witness of actions", he says, will gain the Church's social message greater credibility than will its internal logic and consistency. This broader appreciation of the presence of Christ expands the notion of the Body of Christ in the direction of an active witness.

Murphy's next two themes, "Church as Mother and as Feminine after the Model of Mary" and "Solidarity of Humankind Is in Christ and the Church", relate to the preceding remarks. The Church as mother shows itself to be the only place where humanity comes to mean or actually to exist inasmuch as it consistently declares and supports human dignity and rights through loving dialogue and actions in service of the truth of human persons.

The solidarity of humankind, as Murphy notes, is both a means for achieving a public life whose goal is human development and also is a result of the self-awareness formed in dialogue directed to the other. The principle of solidarity is related by the pope in *Centesimus Annus* to Leo XIII's term "friendship", Pius XI's "social charity", Paul VI's "civilization of love". The pope avoids describing solidarity as homogeneity. In *Centesimus Annus* he discusses the diversity of cultures and finds at the heart of culture the attitude a person takes toward the mystery of God. He notes that different cultures are basically different ways of facing the question of the meaning of personal existence.

Elsewhere in the same encyclical he goes on to describe the interaction between human activity and the formation of culture. The formation of culture requires involvement of the whole person, whereby one exercises creativity, intelligence, and knowledge of the world and its people. Furthermore, a person displays his capacity for self-control, personal sacrifice, solidarity and readiness to promote the common good. The Church advances the proper development of culture by preaching the truth both about the creation of the world by God and God's entrusting it to human work and about its redemption by Christ and the consequent unity and mutual responsibility of all people. Difficulties facing the Church's effort to help cultures develop include those societies which experience various forms of alienation that turn people away from each other as well as those persons who refuse to transcend themselves and live the experience of self-giving which entails the formation of a genuine human community and solidarity of people based on the mutual gift of self. On the other hand, solidarity does not necessitate uniformity of cultural expression. In fact, the dialogue which emerges from solidarity seems to presuppose differences among people in society. The aim is a discovery of true identity much like the discovery of self in the original encounter of man and woman in the *Genesis* creation myths.

Nonetheless, as Murphy makes clear in the theme "The Christian Mission Is to Make the Hidden Christ Explicit", the Church's efforts are not reduced to a bland relativism. For example, while the Church respects the legitimate autonomy of the democratic order and refrains from showing preference for particular institutional or constitutional solutions, the Church makes a contribution to the political order by imparting a vision of the dignity of the person as revealed in its fulness in the mystery of the Incarnate Word (*Centesimus Annus*). Murphy's theme "The Church Relates Freely to Social and Political Orders" hits on similar ideas. To go on, in *Centesimus Annus*, the pope refers not just to the Church's mission but to the Christian's as one wherein the Christian upholds freedom and serves it, constantly offering to others the truth which he knows. He pays heed to every fragment of that truth in the culture of individuals and of nations and will not fail to affirm in dialogue with others all that his faith and the correct use of reason have enabled him to understand. The Church's claims to knowledge of the truth through faith and reason are clear but at the same time modest. The Church's stance toward others is supportive rather than coercive. The dialogue in solidarity is thus a real one.

The theme "The Spirit Is in All the World but Only as the Spirit of Christ" sees the Spirit in reference to Christ as prompting every authentic prayer, as preparing for the gospel and at the source of man's existential and religious questioning occasioned by the very structures of man's being. Moreover, Murphy reminds us, the Church found in unbelievers is incomplete unless it is related to the kingdom of God present in the Church. But I wonder who are the unbelievers whose Church is incomplete and how far the universal human existential and religious questioning goes to disqualify pretenders to participation in the kingdom of God. *Centesimus Annus* says the human person receives from God the capacity to move toward truth and goodness but is also conditioned by the social structure in which he lives, by his education, and by his environment. The latter can help or hinder a person's living according to the truth, and the task of replacing structures of sin with more authentic forms of living in community is one that demands courage and patience. Surely, the work of the Spirit outlined in this theme with regard to opening the human up to the gospel is one needed by nonbelievers and believers alike. The Church as repository of truth and champion of human dignity may be variously reflected in the attitudes and action of churchmen. The dialogue about the true human identity in Christ unites both believer and nonbeliever in a solidarity of questing and discovery.

That solidarity or communion of persons was formed out of human solitude at creation with the first man and woman and seems to be deeper that the human somatic structure which is male and female. This being with and for someone in a mutual gift characterizes humanity. The giver and receiver are both enriched in the giving. This relationship is a symbol of Christ's relationship to the Church and God's relationship to humanity (as Murphy reminds us in his treatment of the pope's catechesis on the book of *Genesis*). It is also a symbol of the relationship of solidarity which is a relationship of mutual giving in love and moves both persons to a firmer grasp on the truth of their human identity and dignity. As such, it is a relationship which brings the Church to reality among them.

I will close my remarks now with a word of congratulations to Fr. Murphy for his penetrating exposition of the heart of the pope's thought about the human person and the human person's relation to the Christ, the creative Word. I hope my repetition and restatement of some of his treatment of the pope's anthropological and social teaching did not distort his views and hope that I was able to add some further nuances to those ideas.

THE CHURCH AS LOCUS OF SALVATION

Avery Dulles, S.J.

My assignment, as I interpret it, is to discuss the relationship between the Church and salvation in contemporary Catholic teaching, with special attention to the teaching of John Paul II. In order to set boundaries for this paper I shall limit my consideration to eschatological or definitive salvation, to which Christians aspire as a gift in the life to come. I shall not here explore the ways in which eschatological salvation is attainable within history in anticipatory ways through signs, sacraments, interior grace, and the gifts of the Holy Spirit.

John Paul II repeatedly invokes Vatican II and recent popes as authorities. For this reason I shall not treat his teaching in isolation, but rather in the context of earlier pronouncements. Although much of the secondary literature dwells on the alleged variations of church teaching during the past fifty years, I shall try to bring out the continuity, which I regard as more striking. The present pope, in my opinion, strives to maintain solidarity with his predecessors and to avoid adding materially to the existing body of official teaching. He apparently wants to leave open to theological discussion whatever can be legitimately debated without detriment to the truth of revelation.

In order to grasp the significance of the teachings I shall be summarizing, it will be helpful for the reader to have in mind a grid that lays out the options. The most useful for present purposes may be the spectrum of views set forth by J. Peter

Schineller in 1976[1]. He expounded four basic approaches to Christ and the Church as ways of salvation. For purposes of my own paper, which deals only with the Church, Schineller's options may be described as follows:

1. The Church as the constitutive and exclusive way of salvation. In this approach the axiom "Outside the Church no salvation" is interpreted quite literally. With few if any exceptions, formal membership in the Church is considered to be absolutely necessary for salvation. Leonard Feeney and his disciples were generally understood as holding that only Roman Catholics, and those who explicitly desired membership in the Roman Catholic Church, could be saved. Schineller calls this position "ecclesiocentric".

2. The Church is, under Christ, the constitutive but not the exclusive way of salvation. All grace and salvation are mediated through the Church. Without it no grace or salvation would be possible, but these gifts may, under certain conditions, be given to persons who neither are nor consciously wish to be formal members of the Church. Some adherents of this position speak of a salvific orientation toward the Church; others speak of latent or anonymous Christianity.

3. The Church is the normative way of salvation, but is not constitutive. It proclaims the reality of God's salvific activity throughout the world, but is not the indispensable mediator of grace and salvation. While it mediates salvation to its own members, the Church serves only to point nonmembers to the grace of God that is available always and everywhere. As a divinely given sign, the Church is the norm by which other religious communities may be judged.

4. The Church is one of many legitimate and divinely willed paths of salvation. It is neither constitutive nor normative. For Christians it is the way of salvation, but non-Christians may be

---

[1] J. Peter SCHINELLER, "Christ and the Church: A Spectrum of Views", *Theological Studies* 37 (1976), 545-66.

saved through ways that have no necessary relationship to the Church. This view, corresponding to modern pluralistic thought, has earlier roots. Schineller mentions Thomas Jefferson and Ralph Waldo Emerson as exemplifying this model. In the fourth century, as Arnold Toynbee notes, the Roman senator Symmachus, pleading for the retention of pagan shrines, protested that Christianity should not be the sole legitimate religion of the empire. "It is impossible that so great a mystery should be approached by one road only"[2].

The history of our problem has often been surveyed, and is compactly presented in the recent and up-to-date work of Francis A. Sullivan, *Salvation outside the Church?*[3] Instead of retracing the history I shall here adopt a systematic approach. For the sake of clarity I shall divide my paper into ten sections, each consisting of a set of thesis-like propositions, followed in some cases by commentary. The numbered sections deal respectively with (1) Christ as mediator, (2-3) the mediation of the Church of Christ, (4-6) the role of the Catholic Church, (7-8) the status of non-Catholic Christians, and (8, in part, and 9-10) the status of non-Christians. For the most part I shall content myself with summarizing what I regard as settled Church doctrine, accepted and reiterated by John Paul II both in his writings as Cardinal Wojtyla and in many papal documents. In parentheses and footnotes I shall indicate some of the sources.

---

[2] Arnold TOYNBEE, *Christianity among the Religions of the World* (New York: Scribner, 1957), pp. 111-12.

[3] F. SULLIVAN, *Salvation outside the Church?* (New York: Paulist, 1992). Among the more useful and important studies of our subject one might mention Maurice Eminyan, *The Theology of Salvation* (Boston: Daughters of St. Paul, 1960) and Jerome P. Theisen, *The Ultimate Church and the Promise of Salvation* (Collegeville, Minn.: St. John's University, 1976). For anyone doing historical research on the theological problem of salvation outside the Church the classic study by Louis Capéran, *Le problème du salut des infidèles*, 2 vols., 2nd ed. (Toulouse: Grand Séminaire, 1934), is still indispensable.

Theses and Commentary

1. All human beings since the Fall are in need of salvation, which is obtained by God's bestowal of redemptive grace. Such grace is in every case given through Jesus Christ[4], "the one mediator" (1 Tim. 2:5-7; quoted in LG 28, 49, 60 and AG 7) in whose name alone salvation can be found (Acts 4:12). Whatever might have been true in the state of original justice, it is certain that, in the present dispensation of fallen nature, there is no unmediated grace. No one can come to the Father except through Jesus Christ (Jn. 14:6).

After citing a long series of biblical texts to establish that there is no salvation without the mediation of Christ (RM 5), John Paul II adds that this means the mediation of the incarnate Word. Against some modern theologians who seem to make the saving work of the Logos independent of that of Jesus Christ, the pope asserts: "To introduce any sort of separation between the Word and Jesus Christ is contrary to the Christian faith" (RM 6)[5]. Christ's mediation, moreover, excludes parallel or com-

---

[4] Council of Trent, Decree on Justification, chap. 3 (DS 1523), chap. 7 (DS 1529), and canon 10 (DS 1560).

Besides the abbreviations referring to the writings of Pope John Paul II found at the beginning of this volume, the following abbreviations are employed in the main text:

AG — Vatican II, Decree *Ad gentes* on the missionary activity of the Church.

DS — H. DENZINGER et A. SCHÖNMETZER (ed.), *Enchiridion Symbolorum*, 36th ed. (Barcelona: Herder, 1976). [Collection of official ecclesial documents].

EN — PAUL VI, Apostolic Exhortation *Evangelii nuntiandi* (1975).

GS — Vatican II, Pastoral Constitution *Gaudium et spes* on the Church in the Modern World.

LG — Vatican II, Dogmatic Constitution *Lumen gentium* on the Church.

NA — Vatican II, Declaration *Nostra aetate* on non-Christian Religions.

SC — Vatican II, Constitution *Sacrosanctum concilium* on the sacred liturgy.

SR — K. Wojtyla (John Paul II), *Sources of Renewal*, tr. P. Falla (San Francisco: Harper and Row, 1980).

UR — Vatican II, Decree *Unitatis reintegratio* on ecumenism.

[5] This point is amplified by Cardinal Jozef Tomko, prefect of the Congregation for the Evangelization of Peoples, in an address of April 5, 1991 to the College of Cardinals. According to the published digest of his address, he

THE CHURCH AS LOCUS OF SALVATION

plementary mediation by other agents or agencies. It does not, however, exclude participated forms of mediation that "acquire meaning and value only from Christ's own mediation" (RM 5). Thus the intercession of the saints, the priestly ministry, the Scriptures, and the sacraments must not be seen as derogating from the sole mediatorship of Christ.

The grace of Christ may be mediated not only by divinely established means of grace but also, in indirect ways, by occasional events, such as good example, providential experiences, and the like. The Holy Spirit can act through instrumentalities of his own choosing.

2. The Church exists in order to perpetuate Christ's redemptive work[6]. It is equipped for this task by its apostolic heritage of faith, sacraments, and ministry, together with the promised assistance of the risen Christ, who acts through the gift of the Holy Spirit. The Church of Christ is the "universal sacrament of salvation" (LG 48; GS 45; AG 7; RM 20) and is "the first beneficiary" of salvation, since Christ "won the Church for himself at the price of his own blood", and chose it as his bride (RM 9).

3. Since Pentecost the ordinary way of salvation for all human beings is through believing the gospel and being incorporated in the one Church of Christ (EN 80; RM 55).

Paul VI and John Paul II, in using the term "ordinary", seem to be disapproving the formulation popularized by Heinz Robert Schlette that the Church is the "extraordinary" way of

---

rejected the view of some unnamed Indian theologians: "Taking the distinction between the Christ-Logos and the historical Jesus as the point of departure, it is claimed that there is more in the Logos than in the historical Jesus, so that the Logos can appear in other religions and be hidden in other historical figures. The Christ-Logos would belong to all the religions and be manifested in them. On the other hand, the historical Jesus belongs to the Christian religion and the church. The salvific mediation of non-Christian religions is also tied to the cosmic Christ-Logos". See Jozef Tomko, "On Relativizing Christ: Sects and the Church", *Origins* 20 (April 25, 1991), 753-54, at 754.

[6] Vatican I, *Pastor aeternus*, Prologue (DS 3050).

salvation, whereas the other religions are "ordinary" ways[7]. In English (and perhaps in German) the terms "ordinary" and "extraordinary" are problematic, since we tend to understand them in an empirical, or statistical, rather than a normative sense. In official church usage the "ordinary" way is that which is divinely established and willed for all human beings. The terminology does not say anything about the relative frequency of the two ways.

The proportion of the human race that achieves definitve salvation is not known from revelation. Paul in *Romans* 8:28-33 seems to be confident that the generality of Christians, having been called, will be justified and attain eternal life. Some interpret *Romans* 5:18-21 as teaching that the effects of Christ's redemptive grace will quantitatively outweigh the harm done by Adam's fall. In *Romans* 11:32 Paul marvels at the wisdom of God, who "has consigned all men to disobedience, that he may have mercy upon all".

The Synoptic Gospels, however, are less encouraging. Matthew quotes Jesus as saying in the Sermon on the Mount: "Enter through the narrow gate; for the gate is wide and the road is broad that leads to destruction, and those who enter it are many. How narrow the gate and constricted the road that leads to life. And those who find it are few" (Mt. 7:13-14). Elsewhere Matthew depicts Jesus as giving the admonition: "Many are called (*kletoi*) but few are chosen (*eklektoi*)" (Mt. 22:14). A similar impression is conveyed by Luke. When asked whether few or many will be saved, Jesus, without directly answering the question, warns his hearers: "Strive to enter by the narrow door; for many, I tell you, will seek to enter and will not be able" (Lk. 13:23-24).

Until rather recently the preponderant opinion among

---

[7] Heinz Robert SCHLETTE, *Towards a Theology of the Religions* (New York: Herder and Herder, 1966), pp. 80-82; cf. Sullivan, p. 188.

theologians was that only a minority of the human race is saved[8]. In the Western church since the time of Augustine this opinion was all but universal. Today many seem to assume the opposite, and some even speculate that no one suffers eternal loss. The argument is often made that if God is all-powerful and all-good he will find ways in which to bring everyone, or the large majority, to that faith and repentance which they need to qualify for salvation. While the final outcome remains hidden in the divine counsels, two affirmations may be safely made: that God will not afflict greater suffering upon anyone than what that person's sins deserve; and that a real possibility of achieving eternal life is given to everyone (or at least to all who attain to the use of reason: the salvation of unbaptized infants is another question, too complex to be addressed here). Both these statements have been often repeated since Pius IX made them in 1863 in *Quanto conficiamur moerore* (DS 2866).

4. To be fully incorporated in the Church of Christ it is necessary, but not sufficient, to be a baptized Christian in union with the bishops who are in communion with the pope, the successor of Peter; in other words, it is necessary to be a Catholic. Full incorporation in the Church involves, positively, maintenance of the bonds of professed faith, sacramental participation, and ecclesiastical government, and the negative condition of not being legitimately excommunicated for grave sin (*Mystici corporis* [DS 3802]; LG 14). Yet even Catholics who maintain these external bonds are not fully incorporated unless

---

[8] Albert MICHEL, in his article "Élus (Nombre des)" (DTC 4:2350-78), gives an imposing list of fathers and scholastic doctors who hold that the majority of the human race is damned. Thomas Aquinas shares this view (*Summa theol.* 1.23.7 ad 3). But Michel believes that there is no binding tradition against the opposite view, which is still theologically tenable. Hans Urs von Balthasar, in his *Dare We Hope "That All Men will be Saved"?* (San Francisco: Ignatius, 1988), mentions a number of recent and contemporary theologians, including Henri de Lubac and Karl Rahner, who agree with him that one may hope for the salvation of all.

they possess the gift of the Holy Spirit, nor can they be saved unless they persevere in charity (LG 14). According to the present pope, writing when he was still a cardinal: "It is clear that membership of the Church may itself be merely external, lacking the interior elements which denote membership of the People of God and give man his place in the order of salvation" (SR 127).

The Catholic Church, as the institution in which the Church of Christ subsists (LG 8), has the fullness of the means of grace (UR 3), but these means do not bring about salvation automatically; they are fruitful only when used by persons having the right dispositions.

5. All human beings have in principle a right to hear the proclamation of the gospel (EN 80; RM 11). Those who know the truth regarding the divinely instituted way of salvation are obliged to bear witness, and will be judged the more severely if they fail to do so (LG 14; RM 11). Neither Vatican II nor the present pope bases the urgency of missionary proclamation on the peril that the non-evangelized will incur damnation; rather, they stress the self-communicative character of love for Christ, which gives joy and meaning to human existence (RM 10-11; cf. 2 Cor. 5:14). The new life that Christians receive as a gift from God in Christ stirs up generosity in the hearts of its recipients. "For he who loves desires to give himself" (DIM 7). The mystery of Christ "obliges me to proclaim mercy as God's merciful love, revealed in that same mystery of Christ" (DIM 15).

6. For all who are in a position to discover the necessity of the Church and the steps to incorporation, membership in the Catholic Church (through the bonds of professed faith, sacraments, ecclesiastical government, and communion, as described above) is in principle obligatory for the sake of salvation (LG 14; SR 126). Vatican II did not explicitly take up the question whether the Catholic Church is necessary for salvation with a necessity of precept alone (i.e., because God so commands) or also with a necessity of means (i.e., as bestowing a needed help). But the council declared that Christ, "by insisting on the need for faith and baptism... at the same time confirmed the need for the

Church into which people enter through baptism as through a door" (LG 14). The analogy with faith and baptism, both of which are regarded as necessary means, suggests that the Catholic Church, likewise, must be required with a necessity of means. But, as regards actual membership in the Catholic Church, the necessity of means can only be a *relative* one because, as we shall presently see, some means of grace (ordinary and extraordinary) are available to Christians in other churches and ecclesial communities and even to non-Christians.

7. Other Christian churches and ecclesial communities have some divinely instituted means of grace, such as Holy Scripture, certain sacraments, apostolic ministries, prayers, and spiritual traditions (LG 15). All these ecclesial elements "properly belong to the one Church of Christ" (UR 3) and "give an impulse toward catholic unity" (LG 8). They derive their efficacy as means of salvation "from that fullness of grace and truth which has been entrusted to the Catholic Church" (UR 3). The sacred actions performed in these churches can truly engender the life of grace and can give access to the community of salvation (UR 3; cf. SR 128, 316). Baptized believers who are members of churches or ecclesial communities separated ("seiunctae") from the Catholic Church are in a state of partial or incomplete communion ("In quadam cum ecclesia catholica communione, etsi non perfecta, constituuntur", UR 3). Paul VI declared that the Orthodox churches are "in almost complete communion" with the Catholic Church — a formula that John Paul II has repeated[9]. It would seem that the salvific means of grace in these churches and communities are those that bring them into communion (albeit

---

[9] PAUL VI, Letter to Patriarch Athenagoras of Constantinople, Feb. 8, 1971; text in *Tomos Agapes* (Rome: Polyglot Press, 1971), 614. In his 1979 address for the Week of Prayer for Unity, John Paul II said: "With the Orthodox Churches of the East the dialogue of charity has made us rediscover a communion that is almost full, even if still imperfect"; text in Pope John Paul II, *Addresses and Homilies on Ecumenism 1978-1980*, ed. John B. Sheerin and John F. Hotchkin (Washington, D.C.: U.S. Catholic Conference, 1981), pp. 5-9, at 8.

incomplete) with the Catholic Church and not those that separate them (albeit partially) from it. In a sense, therefore, the Catholic Church is operating through them.

8. In ways known to God, persons inculpably ignorant of the necessity of the Church have the possibility of attaining salvation, through God's grace, by means that are in the technical sense "extraordinary" (AG 7; GS 22; EN 80; RM 10).

Building on the analogy of the reception of the sacraments *in voto* (as taught by the Council of Trent in its Decree on Justification; cf. DS 1524, 1543), Pius XII stated that non-Catholics may be "ordered" (*ordinentur*) to the true Church by an "unconscious will and desire" ("inscio quodam voto ac desiderio"; *Mystici corporis* [DS 3821]) to be incorporated in it. The Holy Office, dealing with the so-called Feeney case in 1949, spoke of an implicit *votum* that was contained in that disposition of soul whereby a person wanted his or her will to be conformed to the divine will (DS 3870). To be efficacious for salvation, according to the Sacred Congregation, this *votum* must be accompanied by supernatural faith and informed by perfect charity (DS 3872).

Pius XII's doctrine of the unconscious or implicit *votum* was not taken up, at least in so many words, by Vatican II. The council acknowledged that non-Catholic Christians, inasmuch as they have access in their own churches or ecclesial communities to certain divinely established means of grace, can attain union with God through regularly appointed means of grace and not by virtue of a mere *votum*. Yet the means of grace, as already noted, "give an impulse toward catholic unity". This dynamism toward the plenitude that subsists in Catholic Christianity may, in my judgment, be regarded as a kind of *votum* for the Catholic fullness. Where this *votum* is present, at least in an implicit way, the sacrament can confer sanctifying grace[10].

---

[10] Thomas Aquinas holds that anyone who receives baptism with the right disposition by that very fact receives the Eucharist *in voto*, inasmuch as baptism, as the *ianua sacramentorum*, is objectively ordered toward full incorporation

Taking up the status of non-Christians, Vatican II taught in several important texts (LG 16, AG 7, GS 22) that the grace received by such persons produces a positive relationship ("ordinatio") toward the Church (LG 16). This language is fully compatible with the *votum* theory[11]. Respecting the mystery of God's extraordinary dealing with such persons, the council did not attempt to specify how God brings them to salvation. Several texts, however, contain interesting suggestions.

GS 22 asserts that Christ has "united himself in some sense to every human being", a statement that recalls the teaching of some of the Greek fathers on the ontological consecration of humanity as a whole by virtue of the Incarnation. The same Constitution taught that "since Christ died for everyone, and since the ultimate calling of all human beings is one and divine, we are obliged to hold that the Holy Spirit offers everyone the possibility of sharing in this Paschal mystery in a manner known to God" (GS 22). Pope John Paul II has frequently quoted these two texts (e.g., SR 79-80; RH 13; RM 6, 10, 28). Throughout his writings this pope returns many times to the idea that since "in Jesus Christ the visible world was created for humanity" (RH 8) and since all men and women have the same divinely given destiny, human beings cannot understand their world or themselves, or achieve their true destiny, apart from Christ.

Some theologians conjecture that by a kind of divine illumination at the moment of death, an explicit decision for Christ and the Church might be made possible, and therefore

---

into the Church (and thus toward the Eucharist as the sacrament of full incorporation); *Summa theologiae* 3.73.3c. Whereas I believe that this theory of the *votum* accounts well for the position of Vatican II on the salvation of non-Catholic Christians, Sullivan takes the position that after the 1963 draft, the Constitution on the Church abandoned the view "that the salvation of other Christians must also come through the Catholic Church, in view of their implicit desire to belong to it"; *Salvation*, p. 145.

[11] See Avery Dulles, *The Reshaping of Catholicism* (San Francisco: Harper & Row, 1988), pp. 138-141. See also Sullivan, *Salvation*, pp. 151-52.

also required. Maurice Eminyan judges that "it is highly probable that God, in His mercy, does grant such an interior
inspiration to every infidel at the moment of death"[12]. This view
has the merit of reconciling the modern teaching that God's
salvific will extends to every individual with the thesis, supported
by Augustine, Aquinas, and most scholastic theologians, that no
one can be saved in the Christian era without explicit belief in the
Trinity and the Incarnation. Even if (as is rather commonly held
today) a more implicit type of faith suffices for the salvation of
the unevangelized, still it seems likely that God's grace may give
special lights and attractions that favor a salvific option at the
moment of death.

Karl Rahner and others speak of unevangelized persons who
are "anonymous Christians". This term is acceptable if it is taken
to mean that whatever graces such persons receive are in fact
gratia Christi, even though the recipients do not recognize this.
In saying Yes to the demands of conscience as influenced by
grace, they are in effect saying Yes to the call of Christ in the
form in which it comes to them. But the terminology of "anonymous Christianity" is sometimes understood as implying that the
real substance of Christianity is available without any explicit
knowledge of, or belief in, the gospel, and that only the name
(*onoma*) of Christian is lacking to the unevangelized who follow
the dictates of their personal conscience.

This second understanding of anonymous Christianity is
difficult to reconcile with the salvific importance that the New
Testament and tradition attach to the proclamation of the good
news and to explicit faith in Christ. The New Testament writers
seem to be convinced that anyone accepting the Christian
message enters a radically new salvific relationship with God.

---

[12] EMINYAN, *Theology of Salvation*, p. 207. Earlier in his book (pp. 80-95)
Eminyan discusses the illumination theories of Canon Palémon Glorieux and
others. For a restatement see Maurice Eminyan, *The Mystery of Salvation*
(Valletta: Malta University Press, 1973), pp. 172-76.

Theories of "anonymous Christianity" that depreciate the salvific importance of Christian proclamation and explicitly Christian faith are questionable. Yet there are good grounds for affirming the common doctrine that God will treat an implicit desire or tendency as an acceptable substitute in the case of persons who, moved by grace, desire with their whole heart to do what God requires of them but who are inculpably impeded from making acts of explicit Christian faith and from physically receiving baptism.

9. Saving grace is always ecclesial. As I have noted in the preceding section, those who receive grace without coming into historical contact with the Church are "oriented" or "ordered" (*ordinati*) to the Church by grace itself (*Mystici corporis*, DS 3821; Holy Office, Letter to Cushing, DS 3869-71; LG 16). The translation "related to the people of God" in the Abbott, Flannery, and Tanner versions of LG 16 seems too weak to do justice to the Latin *ordinati*, especially when this term is seen against the background of the previous documents from the pontificate of Pius XII. The "ordering" in question is a dynamic tendency toward the Church as its goal. Thus the Church is involved in the salvation of non-Christians by way of finality[13].

It seems probable that the Church is involved not only by way of final causality but also as a kind of instrumental efficient or meritorious cause of grace for such persons, in the sense that grace is dispensed to them through the active mediation of the Church. This instrumentality of the Church seems to be implied in the teaching of the Holy Office and of Vatican II that the Church is an "all-embracing means of salvation" (*generale auxilium salutis*, DS 3870; cf. Vatican II, UR 3) and in the doctrine

---

[13] Yves CONGAR in his article "Hors de l'Eglise, pas de salut", (*Catholicisme* 5:948-56, at 955), reached the conclusion: "The Catholic Church remains the only divinely instituted and commanded institution (*sacramentum*) of salvation, and the grace that exists in the world is attributed to it by finality if not by efficacy". For discussion see Theisen, *Ultimate Church*, pp. 75-81 and Sullivan, *Salvation*, pp. 155-56.

of Vatican II that the Church is the "universal sacrament of salvation" (*universale sacramentum salutis*, LG 48; cf. AG 1 and GS 45). A sacrament is by nature an efficacious sign, one that confers the grace that it signifies. Thus the Church is also called "an instrument for the redemption of all" (LG 9). The Church preaches the gospel to all whom it can reach; but it offers prayers and sacrifices, including the Mass, also for those whom it cannot effectively reach with its proclamation. The Constitution on the Liturgy declares that the Church, by its prayer and eucharistic sacrifices, unceasingly intercedes with the Lord for the salvation of the whole world (SC 83)[14]. John Paul II, in a paragraph on "The Church as Sign and Instrument of Salvation", reaffirms the general teaching of Vatican II just summarized (RM 9).

10. Although non-Christian religions (or at least nonbiblical religions) can claim no authoritative Christian warrants as ways of salvation, it is evident that the Holy Spirit can act in an "extraordinary" way (not necessarily rare) through such religions to the extent that they are vehicles of truth and goodness. Vatican II expressed its esteem for the truth and grace given through "the particular rites and cultures of peoples" (AG 10). Speaking of religions such as Hinduism and Buddhism, the council declared that the Catholic Church "rejects none of those things that are true and holy in these religions" (NA 2); it acknowledged that non-Christian religions contain "seeds of the Word" (AG 11; cf. 18) and reflections of that light that illumines the whole world (NA 2). The council did not, however, attempt to settle the question whether the good things in these other religions were merely natural or were due to divine grace and revelation.

Paul VI in many pronouncements limited himself to the human and natural aspects of these religions, calling them "natural religious expressions most worthy of esteem" (EN 53).

---

[14] DULLES, *The Reshaping of Catholicism*, pp. 140-41; Sullivan, *Salvation*, pp. 157-59.

John Paul II, without going so far as to call the nonbiblical religions "means" or "ways" of salvation, holds that "every authentic prayer is prompted by the Holy Spirit" (RM 29), who offers everyone the possibility of sharing in the Paschal mystery (AG 22). The Church's respect for non-Christian religions, he declares, is twofold: "respect for man in his quest for answers to the deepest questions of life, and respect for the action of the Spirit in man" (RM 29). Whatever the Holy Spirit brings about in any culture or religion serves as a "preparation for the gospel" (ibid.). The possibility of salvation for persons in other religious traditions comes from the grace of Christ, which enlightens them in a way accommodated to their situation (RM 8).

In some recent literature the various religions are depicted as alternative routes to salvation, all of them willed by God. The Protestant theologian John Hick, for example, holds that Christianity must abandon its claim to ultimate religious superiority and must view itself "in a pluralistic context as one of the great world faiths, one of the streams of religious life through which human beings can be savingly related to that ultimate Reality Christians know as the heavenly Father"[15]. This recognition, he says, would mean a move from the inclusivism of Vatican II and the recent popes to a pluralism that sets all the religions on a plane of fundamental equality[16]. Similarly, the Catholic Paul Knitter, after paying tribute to the pluralistic theocentrism of theologians such as Hick, concludes that Christians "need not insist that Jesus brings God's definitive, normative revelation"[17].

These pluralistic theories, widely disseminated among American Catholics today, raise fundamental questions about the criteria of religious truth. Within the perspectives of the

---

[15] John HICK, "The Non-Absoluteness of Christianity", in *The Myth of Christian Uniqueness*, ed. John Hick and Paul F. Knitter (Maryknoll, N.Y.: Orbis, 1987), 16-36, at 22.

[16] *Ibid.*, 20-23.

[17] Paul F. KNITTER, *No Other Name?* (Maryknoll, N.Y.: Orbis, 1985), p. 205.

present paper it may suffice to say that they are not reconcilable
with the obvious meaning of many biblical texts, which depict
Christ as the only-begotten Son of God and as the one mediator,
in whose name alone salvation can be found. Nor are they in
harmony with the Christology of the councils and popes of all the
centuries. Most recently, John Paul II has included in his
encyclical on missionary activity a first chapter entitled, "Christ,
the only Savior", in which he emphatically teaches the "uniqueness of Christ, which gives him an absolute and universal
significance whereby, while belonging to history, he remains
history's center and goal" (RM 6). In a later chapter of the same
encyclical the pope explains that interreligious dialogue must not
detract "in any way from the fact that salvation comes from
Christ and that dialogue does not dispense with evangelization"
(RM 55). It is hard to see how Christianity, without denying its
own basic teaching about the Trinity and the Incarnation, could
adopt the kind of pluralism suggested by Hick and Knitter[18].

Conclusion

This survey of contemporary official teaching reveals, in my
opinion, that the Catholic does not have to stand paralyzed
before the four options set forth in Schineller's article, mentioned at the opening of this paper.

The first option is not tenable. Whatever may have been
true in previous centuries, Catholics since Pius XII are not free to
hold that only members of their own Church can be saved.
Formal entrance into the Catholic Church, or for that matter into
any Christian church or community, is not a absolute precondi-
tion for salvation. In the light of recent official teaching it seems
highly improbable that an explicit desire for membership in the
Church is indispensable for salvation. Yet entrance into the
Church is a requirement for the salvation of anyone who is in a

---

[18] In the address quoted above, Cardinal Tomko also repudiated "pluralistic theocentrism"; *Origins* 20 (April 25, 1991), 754.

position to know the truth of the Christian or Catholic faith and to become a member of the Church.

Likewise unacceptable is the fourth position, which denies the established doctrine that Christ is the sole mediator of all grace to fallen humanity. From the sole mediatorship of Christ it follows that the Church, which proclaims Christ and perpetuates his work, has a unique legitimacy, although other religions may play a providential role às occasions of grace for persons who adhere to them in good faith. God is capable of working through these religions insofar as they contain elements of truth and goodness, mingled though these be with error.

The third position, which depicts the Church as a sign but not an instrumental cause of grace, is not so clearly excluded, but it is in my opinion difficult to reconcile with current Catholic teaching about the Church as "universal sacrament of salvation" and an "instrument for the redemption of all". The position seems to underestimate the efficacy of the sacrifices and prayers of the Church for all human beings. Finally, it unduly separates the action of Christ as head from that of his body, the Church, which constitutes together with him the "whole Christ". While Christ as head is always the principal minister, it is difficult to conceive of him dispensing grace without the instrumentality of the body which he has indissolubly conjoined with himself.

The most acceptable position of the four, in my judgment, is the second. The Church of Christ, I would hold, is constitutive in the sense that all grace and salvation are somehow mediated through it. Christians are the first and primary beneficiaries of the means of grace committed to the Church, but they are not the sole beneficiaries. Those who receive grace without being incorporated in the Church are oriented toward the Church by grace itself. They may be said to have a *votum* or desire for membership, even though they are not conscious of this orientation.

When it is said that the Church of Christ is the universal sacrament of salvation, the statement applies without qualification to the Catholic Church, in which the Church of Christ "subsists" (LG 8) in such a way that "in the Catholic Church alone... the fullness of the means of salvation can be obtained" (UR 3). But other churches and ecclesial communities participate in various degrees in the reality of the Church as sacrament, to the extent that they preserve and make use of means of grace committed by Christ to his Church. These means of grace, as we have seen, have a dynamism toward Catholic unity and derive their efficacy from the plenitude of grace and truth that has been entrusted to the Catholic Church.

The teaching of John Paul II in all essentials agrees with that of Vatican II and Paul VI. In comparison with Pius XII the present pope, like the council, gives a more positive appraisal of non-Catholic Christianity and of the non-Christian religions, and a greater willingness to assume the presence of grace and good faith among those who err. But the teaching of Pius XII on the necessity of accepting the Catholic Church as "all-embracing means of salvation" still stands.

THESES ON CHURCH AND SALVATION

1. Jesus Christ, the incarnate Son of God, is the one mediator of all grace and salvation.

2. The Church of Christ, as sacrament, perpetuates Christ's redemptive work.

3. Membership in the Church is today the ordinary way of salvation.

4. Only members of the Catholic Church are fully incorporated in the Church of Christ.

5. All Christians are obliged to bear witness and to help others find their way to the Church.

6. Membership in the Catholic Church is required with a necessity both of precept and of means, but this necessity is not absolute.

7. Other Christian churches possess some means of grace, which derive their efficacy from the fullness of grace and truth entrusted to the Catholic Church.

8. Non-Christians in good faith may by the grace of Christ be saved through an implicit *votum* which orders them to the Catholic Church; in the case of non-Catholic Christians, this *votum* is fortified by the means of grace available in their communities.

9. The Church of Christ is involved in the salvation of non-Christians not only by way of final causality but also as instrumental cause.

10. The Holy Spirit can act in extraordinary ways through the nonbiblical religions, but these religions should not be regarded as mediating salvation without dependence on Christ and the Church.

THE CHURCH AS LOCUS OF SALVATION

A Response

BRIAN E. DALEY, S.J.

I. I once heard Gov. Mario Cuomo, at the start of a graduation address, remark that his position in the ceremonies was something like that of the corpse at an Irish wake: you don't have to say much, but they can't have the party without you! Replying to a paper such as the one we have just heard — Avery Dulles' characteristically clear and comprehensive exposition of the Catholic Church's classical understanding of its role as the place and the means of human salvation — may not be quite as ceremonially canonized as either that of the corpse or that of the commencement speaker, but it *is* even simpler: there is not much one *can* say to add to the paper's rounded fulness: there is even less that I, personally, would want to disagree with or qualify.

Instead, then, of artificially searching out points in Fr. Dulles' synthesis where one might find some grounds for question, it seems to me more useful simply to keep going in the same direction: to offer some further reflections on this very complex and delicate subject from my own, largely patristic perspective, with the hope that some remarks in a second voice on the same theme might be some help to the rest of us as we prepare to discuss it further.

II. The central issue raised by the paper, it seems to me, is that of the claim to uniqueness constantly, if often implicitly, made by Catholic faith and religious practice: the uniqueness of our God, as source of the world's being and goal of its movement; the uniqueness of Jesus Christ as savior; the uniqueness of the Roman Catholic Church as the continuing publicly identifiable body of authentic disciples of Jesus, who see in their common discipleship a unique way of sharing in the life-transforming power Jesus offers. Claims to such uniqueness do not go down well in liberal, post-Enlightenment Western culture: tolerance and even-handed openness are the civic virtues we prize and inculcate above all others, diversity and pluralism are the norms we assume as essential for a healthy society; we are hostile to anything that seems like privilege in the position of others and are embarrassed to claim anything like privilege for ourselves. Yet Biblical religion, as has often been observed, distinguished itself from the other ancient religions of the Mediterranean above all by its intolerance of rival cults, its insistence that those who serve the God of Israel should openly repudiate all other gods. For the Deuteronomist, "going after other gods" was the root of Israel's historical infidelity and the cause of all her woes; for the exilic and post-exilic prophets and psalmists, other gods are simply manufactured idols, "the work of human hands". And the disciples of Jesus, who know him as Israel's Messiah, as risen and living Lord, have recognized him since New Testament times as God's final spokesman and agent within human history, "the Way, the Truth and the Life", by whom alone all human beings must find their way to God. "There is salvation in no one else", Peter tells Israel's elders in *Acts* 4:12, and the very term "salvation" suggests that a much greater urgency is attached to believing in his name than simply enhanced well-being. It is a matter of life and death — of encountering or not encountering absolute reality, the truth that alone sets us free.

The Catholic tradition, however, has come to distinguish levels of finality within the ways this single, life-giving and life-saving absolute reality we call God is "mediated" or made accessible: between *the Mystery* (to use Rahnerian terms), which is God communicating himself to created being, and the various "mysteries" of human symbolic representation and worship which realize that communication of life concretely and respond to it — mysteries the Latin theological tradition tends to refer to as *sacraments*. Salvation, the fulfillment of our natural end as intelligent and loving creatures and the alternative to the self-imposed annihilation involved in rejecting our creaturehood (which we call *sin*), is, for Christian faith, to share in the very life of God — not as something achieved by our own natural energies, but as God's free gift of inclusion, of participation. This gift (which we call grace) is made intelligible to us, historically and dramatically *realized*, in the person and teaching of Jesus, God's Son, who taught us to call God "Father" with him, and it is realized within each of us, and within the community of faith, by the presence of the Holy Spirit, God personally given, "God the gift".

Sharing in God's life in this way — *with* the Son, *in* the Spirit — *is* the Mystery of salvation. But because the Church, as the community that proclaims and receives this Mystery in faith and hope, is the key link between God and an unknowing world, the Church, too, can be called the "sacrament of salvation", in the words of *Lumen Gentium* 42, and the various faith-filled acts by which the Church defines and realizes itself in its members — its Eucharist, its acts of initiation and reconciliation and ordination to office, the consecration of family life and of human mortality, along with a host of more incidental blessings and commemorations — can also be called, in varying degrees, "sacramental". Sacraments, as Fr. Dulles reminds us in his paper, are traditionally understood in Catholic theology as "efficacious signs", conferring the grace they signify: this is another way of saying that they reveal and represent the single, final saving Mystery of God in Christ in such a way that they inevitably draw us into it more deeply, allow us to share more fully in the gift of the Spirit, provided we are willing and ready to be drawn. The important thing to note here, however, I think, is that because *all* the sacraments — including the Church itself — are saving "mysteries" in a secondary and representational sense, they are *signs* of

God's Trinitarian self-communication but *not* that self-communication in its totality. So while the Church itself, and the Church's formal acts, bring us, in a variety of ways, face to face with God's unique self-revelation in Christ, let us drink more deeply of his unique self-communication in the Holy Spirit, none of these "lesser mysteries" can be thought of as monopolizing God's continuing, gracious gift of self — none can be regarded as the *only* way in which human beings find Christ as "the Way, the Truth and the Life". Sacraments, including the Church, are privileged means of access to the life of grace, norms and types, classical *loci*, for the communion to which God calls all men and women; but the ultimacy of these sacraments, their "eschatological" uniqueness and validity, must be distinguished, on a descending scale of importance, from the uniqueness of salvation through Christ in the Spirit.

III. Having said all this by way of background, let me try to articulate anew, in my own way, an understanding of the Catholic Church as *locus* of salvation that will, I think, parallel in meaning what Fr. Dulles has laid out for us, but that will put it in slightly different terms.

1. As Christians, we believe most fundamentally in a God who is unique and who is ultimately, absolutely real. This God, we believe, *is* Father, Son and Holy Spirit. God reveals himself in this way in human history — as the hidden God of Israel, as Jesus the Christ, as the Spirit sent by Jesus upon his Church in fire and wind; and God "saves" human beings by enfolding us in his own reality, by "placing us with the Son" and letting us "dare to call him Father", with Jesus, by the power of the Spirit.

2. Human beings have only come to *know* that the ultimate reality *is* Father, Son and Spirit from the perspective of the community of disciples at Easter and Pentecost: from the perspective, in other words, of the lived self-understanding of the Christian Church. The Roman Catholic community understands itself as the only Christian body fully in continuity with the faith, structure and worship of the Easter and Pentecost community. So the Catholic Church sees itself as a fundamental, indispen-

sable means to humanity's coming to know and share fully in what is ultimately real, and in that knowledge and participation to find ultimate fulfillment. It is the most perfect sacrament we have of the community of salvation.

3. God *saves* men and women by drawing them to be identified with Christ, by incorporating them (in Paul's image) into Christ's body. Yet God remains free to do this in his own ways, and is not *limited* in his saving activity to the historical persons and institutions in which he has revealed and actualized that activity. Let me use a Christological analogy. St. Athanasius, and many other Greek Fathers before and after, insisted that the divine Logos who became flesh in the man Jesus was never *confined*, in his activity, to Jesus' humanity; even during the earthly life of Jesus, the Logos who was the personal core of Jesus' existence was also present and active as God's creative Word in the whole universe, holding it in order and sustaining its life. It is this universal Logos, as Justin and Irenaeus had insisted two centuries earlier, who is the divine principle by which all people of good will act reasonably and well, even if they never knew Christ and were not part of the people who had hoped for his coming — the one by whom Socrates was saved. One can participate in the life of the Logos, in the early apologists' view, by acting "reasonably" (*logikōs*), in the broadest sense; one can share in the life of Christ, one might say, by living in a Christ-like way. So, it would seem, one can belong, in the broadest sense, to the "body" of Christ in the world by allowing the way of life he revealed to become "embodied" in one's own pattern of moral and spiritual choices and commitments; this would be the practical form of what Catholic documents have referred to as an "implicit *votum*" for baptism.

This position seems to have at least two further implications: first, that while a Christian must reject the agnostic religious pluralism of an Aurelius Symmachus, which Fr. Dulles alludes to, or his contemporary counterparts like John Hick and Paul Knitter, one must agree — if one takes the universal role of the Logos seriously — that there is more than one way to share in the mystery of *Christ*; and second, that if it *is* Catholic teaching that membership in the Church is necessary for salvation by a "necessity of means", that necessity must refer to the "Church" in its broadest terms — to the *body of Christ*, to Augustine's "city of God" — which is not the same as the historical Christian or Catholic community, but which is comprised of those who "embody" their faith in the Word in the way they live, even if they cannot share, for various reasons, in the life of his historical, sacramental community.

4. The Roman Catholic Church believes that despite its own historicity, its sinfulness and its constant need for reform, it alone — within a splintered Christendom — reveals and realizes the life of the community of grace in institutional fulness. So *Lumen Gentium* can say, with great precision, that the Church of Christ "subsists in" the Roman Catholic Church (LG 8), because it is the Catholic Church alone, in its continuity with the Church of the Apostles, its unity and dogged holiness and trans-cultural universality, which gives concrete *subsistence* to the more universal body of Christ. Let us return to the Christological analogy, since this language of "subsistence" parallels the classical language of Chalcedon. Just as the natures, the dynamic realities or substances, of God and humanity, *subsist* together historically in one concrete individual, one *hypostasis* or person named Jesus, without being exhausted by that hypostatic human existence, so the universal "body" of those who walk the way of Jesus is *personalized, hypostatized*, given concrete historical expression in the Roman Catholic Church. Yet clearly the community of grace extends more widely, despite the fact that there are no other historical communities in which it subsists as authentically as in the Catholic communion.

5. So the "necessity" of the Church for salvation can be formulated in two senses, depending on how one understands the meaning and extension of the word "Church":

a) In order to come to the fulfillment of human existence, *everyone* must share in the pattern of loving, just, humble, creaturely existence that is made possible by the divine Logos and fully realized in Christ, everyone must be related to God and his or her neighbor in the charity which is God's gift; so everyone must belong, by his or her free assent to love, to the eschatological "body" of Christ.

b) The Roman Catholic Church is the unique historical realization, the concrete "hypostasis" of this community of love and grace, making it known and effectively present in its preaching, structures and sacraments. To understand fully what communion with God in Christ means, to share in its sacramental and historical realization, it is necessary to belong to the Catholic community.

Further, as Fr. Dulles points out well towards the end of his paper, the Church takes a *sacramental* role in the wider community of grace not only as a representative, efficacious sign but as a kind of celebrant or priest: joining with Christ, our sole mediator with God, in his continued intercession for the world. The Church, in its prayer and especially in its Eucharistic sacrifice, joins in the dynamic human process of calling on God in its radical need for salvation, expressing its need for grace — a process that is, in God's providence, the necessary human dimension of the event of reconciliation.

IV. Cyprian of Carthage, in the spring of 256, unaware of the use future generations would make of his phrase, remarked to his brother bishop Jubaianus (Ep. 73.21), *salus extra ecclesiam non est*, as a way of discounting the efficacy of schismatic baptism. He wrote in the context of a local Christian community divided by persecution, troubled by competing claims to authority, and tempted by the Gnostic vision of alternative, non-institutional means of access to God, alongside the dreary realities of hierarchical institutions. His theory of the conditions for valid baptism needed revision, but his underlying point was that there are no end runs around the "ordinary" Church which can lead to the same goal; disgruntled Catholics who desire their own alternative priesthood, perform their own Eucharist, arrange reconciliation on their own terms, have no authentic access to a saving God through these actions, because they are not the sacramental signs that grow directly from the historical order of salvation — from the original experience of salvation in Christ by the disciples of the risen Jesus. Cyprian was concerned here with Church order and internal Church discipline, with sacramental reality, not with God's more fundamental readiness to save whom he will in the way he will. As we, today, confront both problems of anti-hierarchical affect, similar in some ways to those of Cyprian's day, and the very different problem raised by the plurality of world cultures and religions — problems Cyprian never dreamed of — we need both to savor the wisdom in his words, and to move beyond them to a wider view of humanity's relationship to the mystery of God's love. It is the great merit of Fr. Dulles' paper, I think, that it provides us with the categories to do both, faithfully and well.

PHENOMENOLOGICAL EXPERIENCE
IN KAROL WOJTYLA

JOHN H. NOTA, S.J.

To understand the philosophical approach of the author of *The Acting Person*[1] it is absolutely necessary to be aware of his special meaning of experience.

In *The Acting Person* and in his philosophical articles he points himself to the influence of Max Scheler. Although his dissertation on Scheler is rather critical, later on he becomes more positive in his evaluation, and he tries to enrich his thomistic thinking in philosophy with the new approach of Edmund Husserl and especially of Max Scheler. Wojtyla's philosophy is never just abstract, but always practical, prompted by his concern for his fellow human beings. He understood very soon that modern technology with all its wonderful discoveries threatened to become a *technocracy* where human beings become alienated from their own being instead of participating in Being. This happens in the world of capitalism, but the marxist solution in his own country after the war did not do much good for the economy nor did it improve the human condition of the people. The autonomous way of thinking of the neopositivistic philosophers in his country who rejected any kind of heteronomy he considered valuable in their rejection of marxism, but insufficient because of the neglect of deeper dimensions in the human.

---

[1] K. WOJTYLA, *The Acting Person*, tr. A. Potocki (Boston: Reidel, 1979).

So he was attracted by the existential personalism of Max
Scheler, who stressed the importance of person *and* community,
the need to discover the right order of values, social justice in his
philosophy of solidarism, the religious dimension.

Now Scheler is a phenomenologist and you cannot read a
book written by a phenomenologist unless you understand his
phenomenological method. Scheler never belonged to Edmund
Husserl's students, but he owes his method, or, as he likes to call
it, his phenomenological attitude, to Edmund Husserl. They had
a chance to meet each other, during the years that Scheler taught
in Jena and Husserl in Halle, Edith Stein told me. Moreover
Scheler studied the *Logical Investigations*. The "principle of
principles" of phenomenology, according to Husserl, is intuition
or experience, and the important discovery to Scheler is that
Husserl made clear to him that intuition is not limited to intuition
of the senses[2]. Via Eucken, Dilthey and Bergson Scheler had
come close to that insight, but he needed Husserl's approach to
be certain that the "dogma" of Hume and Kant was not true at
all. This is also *the* important issue in Wojtyla's philosophy, that
there is also an experience on the level of the intellect, or more
precisely, on the level of the spirit, to include the knowledge of
the heart.

He explains very clearly what he means by experience. On
p. 46 of *The Acting Person* we read: "Indeed, experience is that
specific form of the actualization of the human subject which
man owes to consciousness". This experience is not phenomenal-
istic, but phenomenological[3] and will reveal to us the *nature* of
the human person. Experience of the senses would only give us
"some sense-perceptible 'surface' of the being I call a human
being"[4].

---

[2] A. HUSSERL, "Ideen zu einer reinen Phänomenologie und phänomenolo-
gischen Philosophie", *Jarbuch für Philosophie und phänomenologische For-
schung* 1 (1913), 36, 43.

[3] Cf. WOJTYLA, pp. 8f., for the meaning of this distinction.

[4] WOJTYLA, p. 9, but in the better translation in the manuscript of Dr.
Teresa Sandok, OSM.

An attentive reader may make the objection that on p. 17 one reads: "...not only because experience is an act and a process, the nature of which is sensuous while the nature of understanding and interpretation is intellectual..."[5] But a more careful reader is going to wonder if this is the correct translation. So I asked Dr. Teresa Sandok, OSM, and she wrote me that the original says exactly the opposite of the English text: "In general, understanding is immanent to human experience but at the same time transcends it, not because experience is a sensory act and process, and understanding and explanation intellectual, but because of the essential character of the one and the other. To 'experience' is one thing, and to 'understand' or to 'explain' (which implies understanding) another". So there is no contradiction in the original Polish text, and this will help us to understand the content better. Moreover, it may explain why there is often misunderstanding about the Pope's thought.

To many people experience, in the limited sense of experience of the senses, is the only experience they know of. This holds also for philosophers who are still in one way or another dogmatically following Hume and Kant, or for theologians who take the experience of empirical psychologists or sociologists as their dogma. As an example one may mention the uncritical acceptance of Hans Küng and his univocal application of Thomas Kuhn's paradigms to all levels of human and superhuman knowledge[6]. Karol Wojtyla is, as a good phenomenologist, a good listener to all contemporary tendencies and so one understands why he writes: "...our prime concern in this study is *to allow experience to* speak for itself as best it can and right to the end"[7].

---

[5] WOJTYLA, p. 17.

[6] H. KÜNG, "Ein neues Grundmodel von Theologie? Divergenzen und Konvergenzen", *Das neue Paradigma von Theologie*, ed. H. Küng u. D. Tracy (Zürich: Benziger, 1986), 205-216; for a critical appraisal and application cf. G. Gutting (ed.), *Paradigms and Revolutions* (Notre Dame: University of Notre Dame, 1980).

[7] WOJTYLA, p. 133.

Subjective and Objective

Outsiders of the phenomenological approach are often wondering how this kind of experience may be anything but merely subjective. Wojtyla explains very well in an article that intends to develop further insights developed in *The Acting Person* that experience is always *subjective* and *objective*. Let me quote from the German translation, because the English translation appears to be less correct and says sometimes the opposite:

> Objectivity belongs to the essence of experience, to experience a human being always means at the same time to experience a "something" and a "somebody". The inclination to withdraw oneself into the "pure subjectivity" is typical of the philosophy of consciousness... To the essence of experience however belongs objectivity and that is the reason why a human being, the subject, is also given in experience in an objective way. Experience drives out in human knowledge the concept of "pure consciousness" and gives all positive aspects of the notion of "pure consciousness" that deepened our knowledge of the human dimension of objective reality[8].

One might be tempted to conclude that Wojtyla identifies phenomenology and philosophy of being. However, sometimes he stresses a real distinction in *The Acting Person* between phenomenology and metaphysics (p. 82), whereas the unity is being stressed on pp. 179f. and confirmed in a note where Mrs. Anna-Teresa Tymieniecka points to the origin of the unity in method with Wojtyla and Ingarden in Max Scheler (n. 59, p. 312). In later articles, later than the original Polish edition of *The Acting Person*, the unity between phenomenology and philosophy of being is becoming more evident to him, I think. As for the phenomenological method he might have quoted the interpreta-

[8] K. WOJTYLA "Person: Subject und Gemeinschaft", in K. Wojtyla et alii, *Der Streit um den Menschen* (Kevelaer: Butzon & Bercker, 1979), 17-68, at 17; cp. the English version: "The Person: Subject and Community", *The Review of Metaphysics* 33 (1979), 273-308, at 273.

tion of Maurice Merleau-Ponty who refused to separate essence and existence, but his own words will be sufficient:

> First of all, *Max Scheler helped me to discover that specific experience, which lies at the basis of the concept "actus humanus"* and which must be identified there always anew. The entire exposition of mine is also a certain *attempt at identification of this experience.* Is this identification phenomenological? I believe that it is, and at the same time I am convinced that this experience "carried being within itself", if it can be expressed that way. In a given case, that being which carries being within itself, "phenomenon", is really the act as a dynamism proper to the human person. And so, the "actus humanus" is identified phenomenologically as a distinctive factor of man's functioning[9].

Once Wojtyla accepts this, he can not only identify the human experience with the human act, but also the human act with the moral act. This approach which Wojtyla shares with Max Scheler is very important for a better understanding of our human behaviour, of ethics and moral theology. A human being, according to Wojtyla's existentialist personalism, is a *moral* being, not as an addition to a neutral ontological reality, but as *such.* Of course, he is aware of the fact that the person in a human being is in the state of becoming, of development, but his metaphysical-phenomenological approach transcends the attitude of the psychologist. As Scheler likes to say: the *seeds* of the person are present in the child, or the person is *hidden*, but present, in the "mental" patient. To use Wojtyla's words:

> The fact that in some cases the human subject or metaphysical subjectivity does not manifest the characteristics of personal subjectivity (as in the case of psychosomatic or purely psychical deficiencies in which the normal human self fails to develop or becomes deformed) does not authorize doubts concerning the

---

[9] K. WOJTYLA, "The Intentional Act and the Human Act, that is Act and Experience", *Analecta Husserliana* 5 (1976), 278.

foundations of this subjectivity, since they are inherent in the essentially human subject[10].

Community

One may still wonder, if this starting-point of phenomenological experience is not the cause of a certain kind of individualism in Wojtyla's philosophy. In the article we just mentioned the author shows that he is aware of a certain shortcoming in this regard: "*The Acting Person* does not contain a theory of community... The last chapter of *The Acting Person* does not sufficiently elaborate the theory of community, although it contains implicitly some elements of this theory. One principal element is the concept of participation..."[11]. This participation is opposed to alienation. Here one should realize that Wojtyla is philosophizing at that time amidst a marxist society that stresses community at the expense of the person. So it is understandable that we read: "This points to the indispensable priority of the personal subject in regard to the community. It is a metaphysical priority and therefore a factual and a methodological one"[12]. In the elaboration of the importance of the community he does not only stress the aspect of the personal relationship in the I-Thou, but he goes beyond it by pointing to the social dimension of the "we":

> The best example is provided by matrimony in which the clearly outlined relation "I-you" as an interpersonal relation receives a social dimension. This occurs when the husband and wife accept that complex of values which may be defined as the common good of marriage and, potentially at least, the common good of the family[13].

---

[10] WOJTYLA, "The Person", 277.
[11] *Ibid.*, p. 288.
[12] *Ibid.*, p. 289.
[13] *Ibid.*, p. 298.

Although Max Scheler has a somehow similar approach, when he says that he prefers to start from the "I" and not from the "we", he would still stress that person is to him always primary. However, that means: individual *and* communal person. Wojtyla on the other hand stresses the *self*, where the other is another *self*, a position he tries to explain in the German translation by referring to the biblical "Love your neighbour as yourself"[14].

Let me conclude my remarks as member of the panel discussion:

1) Wojtyla is starting from the full human experience which enables him to talk as a philosopher on the level of being;

2) The human act is a *moral* act.

---

[14] WOJTYLA, "Person: Subject und Gemeinschaft", 38.

PHILOSOPHICAL CORRELATIONS AMONG
K. WOJTYLA, C.S. PEIRCE, AND B. LONERGAN

Vincent G. Potter, S.J.

My role on this panel is, as I understand it, to compare Pope John Paul II's thought as expressed in his book *The Acting Person* with that of Transcendental Thomism and the American movement known as Pragmatism. The authors from each of those traditions whom I know best are respectively Bernard Lonergan and Charles Peirce. I recognize that they may not speak for all who identify themselves with those movements (at least not in every respect) but, in my opinion, these two represent the best of their respective movements.

This panel's discussion has touched on several themes central to John Paul's philosophy which are also at the heart of both Transcendental Thomism and Pragmatism. They are: 1) the central place of experience in human knowing and willing; 2) the important role of action as *the* characteristic of the human person; and 3) the essential function played by community for understanding properly the acting person. I will say a word or two about each of these points.

1. *Experience*

a) John Paul II:

John Paul II insisted on understanding experience as including all human phenomena — acts of intelligence and acts of will — and not merely acts of sensation. He insisted that the most informative lessons about mankind come from long and careful reflection on all facets of human experience (but especially on mankind's free acts) in order to find an invariant structure. This structure is not extraphenomenal but transphenomenal. It cuts across all presentations of the world to the human person. This structure therefore is not noumenal in Kant's sense nor is it metaphysical in the caricature made popular by the Enlightenment as "something beyond" or perhaps "behind" the phenomena.

b) The Pragmatists (Peirce):

It is widely acknowledged that the American Pragmatists set out to recover experience from the truncated version of it in British Empiricism. Experience for Peirce, James, and Dewey, for example, was the rich matrix from which comes all human knowing and understanding. For Peirce, at least, experience was not to be confined only to the sensuous even if the sensuous is always a part of it; thus Peirce would argue that we directly experience God albeit through symbols. Peirce held that humans cannot transcend experience in the sense of getting outside of it even though he held that the transcendent is immanent in experience. In this I believe he different from both James and Dewey. He differed from James in holding an account of experience in terms of categories (Firstness, Secondness, and Thirdness) rather than one based on "pure experience" which of course cannot be experienced at all. He differed from Dewey in that he rejected a naturalism which precluded any transcendent reality being immanent in the world.

c) Transcendental Thomists (Lonergan):

Lonergan's *Insight* might justly be characterized as an extended treatise on human cognitive experience. Lonergan claims to find across the various manifestations of human cognitive experience (mathematics, physical science, common sense, philosophy, etc.) an invariant pattern: sensuous presentation, understanding, judgment. In the lived human experience of knowing all these elements are always present although in different ways and degrees according to the sort of knowing experience involved. Lonergan's first level of cognitive experience (sensuous presentation) is closest to the empiricist/positivist version combatted by Peirce. Like Peirce, however, Lonergan immediately expands human cognitive experience to include positing questions for intelligence and questions for reflection which yield the two further elements in full human cognitive experience, understanding and judgment respectively. The full unfolding of human cognitive experience moves from presence to understanding of what is present to affirming that presence. When this process is explicitly grasped by the knower the knower's own consciousness is progressively differentiated and his own activities self-appropriated. And this, for Lonergan, is human development. Finally, for Lonergan as for John Paul II, the invariant structure of experience is not outside it (extraphenomenal) but across every experience (transphenomenal).

2. Action:

a) John Paul II:

John Paul II makes a great deal of human action — of human free action as an originating source of activity. He distinguishes clearly between being acted upon and acting. Only the latter is causal efficacy in the sense of originating something new. All other interaction in nature is causal only by analogy: it is merely action and reaction.

This sounds very much like the Kant who seems to say as much himself in various passages of the *Critique of Practical Reason*. In fact Kant argues that we can get to the noumenon through the freedom of moral agency because the free will determines itself to act (while other agents in the natural world are themselves determined to act and so are necessary, not free, agents) and so brings into existence its effects as something entirely new.

Such an emphasis upon human action implies an under-

standing of what it means to be human, which is somewhat
different from, although in my opinion not in conflict with, the
account given by traditional Thomism of the Aristotelian persua-
sion. John Paul criticizes that Thomism for not properly captur-
ing, and so not sufficiently emphasizing, human beings as
persons, as subjects. What is needed according to John Paul II is
a characterization which brings out man's existential subjectivity
which includes the process of growth (decline) dependent upon
moral choices. These choices of good or evil constitute who the
subject is at any stage of its existence.

b) The Pragmatists (Peirce):

The importance of action is at the very heart of pragmatism
of every sort. For Peirce, however, action is important insofar as
it is a way of determining, not the truth of a proposition, but
rather its meaning or intellectual purport[1]. Thus, for Peirce,
pragmatism should not be taken as just another form of empiricism; it does not make truth to consist in "what works", nor does
it reduce human knowing to mere sense perception. Rather it is a
way of determining what is meant by certain claims, namely,
what consequences does it have; it is also a measure of whether
one truly believes a particular claim since Peirce argues that
genuine belief consists in a general resolution to act on that belief
in appropriate circumstances.

What is more, Peirce holds that human agency is free. It is
governed by purposeful resolution and so intentionality cannot
be overlooked in understanding agency in the world, and especially human agency. Peirce denies that the universe is mechanis-
tically determined. Rather he argues that there is a real principle
of spontaneity or change operative in the universe which allows
for true development and for the appearance of new things. Such
a universe is not without order and causality, but that order is

---

[1] C.S. PEIRCE, *Collected Papers of Charles Sanders Peirce*, ed. C. Hart-
shorne and P. Weiss, V (Cambridge: Harvard, 1934), 402, nn. 1, 2, 3.

neither absolutely fixed and unchangeable nor the result of blind and mindless force. Peirce argues strenuously and constantly that there can be no efficient cause without final cause; it would be like having a sheriff without a judge. Perhaps this brief citation will give you a sense of the importance Peirce placed on free human agency: "... it is by the indefinite replication of self-control upon self-control that the *vir* is begotten, and by action, through thought, he grows an esthetic ideal, not for the behoof of his own poor noodle merely, but as the share which God permits him to have in the work of creation"[2].

Peirce's account of the self is more developmental than the usual Aristotelian insistence upon the self as substance, although I think it can be argued that Peirce would admit something like substance to account for the continuity of personal experience.

c) Transcendental Thomists (Lonergan):

Again, action, human action is of central importance. It seems to me that the most important contribution here is made by those Thomists who recognize judgment as a human action and hold that it is in the act of judging alone (hence not in any conceptualization) that existence is grasped. Real existence, actuality, what *is*, is affirmed, not conceived. Kant was correct in thinking that existence is not a predicate insofar as he thought predicates to be universal concepts. Existence is not a universal concept — not even the most universal concept. It is not a concept at all. To the extent that one insists on trying to make it the highest genus one progressively empties it of content so that in the end, as Hegel remarked, it cannot be distinguished from non-Being. Kant's failure was to ignore the special and peculiar human action — judging, affirmation. Too often philosophers have assumed that formulating a proposition and affirming a truth are one and the same act. The first might plausibly be understood to involve simply putting together two concepts (by

---

[2] *Ibid.*, n. 3.

means of the copula verb "to be"); the second cannot be
plausibly so construed. Real existence is act; it is essentially
activity. No existing thing is nor can it be thought to be totally
inert. Our act of affirmation is the co-natural response to the real
as it is presented to us for understanding. Hence, Lonergan for
one argues that the real is what is intelligently understood and
reasonably affirmed — and nothing else is!

Finally, Lonergan thoroughly agrees with John Paul II's
criticism of Aristotelian Thomism's handling of the human
subject. In fact, back in 1968 in a talk to seminarians in
Pittsburgh on the "Future of Thomism" one of his recommendations to make Thomism viable in our time was that it shift
emphasis from a metaphysics of soul, which thought of self as
substance, to the self-appropriation of the subject precisely as
person-in-action and hence as developing through time by its
choices and actions[3].

3. Community:

a) John Paul II:

The very notion of human action as central to human
development implies relations to other things and to other
human beings. Perhaps the most important theme in John Paul
II's anthropology is establishing and promoting human dignity.
To do so supposes one knows in what that dignity consists. It
supposes too that the wide-spread malaise in human society
leading to violence of every kind is due to a deep alienation
which consists in the constant fear of losing human dignity.
According to John Paul II, human dignity is founded upon
respect for one's self and for others. It includes respect for those
things necessary for the quality of human life. Most of all, of
course, it means a relation of personal respect between human
beings which creates community in which all participate and to

[3] B. LONERGAN, S.J., "The Future of Thomism", *A Second Collection*, ed. W.
Ryan and B. Tyrrell (Philadelphia: Westminster, 1974), p. 51.

which all contribute. Hence man is by nature social and his very dignity depends upon a mutual relation of love and trust.

b) Pragmatists (Peirce):

Peirce's conclusions are almost exactly those of John Paul II. Peirce's synechism (a doctrine of continuity) requires that all human beings be related to one another. In fact they cannot not be so related although growth of human potential requires that the relation be one of loving community and not of hating animosity. Peirce would argue that insofar as an individual or group of individuals isolate themselves from their fellows they are mere negations.

Peirce's emphasis on community began with his attempts to understand human knowing. According to him our opinions are fixed rationally neither by mere tenacity nor by sheer authority, but rather by scientific (orderly) investigation. But he claims that such investigation requires a community of inquirers whose sole dedication is to discover the truth. No one can go it alone. And no one or no group can pursue truth perseveringly without good moral character. This is Peirce's doctrine of the normative sciences according to which scientific methodology (logic) depends upon our understanding what ends are fitting for mankind to pursue (ethics) which in turn depends upon our ability to recognize the *summum bonum* (esthetics).

c) Transcendental Thomists (Lonergan):

Again, Lonergan comes to substantially the same conclusion. He argues, for example, that for human growth and development there must be a series of conversions in each one's life including at least the following: intellectual, moral, and religious. These conversions are usually not events which take place once and for all but dispositions which need constantly to be nurtured and renewed. The point for us, however, is that each of these conversions involves a radical changing of mind with respect to one's understanding of self and of others. It requires overcoming certain biases which prevent human beings from forming a genuine community and so foster ever greater alienation. Those of you familiar with *Insight* will recognize the biases there analyzed: dramatic, individual, group, and universal. Lonergan proposes a "cosmopolis" as the kind of society which would have overcome these biases and which would provide the means to prevent them from recurring.

Like Peirce, Lonergan requires more than intellectual conversion. He also demands moral conversion in which one's notion of the good expands to include the good of others, from a self-regarding ethic to an other regarding code of conduct. Lonergan also argues that this moral conversion (and so intellectual conversion) is not possible without religious conversion and this because of the mystery of evil.

Conclusion

That three thinkers from rather different philosophical backgrounds should come (independently so far as I can tell) to such strikingly similar conclusions lends support at least to the supposition that those conclusions might be true or close to the truth. The issues certainly are absolutely central to contemporary thought and debate.

THE IMPLICATIONS FOR THEOLOGY OF *THE ACTING PERSON*

David Stagaman, S.J.

Introduction

The task assigned for this article (the implications for theology of *The Acting Person*) has not come easy. The book itself is extremely difficult to read. The writing is abstract in the extreme. One looks in vain for an example or two or even three. The author has laid down stringent demands for the reader as he attempts to lay out the general structure of the human person, a person whose essential self is revealed only in moral acts. Because the book operates at such a high level of abstraction, the structures of the human person that are uncovered translate into general principles that could admit of several theological applications.

If Karl Rahner is correct (and I think he is)[1], method in theology is a practical endeavor. Thus, the movement from general philosophical principles and concepts to theological implications and conclusions involves a process whereby the philosophical foundations are profoundly and internally affected by the data that emerge from scriptural, patristic, and magisterial teaching as well as what we learn from other theologians and the experience of our fellow believers. These data transform the

---

[1] Karl RAHNER, *Theological Investigations*, IX, trans. G. Harrison (London: Darton, Longman & Todd, 1972), Part One.

principles in such a way that the transition from philosophical beginnings to theological reflection requires observation and not prediction from the onlooker. One thinks of the early work of Rahner: *Spirit in the World* and *Hearer of the Word*. While one can readily see echoes of these earlier books in the several volumes of *Theological Investigations* and his masterwork, *Foundations of Christian Faith*, one must also acknowledge the genuine surprises that emerge in these later, clearly theological texts.

The Acting Person poses one further difficulty. It combines two quite different, not altogether consistent, methodologies[2]. Clearly, the overarching method is that of phenomenology. The book reflects the author's doctoral thesis on Max Scheler's ethics. It demonstrates his profound indebtedness to Scheler and shows how well he learned Scheler's method. Much of the terminology, however, comes from Thomistic metaphysics. *The Acting Person*, then, has also as its source what John Paul learned at the Angelicum in Rome while doing his first doctorate. It is important to note here for future reference that the Thomism in question is one which emphasizes the impact of Augustine (rather than Aristotle) on Aquinas.

The Polish original of *The Acting Person* appeared in 1969. At the time the author was already Archbishop of Cracow. As a result, the body of his theological writings must be read with great caution since they were written by a pastor, and not by a professional theologian. This pastoral emphasis does not imply that his episcopal letters and papal encyclicals, instructions, etc., are not theology of a high order; but we do need to remember that these works probably do not reveal to us Wojtyla the theologian's most speculative, and venturesome thinking.

A glance at the encyclicals introduces us to an ecclesiastic who takes the documents of Vatican II with supreme seriousness.

---

[2] Karol WOJTYLA obviously thought the two methods were happily synthesized. This reader found them occasionally discordant.

He has learned the lessons of the Council well. His favorite sources in the papal letters are manifestly the Scriptures. In fact a superficial glance might lead one to wonder whether the phenomenologist who gave us *The Acting Person* has vanished. But, then, one notices the appeal implicit in his encyclicals, viz. to the reflective man or woman of good will, is the same as that in the pages of his book. *Redemptor Hominis* is an exemplary instance. The encyclical presents a majestic view of the Christian mystery; nonetheless it presents this mystery as an invitation to all men and women to find their best selves therein. When John XXIII addressed *Pacem in Terris* to all people of good will, and not simply to his Roman Catholic flock, that address was a novelty. Not so for the present Pope. He consistently writes for that broader audience.

The thesis of this essay is that *The Acting Person* can be read as laying the groundwork for his papal theological writing; it functions in a way not dissimilar to the relationship between *Spirit in the World* and *Hearer of the Word* to Rahner's subsequent theological endeavors. While the remainder of this article will demonstrate the credibility or incredibility of this thesis, the tentative character of the claim being made requires emphasis. The pastoral nature of the theological writings plus the use of conciliar and scriptural sources with rare acknowledgement of philosophical influences render the claim highly hypothetical. The evidence adduced is necessarily of a circumstantial character.

The Acting Person

The acting person is an integrated, self-possessed person. This person's consciousness consists of a cognition that has integrated not only bodily awareness and activity, but also affective life. In the course of a lifetime, this person has become aware of objective moral values and has developed the appropriate human and humane skills to embody these values. The acting person can concentrate the whole of his or her energies in

conduct and behavior that fulfills him or her as a self. The acting
person is not a cluster of drives, reactions, and capacities; nor,
for that matter, simply several levels of consciousness. He or she
is a sovereign actor who abides in his or her acts.

The acting person is free. Such a person is not being coerced
recognizably or subliminally; nor does he or she act out of
conformity to socio-political pressures. In *The Acting Person*, the
argument for human freedom is not based on foundations readily
familiar to those of us who live in the West. Freedom is not, as
liberal individualism would have it, a political right. Rather, it is
a metaphysical datum, a given of the structure of human being
uncovered through phenomenological description. This description also reveals that freedom is, of necessity, open to a
normative ethic and Absolute Truth.

Furthermore, human freedom is opposed to any kind of a
totalism where the collectivity precedes and can cancel out the
individual. The free human being is not motivated by the
imperatives of class struggle or a sense of class interest. The free
person is conscious, rational, and responsible as an individual in
community whose wisdom comes out of a tradition where norms
are objective and perennial.

Thus, the acting person is a social being. The first and
fundamental right of human being is the right to participate in a
community. Such a person acts out of and for the common good.
His or her categorical imperative is "love one another". For him
or her, human fulfillment comes only in moral acts where the
individual acts with responsibility to and for oneself, but also in
communion with other like-minded actors. Responsibility to
oneself, i.e. to one's best self, can only be achieved when it is
simultaneously responsibility to the neighbor, to truth, and,
finally, to God[3].

---

[3] In composing this section of the article, I found very helpful George
Hunston Williams' *The Mind of John Paul II; Origins of His Thought and Action*
(New York: Seabury Press, 1981).

As one reads through *The Acting Person*, one cannot help but suspect that the person of Jesus Christ lurks between the lines on each page. For John Paul, Jesus Christ reveals not only who God is, but who the human person is and how that person ought to exist. Only he is the acting person fully alive, able to integrate all of his capabilities and energies in a deliberated act which is complete self-donation. For the author of *The Acting Person*, only the acting person is capable of genuine self-sacrifice.

The ideal of the book is fulfilled in Christ Crucified. There the whole life and mission of Jesus are consummated in a single moral act where he lays down his life for the values he believes in and for his friends that he loves and gives himself over completely to his Father or Absolute Truth.

Some Theological Implications

Within the spectrum of current theological debate, the author of *The Acting Person* would almost certainly fall in among those who regard faith as orthopraxis[4]. While faith would include intellectual assent (as any moral act includes careful deliberation and judgment), such assent would not be the primary factor in religious belief. Belief or faith would be preeminently a moral act. One believes by making one's behavior consistently a response to the God revealed in Jesus Christ. The Crucified One would become one's teacher along the path towards total self-sacrifice. Following Christ would be the means of human enlightenment.

---

[4] *Orthopraxis* is a term that is overly and often loosely used. When I apply it to Karol Wojtyla, I do not mean to infer that he is a liberation theologian or to ally him to any other group of theologians who use the word today. My purpose is to focus attention on the fact that he would probably not align himself with the traditional neo-Thomist position that faith is first and foremost an intellectual assent. Also, intellectual assent vs. orthopraxis is a question of emphasis. The former acknowledges that intellectual assent leads to appropriate action; for Wojtyla the moral act of faith comes after serious deliberation and reflection.

As a theologian, the author of *The Acting Person* would probably have developed his theology as anthropology. A dialectical relationship would have obtained between our knowledge of God and self-knowledge, between the mighty acts of God and our own moral acts. Creation would, then, find its ultimate meaning and purpose in redemption. Any human being would recognize his or her best self in becoming a son or daughter of God. The encyclical, *Redemptor Hominis*, illustrates this theology-as-anthropology bent. The person of good will is invited to find the authentic self within the historical unfolding of the Triune God's salvific plan.

Religious freedom would never be simply the endowment of the individual believer. This freedom involves more than the absence of coercion or the ability to choose. It is realized fully through moral action in a community. Like Thomas Aquinas, the author of *The Acting Person* would probably locate the ideal of freedom in acts of friendship — friendship with other acting persons and with God.

The encyclical, *Redemptor Hominis*, fills out this picture. There, the reader cannot help but notice the profound preoccupation with sin and evil in the world. Sinfulness is so pervasive that even freedom itself is corrupted by the constant presentation of itself in illusory forms. Freedom, thus, is seriously threatened and requires the grace of God to overcome these illusions. In the discussion of evil in this encyclical, John Paul's Augustinianism is amply in evidence. Where sin abounds, there does the divine graciousness more abound.

Finally, the Church for the acting person would not be a free association which the believer might or might not join. The acting person is made for ethical community, and only in a community with a tradition of ethical reflection can this person find fulfillment. In the Roman Catholic Church, it is especially its natural law tradition which makes it an ethical community. The Church, however, is not just a collection of individuals nor a collectivity whose good supersedes that of the individual absolutely or which could use the individual as a means. It is rather a *koinonia* in which the individual participates by a fundamental right of belief. The believer is both nourished by the Church's ethical teaching and contributes to the building up of that community through ethical action.

Conclusion

The labels that are often used to describe the Pope's thought are not terribly helpful. In my opinion, calling him a conservative, a liberal, or even a middle-of-the-roader is not very illuminating. His actual theological thinking ranges across a broad spectrum. Reading John Paul's teaching on human sexuality might lead to the conclusion that he is a theological conservative. The reader of *The Acting Person* would not be totally surprised. There he had made known his great respect for and love of the natural law tradition. If one were to read only *Laborem Exercens*, however, one might consider him a radical. There John Paul attempts to frame a consideration of freedom which depends neither on the liberal individualism of the Enlightenment nor on the collectivist dialectical materialism of Karl Marx. He explores freedom in a manner which is genuinely novel. The Pope who emerges from the encyclicals is a quite supple thinker who dares to cast his reflections in a way that is attractive to believer and non-believer alike even though he seems aware that much of the world would think and act otherwise.

The Acting Person is a piece of solid philosophical reflection. I recommend it to the reader of a philosophical bent in spite of my previous remarks about difficulties in reading it. Had Karol Wojtyla not already been a bishop when it was published, the book would have received more notice for its introduction of a philosopher of great promise. In Poland the book was so celebrated. The book does have some shortcomings. Had his career not taken him to a leading role in the Polish hierarchy and now in the universal Church, he hopefully would have elaborated and revised his discussion of the body and especially the affective

life. The latter is treated in the faculty psychology approach that
was once common among Thomists. *The Acting Person*, however, is well worth reading. To paraphrase Paul Ricoeur, the
reading gives rise to reflection.

REDEMPTOR HOMINIS

RAYMOND T. GAWRONSKI, S.J.

Few Catholics in any part of the world have escaped the question: "Have you been saved?" urgently posed by sectarians. Yet the word "redemption" brings to the modern Catholic imagination a musty odor of Gothic cloisters, a haze of Church Fathers, somehow disappearing in the far more insistent issues of much contemporary Catholic theological discourse.

It was therefore surprising, as usual, that Pope John Paul II's inaugural encyclical, issued on March 4, 1979, should have been entitled *Redemptor Hominis*, "The Redeemer of Man". In light of the recently held Jesuit conference on the thought of John Paul II, this essay will attempt to sketch the main themes treated in *Redemptor Hominis* and will then consider some of the issues which emerged during the discussion of this encyclical.

One participant at the discussion observed that the thought of the Holy Father was much like the movement of a school of fish — now here, now there, all together, all themes included in each new location. Four theological themes suggest themselves as aids to structure this fluid movement of thought: God, Man, Church and World. In the three latter areas there is much movement between light and shadows in the Pope's understanding of the situation.

God

Carefully situating himself in this moment in the history of the Church, the Papacy and the world, in light of 2,000 years of Christian history, the Pope asks:

> How, in what manner should we continue? What should we do, in order that this new advent of the Church connected with the approaching end of the second millennium may bring us closer to him whom Sacred Scripture calls "Everlasting Father", "*Pater futuri saeculi*"?[1].

The Father of the Age to Come manifests Himself in creation and in His eternal love (9), a "love that is always greater than the whole of creation" (9). The God of creation is the God of redemption (9), a redemption that, as we shall see, is being effected in Jesus Christ. Seeing Christ we see the Father (7).

Christ is both God and Man. This commonplace of orthodox Christology permeates the encyclical which insists on the inseparability of the two natures in one Person. The Son is the center of the universe and of history (1), the source of wisdom, love and of the Church (8). In time, and for eternity, He entered man's heart (8), becoming, in history, the form and name of love and mercy (9). As the man who is the form of love, as the Word Incarnate in whom God became an actor in the cosmic drama (1), Christ fully reveals man to himself (8, 10). This revelation is His mission from the Father, a mission to transmit the truth (19). As the Word, He is entrusted with this transmission to man; as the Word Incarnate, He becomes the "center of the mission that God Himself has entrusted to man" (11).

The Spirit, the Counsellor, is given to the world as the Spirit of truth (7, 9), the Spirit of truth that is not limited to any

---

[1] RH 7. All translations are the author's own from the Polish original *Encyklika Redemptor Hominis* (Roma: Editrice Vaticana, 1979). All numbers in parenthesis refer to the corresponding paragraph in *Redemptor Hominis*.

ecclesial form but which is active outside the visible confines of the Mystical Body as well (6). As spirit, it has priority over matter (16) and is opposed to contemporary materialisms (18).

The Pope's presentation of God has a strikingly Trinitarian character, although given the nature of the subject here treated the focus is naturally on the Son.

Man

A well-known study of the Pope's philosophy is entitled *I-Man*: anthropology is at the center of his work. The center of man, for the Pope, is the heart, place of man's "inward mystery" (8). Citing Augustine on the *cor inquietum* (18), the Pope celebrates the creative restlessness of man while warning against his materialistic insatiability (18). A key concern of the encyclical is the dignity of man — so much so that the Good News for man takes the form of amazement at his own worth and dignity (10). The Pope applauds the endeavor to make human life more "human", to make every element correspond to man's dignity (15). True freedom (and not the illusory freedom of materialism or consumerism) is the condition of man's dignity (12).

The Pope insists that the man of whom he writes is the concrete, historical person, and not any "abstract man" (13). It is this concrete individual who is the "way for the Church". He shudders at contemporary collectivisms (16) with their dystopic visions of ant-hill mass societies. John Paul thus emphasizes the uniqueness of Christ (1) and of Mary.

Yet the individual is part of society, a society that should be characterized by human solidarity (16), as against the contemporary divisions of rich and poor, the Dives-Lazarus phenomenon (16). Man's life in community must be characterized by justice and human rights. The absence of justice leads to war (17). Social love and respect are contrasted to selfish exploitation and domination of others (15). There is definitely a need to transform economic structures, yet without being dominated by economic development (16). In this context, the Pope states that the twentieth century has been a century of moral calamities for man (17). Man's true kingship consists in nobility of service, a service which seekes to produce a mature humanity in each: it is a kingship which desires to "be more" rather than to "have more" (16).

To find himself, man needs to appropriate and to assimilate the Incarnation and the Redemption (10). He cannot live without love: life is absurd without the revelation of and encounter with love (10). Prayer is such an encounter. The measure for human acts is *Matthew* 25 (16) where Christ identifies Himself with "the least of His brethren".

Humanity needs correct limits, without which sin dominates. The Pope condemns the programmatic atheism of some societies (17) and warns against a concern for human rights which focusses on the letter rather than on the spirit.

Man's situation is characterized by great progress in technology (8) which is increasingly accompanied by man's fear of his own creatures (15). Thus, the optimism of earlier decades takes on a much darker shade in this encyclical, where man is seen as under threat and afraid. We shall see more of this in the section on the world.

Church

As this is his first encyclical as a new Pope, the Holy Father is especially careful to describe the condition of the Church. The Church is in a new stage of the post-Conciliar era. As taught in Vatican II, the Church is a "sacrament or sign and means of intimate union with God, and of the Unity of all mankind" (18). The Church which, as the guardian of freedom (12), seeks universal openness (4), has suffered from "an excessive self-criticism" (4) which in its turn was a reaction to an earlier triumphalism. Although rejecting indifferentism and the loss of truth of a false ecumenism, the Pope insists that unity is the will of Christ (6) and that ecumenism remains indispensable if one is to serve Christ. He suggests a unity of the churches in mission

(11), a unity of "openness *ad extra*" in the face of "critical attitudes attacking *ab intra*" (4). The Church continues the mission of her Founder, a mission characterized by esteem for other cultures (12). Indeed — and one suspects a wistful smile here — other religious traditions can remind Christians of the best in their own religious and moral traditions which they may be in danger of forgetting.

The Church is the "social subject of responsibility for Divine Truth", whose

> fundamental function in every age and particularly in ours is to direct man's gaze to point the awareness and experience of the whole of humanity towards the mystery of God, to help all men to be familiar with the profundity of the Redemption taking place in Christ Jesus. At the same time man's deepest sphere is involved — we mean the sphere of human hearts, consciences and events. (10)

The attempt to "direct man's gaze" has a contemplative flavor which suffuses the work, and yet this turning one's gaze to the mystery of God means being attentive to the work of the Spirit of truth on mission in God's world.

The "way for the Church" is man, it is the union of Christ with each man (14). The Church, the People of God which is Christ's Mystical Body (18, 21), is composed of unique individuals, each of whom has a vocation. It is not merely a social organism with "social membership".

Man's priestly role is to restore man and the world to the Father (20): this is the Church's sacramental function. The Eucharist is the "ineffable sacrament of unity" (20). It must be safeguarded against liturgical abuses. The Eucharist invites to conversion and repentance, and so penance is crucial. Christ and the human subject have a right of individual encounter which is not adequately respected in general absolution (20).

The prophetic role is especially addressed in the work for truth of the theologian. Theology is an *intellectus fidei*, which is a service of the Church's Magisterium, not the propagation of "personal ideas of some theologians" (19). The saints are key models (19). Mary's divine Motherhood is recalled (22), Mary, who is Mother of the Church.

As noted, the Pope links his papacy with all preceding popes, giving special mention to Paul VI, the "helmsman when the Church was shaken from within" (3). The Papacy is a universal service (1) offering unity for all Christians (21). The episcopate is characterized by its collegiality and synods (5). The laity are distinguished by the vocation of each (21).

World

Finally, the world is seen in light of the approach of the year 2,000. Creation is good (8): redemption show this in a new way. Redemption is thus the new creation in which creation is linked with the divine wisdom and love in Christ (8). The drama unfolding before us is one of creation, redemption and the struggle for justice (16). The United Nations receives special praise for its work in the struggle for human rights.

However, creation was "subject to futility" in sin, a futility seen in the various threats which have emerged along with man's recent technological progress. Technology ignores morals and ethics (15). Thus, in the midst of such advance, man faces grave ecological and environmental problems. There are global famine, economic domination, abortion, arms sales and an arms race, which cruelly exploit the hungry, and maldistribution of wealth. In short, man's great progress in technology is used for domination and is unaccompanied by a moral progress in which man is a king who serves, a king with the correct priorities of ethics over technology, person over things, and spirit over matter (16).

In light of all these considerations, then,

> the redemption of the world — this tremendous mystery of love in which creation is renewed — is, at its deepest root, the fullness of justice in a human Heart — the Heart of the First-born Son — in

order that it may become justice in the hearts of many human beings, predestined from eternity in the First-born Son to be children of God and called to grace, called to love (9).

The Discussion

The freshness of style and content which characterize the encyclical caught the attention of the group which reflected on *Redemptor Hominis*. The Augustinian "restless heart" with which the Pope characterizes humanity serves to describe him as well. His thought is seen as dialectical, a way of thinking which insists on keeping polarities in tension. It is a logic which evades tidy resolution, and yet it is a logic for all its plasticity. Hence the colorful — and apt — description of the Pope's style as that of a school of fish, now here, now there, but all elements together all the time. The traditional penumbra surrounding the Pope breaks open into surprising new vistas. Thus, one expects a treatise on the Redemption — perhaps a scholarly overview of the tradition, focussed on the Passion of Christ — and instead one finds a reflection partly addressed to Christ, in the manner of the *Confessions* (sec. 1) which is chock-full of social analysis. That is to say, the encyclical is unsettling to North American sensibilities which presume a clear separation of religion from public life.

In this lies much of the Catholic nature of the document which speaks much of "rights" but in a way which is different from the individualistic tradition of the Anglo-American world. Rights are intimately connected with culture, for the Pope. Culture is the vehicle in which the Church transmits the truth, which is her mission — and the encyclical strongly criticizes the available vehicles of individualistic consumerism or collectivistic Communism.

So far from encouraging individualism, the Pope seems to insist that there is no way to speak of redemption without speaking of world transformation as well. Again, this is difficult for those from an individualistic culture where individual faith and common life are radically disjointed. One participant observed that the integral approach of the Pope allows for no "smorgasbord reading of the gospel"[2]. Contemporaries want to pick and choose, keeping their distance from what is prophetic until such time as the public sector approves. The example was cited of *Humanae Vitae*, long ignored, but now coming into scholarly study and so sure to draw the interested attention of the faithful.

Such a prophetic spirit is present in this letter, especially insofar as it encourages believers to struggle for "the right to foster radical *communio*". That is to say, the Catholic tradition of rights is less concerned with individual rights than with the common good. Grounding rights language in the individual has led us to conceive rights almost exclusively politically. But man's basic orientation to God means that people should be able "to create a milieu of faith". In the Catholic view, there cannot be an autonomous individual outside of culture, of faith — and outside of community.

The vocation which the Pope teaches each person is given implies the right to answer that call, which comes from God. Moreover, for intelligent choices to be responsibly made, one needs more than mere freedom. Here God's desire for our love is seen when our freedom imitates His freedom: as one member observed, by our choices we "ratify His freedom".

The reality of freedom allows the possibility of radical evil. As Auschwitz and the nightmare that took place there are located in what would later be the metropolitan see of Cardinal Wojtyla, it is natural to ask how the Holocaust has affected the Pope's thought. It is here perhaps that deepest entry is gained into the Pope's writing, in which light and shadow so quicky follow one another, like the intensely blue sky which can surround thunderclouds. One member of the discussion insisted that the Pope's thought is extremely pessimistic about the world,

---

[2] All quotes in this section are taken from the participants in the group discussion.

in the broad, systemic issues — while being, at the same time, profoundly optimistic, for "Christ has given humanity a dignity that nihilating forces cannot snuff out". In his deep sense of suffering, the Cross is seen as the sign of triumph. Another participant observed that in the paradoxical mystery of love "the abyss of evil begins to draw out of God a depth of love we hadn't dreamed of". It should be noted as well that it would be inadequate to focus on the Aristotelian roots of the Pope's Thomism without giving at least equal attention to the Augustinian roots of that thought as well.

If the Pope is "realistic" about the world situation, he seems more optimistic about the individual human, whose perfection has been revealed in the human actor Jesus Christ, the alienated, crucified human actor. But perhaps the notion of human perfection revealed in Christ crucified is better seen not as perfection, so tied in to the Greek notion of *arete* as that word is, but rather as self-donation. The fullness of person is given in a wholly new communion, a gift, as the water from Christ's pierced side. The Passion of Christ, the experience of abandonment, gives sense to suffering, and invites us to an imitating "victim gift". Suffering obedience is integrated into Christ's priesthood.

Thus, the person of faith has no right to run away from the serious problems of the world. One is sober and realistic in the face of the world's evil, but in faith there is reason to hope in ultimate victory.

The year 2,000 is often invoked in the encyclical. Given the astounding events of recent months in Eastern Europe, one wonders what changes in human consciousness (a word he uses often) the Pope envisions for the final decade of this millennium. He is surely aware of the millenarian movements which convulsed the end of the first millennium. In the midst of these turbulent times, he directs the gaze of his readers to Christ.

Conclusion

As he directs the gaze to Christ, the Pope is clear that it is the "Redemption taking place in Christ Jesus" (29), a Redemption which involves man's deepest sphere. In his own words, by that sphere "we mean the sphere of human hearts, consciences and events". For a christological document, *Redemptor Hominis* is amazingly anthropocentric. In this, the Holy Father is grounded in the text of Mt. 25, which suggests itself as the key text for the Church in our day. Christ reveals the Father in a human face. To see and to serve Him, which is the goal of our life, we turn to the suffering, alienated humanity around us in a service worthy of kings, following the example given by Christ in history. The Church is witness to the truth about God Incarnate, the truth about man, in a world which would remove man's freedom and so assault his dignity. The Redeemer of Man is God and Man, and humanity is the way for the Church to her God.

LABOREM EXERCENS

Benjamin Fiore, S.J.

The rather free ranging comments over the course of the two workshop meetings have been summarized and organized here under appropriate headings. Some of these headings arose from the chair's opening remarks. To open the discussion on the encyclical, the chair commented on three aspects of context and background in Poland to which the letter could be seen to relate: the Church's debate with Marxism, the actual situation in Poland (the indirect employer, the Solidarity Union, the intellectual-worker relationship), and Polish National Messianism. These points were raised to introduce the encyclical and to open further discussion.

The first aspect is the Polish Church's debate with Marxism. The post-war situation in Poland found the Church philosophers (largely Thomists) and Polish philosophers in general unprepared to launch an effective counter to the officially promoted Marxist philosophy. This was a result of their longstanding disdain of Marxism as unworthy of serious study when it appeared earlier in the century. This encyclical manifests the effort to address the situation of the worker with Christian principles as an alternative to Marxist interpretation. Subsequent discussion in this area raised the questions as to how much the encyclical could be said to be using Marxist analysis. The issues and categories in the encyclical seem rooted in a Marxist environment: e.g., the opposition of capital and labor, labor as the source of value and of capital, the restricted right to private property. The analysis, however, which is personalist and Christian, sets itself apart from the principal features of Marxist thought: e.g., materialism, class conflict. The question of whether, conversely, the encyclical is influenced by capitalist analysis produced no agreement in the group.

The second aspect of context noted is the actual situation in Poland where the "indirect employer" could be seen as a reference to the socio-economic system which creates and organizes work. The deficiencies of the command economy and its bureaucratic structures, the resulting degradation of the work situation and the exploitation of the worker can be seen as objects of the encyclical's critique. Subsequent discussion of the term "indirect employer" saw its international implications and its application to a variety of economic systems. The term was seen to apply to public and private agencies, governmental departments, laws, collective bargaining agreements, trade treaties, unions, transnational companies, cartels, in short, all those entities which form today's complex web of forces which affect the situation of work in the world. The *maquillador* phenomenon along the Mexican border with the US is a concrete example. Here Mexican plants are established with substandard (from a US perspective) pay and working conditions, cost US jobs, but keep American companies viable in the international marketplace. The subordination of national governments, even our own, to the powerful forces in today's transnational economic structures raises questions of independence and real control over economic and, therefore, labor policies within any individual country. The developing Europan Economic Union is a new response to the situation.

Another reality in the Polish context to which the encyclical has reference is the Solidarity Union Movement. The letter's affirmation of the workers' rights, including the right to association and to strike, echoes ideas articulated by the Pope on his 1979 trip through Poland. One consequence of the trip was an acceleration of the protests in Polish society against prevailing government structures and the eventual formation of the Independent Solidarity Union. Discussion focused on the difference between the idea of a union as described in the encyclical and that in the US union experience. The role of unions described in the encyclical and practiced by Solidarity as quasi-political entities with social-critical responsibilities in their function as spokesman for the national well-being, contrasts with the rather restricted, adversarial, pay and benefits orientation of US labor unions. The US union structures and contractual work rules, as part of the "indirect employer", could even be seen as at times detrimental to the deepest interests of the workers and their personal development. The reduction of union interest to pay and benefits might even share in the economist fallacy criticized in the encyclical.

The topic of unions highlights the encyclical's view that work not only develops the individual but also unites people. This unity is a legitimate source of social change, from the bottom up. The question arose in discussion whether what the encyclical countenances as an approved mode of social transformation in one context (e.g., Poland) is held in suspicion by papal pronouncements in other contexts (e.g., Latin America). It was asked whether a certain backstepping from the idea of social change from the bottom up could be detected in the more recent social encyclical "On Social Concerns".

Be that as it may, this change from the bottom up was recognized in discussion as not totally spontaneous but, in the Polish context, as resting in part on the Church's concerted effort at raising the Polish national consciousness to religious, ethical and social values and responsibilities in preparation for the 1966 celebration of the millennium of Christianity. This continued in subsequent efforts of the Church to foster discussion of ethics and national culture. Similarly, Latin American ecclesiastical communities have turned to group consciousness raising as a vehicle for social transformation. The question arose why the Jesuits in the US have not created a common program around which they might focus efforts to raise public consciousness and to promote social justice. The papal encyclical and the US bishops' pastoral on economic justice (on which several Jesuits worked) were recognized as just such documents, with already formulated perspectives on social justice. The cultural diversity in the US, however, and the diverse views of economic goals and the ways to reach them seem to mitigate against a concerted and unanimous Church, or even Jesuit, effort to develop a consistent line of thought and action on questions of social and economic justice. The diverse reaction to the bishops' pastoral "Economic Justice for All" exemplifies the problem. From "trickle down" theorists to social activists, even we in the Society of Jesus do not agree on the processes and thus it is hard to take the economic pastoral as an agreed on blueprint for action in the near future. Admittedly, though, US Jesuits and Jesuit institutions have taken up the challenge from the pope and the US episcopacy and have made some progress. We have assumed the categories and have been directed to the problem, albeit with diverse conclusions and plans of action.

A related Polish reality is the relationship between the intellectuals and the workers as these are ordinarily understood. The encyclical sees inherent links between these classes of people, traditionally separate in European society. The encyclical ascribes a common understanding of work and its positive benefits to both and also relates the contemporary situation of proletariatization and exploitation to the intellectual as well as to the physical laborer. The articulation of this idea expresses the social reality in Poland. In fact, the recognition of their common plight and the united action taken in consequence of this realization by intellectuals and workers presented the government with a united front for the first time in the post-war succession of mass upheavals, either by workers or by intellectuals but never by both in concert. This ushered in the Solidarity Labor Union Movement.

A third aspect of the letter as related to the Polish context is found in the concluding section on the spirituality of work. Here the acceptance of the suffering of "toil" in the example of the suffering and resurrected Christ could be seen in relation to the

Polish national self-image as "Suffering Christ Among the Nations". This notion of national Messianism, promoted in the works of Polish Romantic authors like Adam Mickiewicz and still espoused today, is the idea that the Polish nation, through its sufferings in imitation of Christ, will one day rise from its degradation and be a focal point of renewal among the nations of Europe. The section on the spirituality of work, therefore, is not just tacked on to the letter but relates the social critique to the spiritual advancement of humankind.

In the group discussion paragraph 19 of the encyclical was given close attention. That paragraph raises the issue of the family wage and discusses family values in general. A new scheme for taxing and reallocating funds for education, social development and welfare through direct, universal payments to families, an "investment capital" which would subsequently be paid back by the recipients, was analyzed. The current US government's misappropriation of the social security fund, the negative impact on individuals and families of the current national and state welfare systems, the tendency of government-run programs and institutions to fall woefully short of their aims and even to intrude upon individual freedom, all have seriously undermined the US family and the progress of individuals within families. A new approach to financing education and meeting basic needs of US families is needed. Personal freedom and the principle of subsidiarity have been sacrificed by state initiatives and programs. Government will, however, to make the necessary changes is not in evidence.

Contributing to the undermining of the family have been vocal groups whose agenda and aims, at times advanced by some Jesuits, are directly counter to traditional family values. These tendencies are abetted by mass media programming and reporting. The failure of the US church generally and the Jesuits in particular to develop and promote effective structures and programs for the support of families was lamented. While paragraph 19 was agreed on to be a critically important paragraph, some difference of opinion developed as to whether it contained the most important ideas of the letter or important family ideas in a letter whose primary focus rests on other aspects of labor and the development of the person.

Another issue addressed was the consequences for work of technology. Market competitiveness calls for ever refined technologies and consequently decreasing numbers of workers to keep costs down and efficiency up. The result is a challenge to maintain employment levels in the face of these pressures. What are people to do as they become irrelevant to the production process? How will wealth be produced, by whom, and for whom? The encyclical, with its view of work as essential for self-development, foresees that all should be workers and that the worker should be elevated by the work. A particular problem arises when work dehumanizes the worker (e.g., in sweatshops or on assembly lines). This goes beyond the issue of adequate compensation, although that is also included.

Tied with the problems raised by technology is the pope's critique of the North/South economic and technological split which is alluded to in this encyclical but expressed more clearly later, e.g., in "On Social Concerns".

Another issue raised in this encyclical is that of freedom. While the deprivation of freedom has been clear in Marxist contexts, capitalist situations present a more subtle form of the same problem in their manipulation of the public to embrace particular values and choices. The encyclical's key opposition was found to be against materialism, whether in its Marxist or capitalist expressions.

The encyclical's idea that work is the way to find and express human values was noted as relatively new in Western thought. Until relatively recently (from the time of Kant) leisure and not work was upheld as the context in which full humanity was achieved. Today, in fact, leisure has taken on a different meaning in a consumption-oriented society like that of the US. We are driven to keep consuming, to maintain a life-style, and this drive has taken over our Sabbath. The drive to consume also sheds light on the value work has for us, a value often at odds with that of the encyclical.

MULIERIS DIGNITATEM

Paul V. Mankowski, S.J.

At the core of *Mulieris Dignitatem* is a theme which the Pope has been years in developing through homilies and pastoral writings, that of the nuptial significance of the body. It was given a new impetus by the recent synod on the role of the laity in the Church, of which the Pope writes, "One of the[ir] recommendations was for a further study of the anthropological and theological bases that are needed in order to solve the problems connected with the meaning and dignity of being a woman and being a man. It is a question of understanding the reason for and the consequences of the Creator's decision that the human being should always and only exist as a woman or a man"[1]. We come, it is suggested, to this understanding in the act of the male contemplating the female, and vice-versa. Contemplation of the other means "coming to know" the other. This knowledge is bound up inextricably with what we mean when we speak of "knowledge in the Biblical sense" — i.e., sexual knowledge, sexual love. Even in the Bible this is more than simply a euphemism; this knowledge is what elevates sexual congress above the status of one more event of mammalian biology: it connects sexuality with creation, with *this* particular human being as a person, with the female or male sex in general, with

---

[1] All numbers in parenthesis refer to the corresponding paragraph in *Mulieris Dignitatem*. This quotation is from paragraph 1.

being human simply. (Beasts, in the Old Testament, do not "know" each other). C.S. Lewis has expressed this point in an extraordinarily beautiful passage in his book *The Four Loves*, in which he suggests that for us human beings, the clothes we wear serve to individuate us, they help to express and preserve uniqueness, and that in laying aside their clothes lovers do not so much abandon their individuality as they acquire a kind of universality, they take on roles larger than themselves, they become Man and Woman in an archetypal, even sacramental, sense. Lewis says lovers "put on" nakedness as a kind of garment. I know of no clearer statement of what the Pope points to as the nuptial significance of the body. Our bodies make us aware of a wedding which has already taken place, a marriage in which the mystery of our destiny and human nature is realized, in which our "supreme calling is made clear" (2) in the words of the Pope, himself echoing *Gaudium et Spes*.

John Paul proceeds to draw out the implications of the nuptial character of man and woman:

> God, "who allows himself to be known by human beings through Christ, is the unity of the Trinity: unity in communion. In this way new light is also thrown on man's image and likeness to God, spoken of in the Book of Genesis. The fact that man 'created as man and woman' is the image of God means not only that each of them individually is like God as a rational and free being. It also means that man and woman, created as a 'unity of the two' in their common humanity, are called to live in a communion of love and in this way to mirror in the world the communion of love that is in God, through which the three Persons love each other in the intimate mystery of the one divine life. The Father, Son and Holy Spirit, one God through the unity of the divinity, exist as persons through the inscrutable divine relationship (7).

Thus, in creating us man and woman, God not only provided for the "revealing of man to himself" but for the revealing of God to man, even God's inner life. "This 'unity of the two', which is a sign of interpersonal communion, shows that the creation of man is also marked by a certain likeness to the divine communion... this likeness... is also a call and a task" (7). In other words, the fact that the human being is not self-contained, as it were, but divided into man and woman makes for two possibilities: on the one hand, the possibility of competition, strife, dominance and slavery — a state which teaches us nothing; on the other, the possibility of unity, love, communion — a state which gives us a glimpse into the mystery of God's life: the life of one God in three Persons.

And this likeness which we bear to God is also, the Pope claims, a call and a task. What is the nature of this call? "In the 'unity of the two', man and woman are called from the beginning not only to exist 'side by side' or 'together', but they are also called to exist mutually 'one for the other'" (7). That is, not simply as mess-mates in the same battalion, but as brothers and sisters in a living family; not merely "partners" in the mystery of redemption, but oblates of one another, each subjecting himself to the other not out of duty but out of love.

Having spoken of the human being in relation to the Creator, *Mulieris Dignitatem* proceeds to address the specific dignity of women. We are presented with a remarkably comprehensive vision of women, based on Scripture, which spans the Bible from *Genesis* to *Revelation*. The entire drama of redemption is focussed on the Woman in this scheme. The Woman is, in the first instance, she of the "Proto-Evangelium" or Prefigured Gospel, that is, the first announcement of our salvation, "the first foretelling of victory over evil" (11). At *Genesis* 3:15, after the serpent has deceived Eve and mankind has fallen, God addresses the serpent thus, "I will put enmity between you and the woman, and between your seed and her seed; he shall bruise your head, and you shall bruise his heel". The woman, here, prefigures the woman of the Apocalypse, the "woman clothed with the sun" who stands before the serpent who is waiting to devour the child she is bringing to birth. The victory of this woman is our victory, the final triumph. The woman of *Genesis* was Eve, and the woman clothed with the sun is the mother of God. The fidelity and obedience of Mary — her *fiat*, her "let it be done to me", not only undoes the damage of Eve, but signals the ultimate consummation of the cosmic battle of evil and good. The Pope connects this notion with the larger drama of redemption: "Is not the Bible trying to tell us that it is precisely in the 'woman' — Eve-Mary — that history witnesses a dramatic struggle for every human being, the struggle for his or her fundamental 'yes' or 'no' to God and God's eternal plan for humanity?" (30).

The point of this digression is not to pillory one more ideologue, but to bring us, albeit through a kind of back-door, into the center of the John Paul's message on the unique vocation, the unique dignity, of women. Mary's obedience, her fundamental "Yes!" to God, made it possible for God to entrust his own Son to her in an unutterably intimate and personal way: she bore Him in her womb. In so doing Mary is an exemplar of the trust extended to every woman:

> The moral and spiritual strength of a woman is joined to her awareness that God entrusts the human being to her in a special way. Of course, God entrusts every human being to each and every other human being. But this entrusting concerns women in a special way, precisely by reason of their femininity, and this in a particular way determines their vocation... A woman is strong because of her awareness of this entrusting, strong because of the fact that God "entrusts the human being to her", always and in every way, even in the situations of social discrimination in which she may find herself (30).

Dr. Joyce Little has explained this well:

> While it may initially surprise us that the Pope locates entrusting, in its most basic sense, in the mother-child relationship rather than in our relationship to Christ or to the Father, a moment's reflection will indicate why he does. Every child is entrusted to the care of a mother before that child is called to entrust himself to anyone, God included. For the first nine months of his life, he knows directly only his mother, and in most instances and for some time to come after the umbilical cord is severed, he meets others, including his own father, through and under the watchful

eye of his mother. Therefore, the Pope points out, parenthood, even though it belongs to both fathers and mothers, "is realized much more fully in the woman, especially in the pre-natal period". For this reason, the man — even with all his sharing in parenthood — always remains "outside" the process of pregnancy and the baby's birth; in many ways he has to learn his own "fatherhood" from the mother.

Now this vocation, this dignity, which is indissolubly connected to entrusting, is so profound that it applies to every woman — even those who will never bear a child. Paradoxically, the vocation of entrusting, which takes motherhood generally — and the maternity of Mary pre-eminently — as its example, is realized in another way in consecrated virginity. Once again it is the Pope's "theology of the body" with its insistence on the nuptial significance of the body which bridges these two outwardly contrary states of life. It is the nuptial, the spousal, character of the body which "informs" or puts its special stamp on the love which women show and which shapes their vocation. "One cannot correctly understand virginity —" he writes, "a woman's consecration in virginity — without reference to spousal love... through the Holy Spirit's action a woman becomes 'one spirit' with Christ, the Spouse... Spousal love always involves a special readiness to be poured out for the sake of those who come within one's range of activity. In marriage this readiness, even though open to all, consists mainly in the love that parents give to their children. In virginity this readiness is open to all people, who are embraced by the love of Christ, the Spouse" (20-21).

Finito di stampare il 5 marzo 1993
Tipografia Poliglotta della Pontificia Università Gregoriana
Piazza della Pilotta, 4 – 00187 Roma

FROM THE SAME PUBLISHER

1990

AA. VV.: *Human Rights and Religions.* (Studia Missionalia, 39).
1990. pp. VIII-460. ISSN 0080-3987.   L. 65.000

RULLA, Luigi: *Depth Psychology and Vocation. A Psychosocial Perspective.* 3ª ristampa.
1990. pp. 438. ISBN 88-7652-374-X.   L. 42.000

1991

AA. VV.: *Faith and Culture. The Role of the Catholic University.* (Inculturation, XI). 1ª ristampa.
1991. pp. XII-148. ISBN 88-7652-604-8.   L. 15.000

AA. VV.: *Women and Religions.* (Studia Missionalia, 40).
1991. pp. VIII-368. ISSN 0080-3987.   L. 65.000

BATE, Stuart C.: *Evangelisation in the South African Context.* (Inculturation, XII).
1991. pp. XIV-118. ISBN 88-7652-635-8.   L. 19.000

BIERNATZKI, William E.: *Roots of Acceptance: The Inculturation Communication of Religious Meanings.* (Inculturation, XIII).
1991. pp. VIII-188. ISBN 88-7652-640-4.   L. 23.000

CONN, James J.: *Catholic Universities in the United States and Ecclesiastical Authority.* (Analecta Gregoriana, 259).
1991. pp. XVI-348. ISBN 88-7652-639-0.   L. 45.000

CRUZ AYMES, Maria de la – BUCKLEY, Francis – NYAMITI, Charles – BIERNATZKI, William – DE NAPOLI, George – MAURER, Eugenio: *Effective Inculturation and Ethnic Identity.* (Inculturation, IX). 1ª ristampa.
1991. pp. XII-128. ISBN 88-7652-572-6.   L. 20.000

ROEST CROLLIUS, A. A. – NKERAMIHIGO, Theoneste: *What is So New about Inculturation?* (Inculturation, V). 1ª ristampa.
1991. pp. XI-54. ISBN 88-7652-608-0.   L. 7.000

1992

AA. VV.: *Religious sects and movements.* (Studia Missionalia, 41).
1992. pp. VIII-392. ISBN 88-7652-650-1.   L. 65.000

AA. VV.: *Cultural Change and Liberation in a Christian Perspective.* (Inculturation, X). 1ª ristampa.
1992. pp. XII-64. ISBN 88-7652-578-5.   L. 12.000

MALPAN, Varghese: *A Comparative Study of the Bhagavad-Gītā and the Spiritual Exercises of Saint Ignatius of Loyola on the Process of Spiritual Liberation.* (Documenta Missionalia, 22).
1992. pp. 444. ISBN 88-7652-648-X.   L. 48.500

VAN ROO, William A.: *The Christian Sacrament.* (Analecta Gregoriana, 262).
1992. pp. VIII-196. ISBN 88-7652-652-8.   L. 25.000

1993

HARTEL, Joseph Francis: *Femina ut Imago Dei. In the Integral Feminism of St. Thomas Aquinas.* (Analecta Gregoriana, 260).
1993. pp. XVI-354. ISBN 88-7652-646-3.   L. 45.000

Orders and payments to:

AMMINISTRAZIONE PUBBLICAZIONI PUG/PIB
Piazza della Pilotta, 35 – 00187 Roma – Italia
Tel. 06/678.15.67 – Telefax 06/678.05.88
Conto Corrente Postale n. 34903005 – Compte Postal n. 34903005
Monte dei Paschi di Siena – Sede di Roma – c/c n. 54795.37